# Agriculture and Water Quality

# Agriculture and Water Quality

## International Perspectives

edited by
John B. Braden and
Stephen B. Lovejoy

Lynne Rienner Publishers  •  Boulder & London

*Publication of this book was made possible by the financial support of the Office of Policy Planning and Evaluation, U.S. Environmental Protection Agency, the Economic Research and Soil Conservation Services of the U.S. Department of Agriculture, and the Center for International Food and Agricultural Policy of the University of Minnesota. Views expressed in the book do not necessarily represent the policies or positions of the sponsoring organizations.*

Published in the United States of America in 1990 by
Lynne Rienner Publishers, Inc.
1800 30th Street, Boulder, Colorado 80301

and in the United Kingdom by
Lynne Rienner Publishers, Inc.
3 Henrietta Street, Covent Garden, London WC2E 8LU

**Library of Congress Cataloging-in-Publication Data**
Agriculture and water quality : international perspectives / edited by
  John B. Braden and Stephen B. Lovejoy.
     p.   cm.
  Includes bibliographical references.
  ISBN 1–55587–183–6 (alk. paper)
  1. Water quality management—Government policy. 2. Water—
Pollution—Prevention—Government policy. 3. Agricultural
pollution—Prevention—Government policy. I. Braden, John B.
II. Lovejoy, Stephen B.
HC79.W32A37 1989                   L8130
363.73'1—dc20                                              89–10811
                                                                  CIP

**British Cataloguing in Publication Data**
A Cataloguing in Publication record for this book
is available from the British Library.

Printed and bound in the United States of America

The paper used in this publication meets the requirements of
the American National Standard for Permanence of Paper for
Printed Library Materials Z39.48–1984.

# Contents

PART 3   ENVIRONMENTAL POLICIES
AND AGRICULTURAL COMPETITIVENESS

# Tables and Figures

# Acknowledgments

This book was initiated and organized through the Consortium for Agricultural, Resource, and Environmental Policy Research. Formed in 1988, the consortium fosters advances in socioeconomic research on policies affecting natural resources, the environment, and agriculture. Its members include researchers, research managers, policymakers, and policy analysts from universities, government, and private research organizations.

The book would not have been possible without the financial support of the Office of Policy Planning and Evaluation, U.S. Environmental Protection Agency, the Soil Conservation Service and Economic Research Service, U.S. Department of Agriculture, and the Center for International Food and Agricultural Policy of the University of Minnesota. A grant from the Farm Foundation was extremely useful in the initial planning for the book. Our involvement with the consortium and our editorial efforts were made possible in part by the Departments of Agricultural Economics and the agricultural experiment stations at the University of Illinois and at Purdue University.

The manuscript was expertly prepared by Sandy Waterstradt, with excellent copyreading assistance from Pedro Hernandez. Pam Ferdinand and Gia Hamilton of Lynne Rienner Publishers provided encouragement and efficient guidance through the publication process.

*John B. Braden*
*Stephen B. Lovejoy*

# Contributors

*Glen D. Anderson* (Ph.D., University of Wisconsin) is senior economist at the Environmental Law Institute, Washington, D.C.

*Sandra O. Archibald* (Ph.D., University of California at Davis) is assistant professor at the Food Research Institute at Stanford University.

*William G. Boggess* (Ph.D., Iowa State University) is professor of agricultural economics at the University of Florida, Gainesville.

*John B. Braden* (Ph.D., University of Wisconsin) is professor of agricultural economics at the University of Illinois at Urbana-Champaign.

*Ann E. DeBossu* (M.S., University of Rhode Island) is staff economist at the Environmental Law Institute, Washington, D.C.

*Alex Dubgaard* (M.S., University of Copenhagen) is an economist at the Institute for Agricultural Economics, Copenhagen, Denmark.

*Gloria E. Helfand* (Ph.D., University of California at Berkeley) is assistant professor of agricultural economics at the University of California at Davis.

*Peter J. Kuch* (Ph.D., University of Minnesota) is staff economist at the Office of Policy Planning and Evaluation, U.S. Environmental Protection Agency, Washington, D.C.

*Karl-Ivar Kumm* (Ph.D., Swedish University of Agricultural Sciences) is state extension specialist in farm management, Research Information Center, Swedish University of Agricultural Sciences, Uppsala.

*Lawrence W. Libby* (Ph.D., Cornell University) is professor of agricultural economics and chair of the Department of Food and Resource Economics at the University of Florida, Gainesville.

*Stephen B. Lovejoy* (Ph.D., Utah State University) is associate professor of agricultural economics at Purdue University, West Lafayette, Indiana.

*Warren F. Musgrave* (Ph.D., University of New England) is professor of agricultural economics at the University of New England, Armidale, Australia.

*Katherine H. Reichelderfer* (Ph.D., University of Maryland) is associate director of the Resources and Technology Division, Economic Research Service, U.S. Department of Agriculture, Washington, D.C. Portions of her chapter were prepared while she was a resident fellow with the National Center for Food and Agriculture Policy at Resources for the Future, Washington, D.C.

*C. Ford Runge* (Ph.D., University of Wisconsin) is associate professor of agricultural and applied economics and director of the Center for International Food and Agricultural Policy, University of Minnesota, St. Paul.

*Kathleen Segerson* (Ph.D., Cornell University) is assistant professor of economics at the University of Connecticut, Storrs.

*Michael D. Young* (M.Ag.Sc. and B.Ec., University of Adelaide) is senior research scientist with the Division of Wildlife and Ecology, Commonwealth Scientific and Industrial Research Organization, Canberra, Australia.

# Overview

JOHN B. BRADEN
STEPHEN B. LOVEJOY

Agriculture is a vital component of all societies, whether they are rich or poor, industrialized or agrarian. The provision of safe and adequate food and fiber products is essential. However, the provision of agricultural commodities leads to some serious problems.

As with any production process, agriculture generates residuals and byproducts. These can pollute surface and ground water, and some chemical residues directly threaten human health. Pollution from agriculture degrades more stream miles, more lakes, more ground-water aquifers, and more coastal areas of the United States than pollution from any other source. And the United States is not alone. Agricultural nutrients are contaminating both freshwater and marine resources in Scandinavia and Europe. The soils of Australia's prime agricultural region, the Murray-Darling Basin, are festering with salts left behind by irrigation water. These are examples of just some of the problems faced in highly industrialized nations. Even more serious problems are faced in some less industrialized countries: witness the blood-red rivers of Brazil or the sliding hillsides of South Asia.

Solutions to agricultural problems confront several obstacles. First, residuals are unavoidable byproducts of all production process, including agriculture. Second, abating pollution is costly because it requires shifting to less valuable crops, using more expensive or complex production practices, or adopting new technologies that alter the commodity/wasteflow ratio. Third, solving one problem through changing production technologies and practices may affect other aspects of hydrologic systems, creating new problems.

This book considers public policies designed to reduce water pollution from agriculture and aims to accelerate international knowledge exchange about policies in a variety of nations. The chapters focus on the successes and shortcomings of policies, and their adaptability across political and cultural boundaries. In addition to reporting on previous policy initiatives, the book points the way toward the next generation of policy options.

As agricultural pollution problems grow in scope and severity, nations are searching for solutions. In the past, many nations have relied on educational programs for farmers and appeals for resource stewardship. However, these approaches have been overwhelmed by the capabilities of modern agricultural

1

technologies and by rising public demands for environmental protection. The result has been recent experimentation with a number of new approaches: taxes on fertilizers and pesticides; requirements for nutrient management plans; cross-compliance between various government entitlement programs for farmers and resource conservation by farmers; intensive agricultural extension involvement in developing pollution management plans; bans on specific types of farming practices in areas where there is a significant environmental threat; erosion standards; and more careful scrutiny of pesticide registrations and tougher standards for their use. This book reviews the experience with several of these approaches and extrapolates from that experience into the future.

Analysis of policies for improving water quality is complicated. First, the environmental property rights of farmers and others are dynamic, yet policy options depend on the nature of those rights. Second, the agricultural causes of water degradation and the effects of that degradation are generally separated temporally and spatially. This makes it difficult to connect causes and effects and to place responsibility for environmental damages. Third, many water quality-based goods are public goods that are not easily separable or tradable; solutions must be collectively arranged. Fourth, the overall lack of information about the extent of water quality damages, as well as the costs of water quality improvements, introduces tremendous uncertainty about the potential gains from policy actions.

In addition to specific policy options, this book considers the economic and political context of agricultural pollution control. The policies do not exist in a vacuum. Farm groups, environmental groups, and, increasingly, fiscal groups are vigorously engaged in the policymaking processes. In addition, the extremely important international trade in agricultural commodities is increasingly intertwined with environmental policies.

## SPECIAL CHALLENGES

Environmental problems associated with farming are special in a number of ways, both practical and political. The problems are widespread—not confined to just a few, easily identified polluters. Moreover, the polluters are interdependent: some of the pollutants running off one farmer's field may actually originate on other fields farther upslope. Under these circumstances, it is almost impossible to keep track of the polluters or to separate their responsibilities. There is little accountability, and this undermines many forms of public policies.

Unlike many types of industrial or municipal situations, there are few pollution control technologies that can be readily identified, purchased, and installed on farms. There are no simple add-on devices for intercepting and neutralizing most agricultural pollutants. Abatement generally requires systematic changes in farming practices, including chemical inputs, tillage practices, crop mixes, and farm field configurations. These changes may need to be supplemented with changes in stream channels or shorelines, such as bank stabilization or buffer strips.

A great many people contribute to agricultural pollution problems, and this adds to the practical and political difficulties. Aggressive policies risk alienating important voter blocks. Moreover, the primary polluters are rarely faceless corporations, but are instead "family farmers" who have long been venerated and supported as a matter of public policy, and whose property rights to use land as they see fit have historically been accorded considerable deference.

Not only is it hard to legislate against farmers, but the objectives sought are not always really compelling. Decreasing the turbidity of streams and lakes, extending the lives of reservoirs, improving the diversity of aquatic biota, and enhancing the quality of recreational experiences are among the results of abatement. Although these problems are widespread and of interest to many people, they do not have the dramatic or health-threatening qualities of a hazardous waste dump, urban smog, or a massive wildlife kill-off from the accidental discharge of toxic chemicals. In fact, many agricultural problems are perennially overshadowed by more flashy if less pervasive environmental concerns.

Public policies must inevitably reconcile the pull of desires for and entitlements to environmental protection and enhancement with the tug of those whose rights and desires would be diminished. Neither set of rights or interests is absolute. Expectations about the proper balance are constantly changing, and they typically are formed amid great uncertainty about the value and cost of the eventual outcome. Only when conflicts and differences of opinion over rights reach compelling levels will the uncertainty be faced, the natural inertia of policies broken, and change undertaken. It is in this fluid context that new policies for agricultural pollution will be set.

The list of special challenges could go on, but the point is clear: These problems are difficult to raise in the public consciousness, to attack politically, and then to tackle with sound and practical policies.


## OVERVIEW OF THE BOOK

Given these challenges, no single nation or jurisdiction has progressed very far down the road toward abating agricultural pollution, but many different aspects of the overall problem are being dealt with around the globe. The specific initiatives must fit local circumstances, although the basic issues, and the principles of policy formulation and implementation, are general. This book begins with three chapters that emphasize these common elements. Chapter 1, by Lawrence Libby and William Boggess, describes both the physical and political dimensions of water quality problems surrounding agriculture. It is followed by chapters on two generic classes of policy instruments: economic incentives and regulations. Incentives for abating agricultural pollution are assessed by Kathleen Segerson in Chapter 2. The basic purpose of incentives is to use economic gain or loss to motivate changes in private decisions without resorting to mandates. The possibilities include subsidies, cross-compliance, taxes, fines, and liability for damages. Segerson thoroughly reviews the options and then draws conclusions about a mix of incentive policies that makes sense for agriculture. Chapter 3, by Glen Anderson, Ann DeBossu, and Peter Kuch, covers regulatory options. These are the mandates that incentive systems attempt to avoid. They include performance, design, or operating standards for production activities, standards for ambient environmental quality, and outright prohibitions of specific activities. There has been considerably more experience with regulatory approaches than with incentive policies. Anderson et al. report this experience in a useful tabular overview of agricultural pollution regulations in Europe and the United States, and draw implications for future uses of regulations toward agricultural pollution.

Part 2 of the book turns away from general considerations and toward specific experiences with a variety of problems and policies. In Chapter 4, Karl-Ivar Kumm examines Sweden's efforts to reduce nutrient pollution from agriculture. These efforts include fertilizer taxes, intensive extension programs, and afforestation incentives. Although the taxes have been good sources of revenues for environmental programs and the extension efforts have been locally helpful, all three policies are overshadowed by others that exacerbate environmental problems. Danish problems with agricultural pollution, the subject of Chapter 5 by Alex Dubgaard, are similarly exacerbated by highly distortionary agricultural policies. Nutrient and pesticide contamination are the paramount problems; input taxes, management plans, and encouragement of greater agricultural diversity are the major policy responses.

The setting shifts to the United States in Chapter 6, by Katherine Reichelderfer. Although surface- and ground-water quality have become galvanizing political issues in recent years, most U.S. federal programs remain tied to erosion control. The use of incentives through cross-compliance has been a major theme in recent U.S. efforts, and Reichelderfer reflects the considerable skepticism that this approach has elicited. The spotlight stays on the United States in Chapter 7, but shifts from the national to the state level. Gloria Helfand and Sandra Archibald assess California's Proposition 65, which creates labeling standards and public exposure restrictions for chemicals used in agricultural production, and provides for both civil and criminal penalties for violators. This proposition is a comprehensive attempt to reduce health threats from pesticides and degradation of water resources by agricultural production, and it may be a precursor of future trends.

The final policy application is to salinization of surface waters and soils in Australia's Murray-Darling Basin. In Chapter 8, Warren Musgrave reviews the physical and political complexities of the Murray-Darling situation, then assesses a proposed, innovative strategy for mobilizing the four Australian states that share the problem. The strategy relies fundamentally on incentives for producers and on new institutional structures.

Part 3 of the book considers agricultural pollution policies from the perspective of their consequences for, and use in, international trading relationships. Ford Runge, in Chapter 9, looks at environmental policies as a relatively new and expanding front in covert trade wars. These policies will play a significant role in future negotiations over trade liberalization, and they have special significance for relations between developed and developing nations. Michael Young, in Chapter 10, takes a different approach, emphasizing the effects of trade policies on the decisions made by farmers, but reaches conclusions similar to Runge's. Together, these chapters provide a fresh and provocative view of the potential for environmental issues to play increasingly important strategic roles in agricultural trade relations.

The message coming from these papers is one of increasing public concern for environmental policies dealing with agriculture. This concern is evident in the many examples of policy approaches being tried and the growing importance of environmental issues in international trade relations, and signals an opportunity to make headway in reconciling agricultural practices with environmental quality. But it also signals a need for rapid progress in order for the agricultural sector to avoid trade dislocations or poorly conceived policies. There are examples of possible approaches around the world, and the policy environment in many nations is ripe for change. At the same time, nations that are not aggressive in addressing environmental problems may be left behind in the competition for international markets for agricultural products.

# PART ONE

# Issues and Policy Options

# ONE

# Agriculture and Water Quality: Where Are We and Why?

LAWRENCE W. LIBBY
WILLIAM G. BOGGESS

Water problems are emerging as the most compelling set of issues facing production agriculture in the 1990s. When U.S. agricultural interest groups assemble to compare notes, take positions, define the enemy, and set priorities, water problems bubble to the surface. In fact, access to *all* natural resources—land, water, even air—is a primary concern for farm groups everywhere. National and local governments in every part of the world are responding to perceived health risks or economic damage with a variety of water quality initiatives. Some of them require farmers to operate differently, reducing their contribution to the quality problem. Farmers are not accustomed to this attention. In nearly all nations with a major agricultural industry, farmers have spent their time and political energies worrying about production methods, prices, and market protection—not environmental matters. But the politics of water are becoming more visible, more urgent, and farm groups must deal with interest groups that they previously had been able to avoid.

This chapter focuses on agriculture's impacts on water quality as a policy challenge for the purpose of establishing a point of departure for more specific discussions of policy options. It identifies the basic physical and policy parameters for water quality and agriculture, covering the major features of this landscape but leaving the important details to others. The water quality problems that will demand attention by university and government social scientists from many nations in coming years are identified and briefly discussed.

## QUANTITY AND QUALITY

Water supply issues tend to be localized, a product of long-term climate and economic development patterns and short-term weather fluctuations. Water allocation limits have been imposed in several important instances. In the United States, adequacy concerns are particularly acute in western states, although they are increasing in high-use eastern areas as well. The U.S. average water availability is far higher than that of many nations. Average per capita water supply in India and China is one-fifth that of the United States.

9

Egypt and Saudi Arabia are 100 times more "water poor" than the United States on a per capita basis (World Resources Institute, 1988). These averages hide acute shortages in localities resulting from rapid population increase or natural scarcity.

For agriculture, water quality issues are more pervasive than water quantity problems. Farmers are a significant polluting source in some areas, and even when they are not, there is concern, even suspicion, regarding them. Agriculture is indeed "part of the problem" in the United States and in other parts of the world (Batie, 1988).

Farmers, foresters, growers, and ranchers are under scrutiny for their use and misuse of water. In the rural United States, local politics are increasingly dominated by people with no particular affinity for farms and farming. Although issues of water quantity and quality have important differences, particularly related to institutional history and policy options, they are integral parts of the larger problem of water allocation. Usable water has a collection of attributes including chemical, biological, and physical factors. Demand for water by various users is responsive to the quality dimension.

In addition to using and degrading water, agriculture itself can be damaged by tainted water. Farm families are more prone than others to consuming water that has been polluted by farm operations. In those cases, the rationale for corrective action on the farm is fairly clear. Consumers are increasingly aware of potential hazards from various pesticides, some of which may come from unintended applications of polluted water.

## WATER USE IN AGRICULTURE

Agriculture impacts heavily upon water use and thus ultimately upon water quality. It is the largest user (withdrawal) of water in the world, accounting for two-thirds of the total freshwater withdrawals in countries from which data are available (World Resources Institute, 1988). Freshwater withdrawals for all uses in the United States in 1985 totaled an estimated 457 million acre-feet, of which 125 million acre-feet were used for consumption and 200 million acre-feet were used for agriculture with 50 percent of that, or 100 million acre-feet consumptive use (Guldin, 1988).

The source of water for irrigation in the United States in 1985 was about 60 percent (114.4 million acre-feet) from surface water and 40 percent (75.1 million acre-feet) from ground water, with a small amount (0.6 million acre-feet) of wastewater reuse. Irrigators in the Great Plains rely most heavily upon ground water, whereas those in the Rocky Mountains and on the Pacific Coast rely most heavily on off-farm surface suppliers (Guldin, 1988). Ground-water withdrawals for irrigation continue to increase across the nation. The Mountain and Pacific regions account for over 50 percent of ground-water use for irrigation. The Great Plains is the next largest user of ground water for irrigation versus dryland farming alternatives. The total value of crops produced with irrigation in the United States was estimated to be $24 billion in 1982; $16 billion of this was attributable to irrigation versus dryland farming alternatives (Day and Horner, 1987).

## Agriculture's Links to Water Quality

Agricultural production processes generate residuals such as manure, fertilizer, pesticides, and soil particles, which can contaminate both ground and surface water. Numerous health and environmental quality problems have been associated with these contaminants. Water is a primary pollutant delivery and transport medium. The joint effects of hydrologic processes and agricultural practices lead to a number of important resource issues that complicate water allocation decisions.

As emphasized by Georgescu-Roegen (1972), the laws of thermodynamics dictate that all production processes generate residuals or wasteflows; for a system to be sustainable, total inflows over time must balance total outflows. The technology used in a production process determines the potential flows of outputs and wastes from that process.

This framework illuminates several important aspects of agriculture's role in water pollution. First, the generation of residuals is an unavoidable byproduct of production. Production processes that generate wasteflows in excess of the environment's assimilative capacity are inherently nonsustainable.

Second, the composition and the timing of agricultural wasteflows can be modified by changing crop mixes, by changing production practices such as input substitution and timing of applications, or by developing new technologies that alter the output/waste ratio. The goals would be to reduce the amount of potential pollutants in the wasteflows and to modify the timing of the outflows in order to reduce the likelihood that the potential pollutants are delivered to a watercourse and/or to mitigate the resulting damages.

Third, the production process affects the spatial and temporal dimensions of water outflows, which in turn affect the delivery and transport of the potential loadings. This introduces important interactions and trade-offs between potential loadings and ultimate delivery to ground or surface waters.

## Sources of Agricultural Pollutants

Residuals from agricultural production activities can be grouped into six major categories: soil sediments, nutrients, pesticides, mineral salts, heavy metals, and disease organisms. Soil erosion is a natural process, which is accelerated by cultivation of land. Five factors have the greatest impact on the rate of soil erosion: rainfall intensity and duration, soil erodibility, field topography, vegetative cover, and tillage practices. These factors have been expressed in a formula—the universal soil loss equation—which is commonly used for predicting erosion from agricultural lands (Wischmeier and Smith, 1978). Agricultural production practices primarily affect the vegetative cover and tillage factors. A great deal of research and effort has been expended to develop and implement production systems (including contouring, reduced tillage, and crop rotations) that help control soil erosion.

Nutrients, primarily nitrogen, phosphorus, and potassium, are commonly applied to agricultural crops as fertilizers to promote growth. In addition, livestock wastes are a source of nitrogen and phosphorus. Nutrient levels in excess of crop uptake are potential sources of pollution of both ground and surface waters. Agricultural production practices to control nutrient losses include modifying the amount, timing, form, and placement of fertilizers or livestock manures applied to agricultural lands.

Numerous chemical compounds are used in agriculture to inhibit growth of various organisms that otherwise would reduce agricultural yields. These compounds, commonly referred to as pesticides, include herbicides, insecticides, nematicides, and fungicides used to control weeds, insects, nematodes, and diseases, respectively. These compounds are potential pollutants of both ground and surface waters. Pesticide losses can be controlled by modifying the amount, timing, form, and placement of the compounds. Important interactions exist among various types of pollutants and control measures. For example, reduced tillage methods are often advocated as a means of reducing soil erosion. However, in many cases these tillage practices are accompanied by increased applications of herbicides and greater rates of water infiltration. The result is a reduction in surface-water runoff and sedimentation, but an increase in leaching and potential ground-water contamination with herbicides.

All surface- and ground-water supplies contain some minerals derived from natural dissolution of rocks and soils (Young and Horner, 1986). When water containing mineral salts is used for irrigating crops, these salts are carried into the soil root zone and are left behind as the water evaporates or is taken up by plants. Rising mineral concentrations in the soil can eventually reach levels detrimental to crop growth (Yaron, 1986). The common solution to this problem is to apply excess water to leach the salts beyond the crop root zone. However, this process also concentrates the salts in irrigation return flows, which negatively impacts downstream users. Salinization is a major problem in arid regions where large quantities of saline irrigation water are applied, and little rainfall is available to dilute and leach the accumulating salts.

Livestock production processes are a source of heavy metals (e.g., lead, zinc, mercury, and arsenic) and disease organisms (coliform bacteria and viruses) in addition to nutrients. Heavy metals and disease organisms are potential pollutants of both ground and surface waters. These pollutant sources can generally be controlled through appropriate handling and treatment of manure.

## Water as a Pollutant Transport Mechanism

Water movement is the key mechanism for transporting wastes from agriculture into receiving water bodies as well as for transporting pollutants into agriculture (e.g., by acid rain or saline irrigation water). Water transports pollutants via four processes: rainfall, surface runoff, percolation/leaching, and irrigation/evaporation. Rainfall impacts water quality in several ways. It transports atmospheric compounds such as nitrogen and sulfates from the atmosphere onto the land. If utilized by crops, nitrogen is highly beneficial; however, if not utilized it becomes a potential pollutant. Sulfur reacts with the rainwater to form sulfuric acid (acid rain), which may kill or retard the growth of plants and may change the leaching patterns of many soils. Nitrogen is a naturally occurring element in the atmosphere, whereas sulfur is not a natural constituent and originates in emissions from coal-burning power plants and other industries.

Water from rainfall or irrigation beyond that taken up by evaporation, transpiration, and storage creates runoff or percolates into the ground water. Runoff water from agricultural lands transports pollutants as solids suspended in the runoff and transported downgradient. Further, chemicals may be picked up in solution and transported offsite in the runoff. Water that soaks into the soil and percolates down into ground-water aquifers may carry chemicals in solution and ultimately contaminate ground water.

In addition to being a potential source of runoff or leaching, low-quality irrigation water transports pollutants onto agricultural lands. Highly saline irrigation water transports mineral salts and occasionally heavy metals onto agricultural lands. Evaporation of the irrigation water causes the salts to precipitate out, and reduction of the kinetic energy in the irrigation flows allows heavy metals to settle out.

Pollutants are often classified by point-source or nonpoint-source origins. Point-source pollutants are those that can be traced to a precise source defined as a "discernable, confined, and discrete conveyance," such as a pipe, ditch, well, or container [33 U.S.C. §1362(14) (1982)]. In agriculture there are relatively few point sources of pollution, although concentrated confinement livestock facilities, confined irrigation return flows, and some greenhouse facilities would qualify as point sources.

Nonpoint or diffuse sources encompass a large areal extent and thus it is difficult to trace such pollutants to a precise source. The majority of pollution from agriculture is classified as nonpoint and arises from runoff and leaching from manure disposal areas and from land used for crop and livestock production.

The distinction between point and nonpoint sources has important implications for the design of pollution control practices. Management of nonpoint-source pollutants is difficult and expensive because the pollution potential of various residuals and the efficiency of control methods tend to be site specific. Furthermore, spatial and temporal variability complicates the assignment of liability for ultimate damages, and thus the choice of institutional framework for controlling nonpoint sources. These issues will be more fully discussed later in this chapter.

Agricultural pollutants can also be classified on the basis of whether they are transported in water as suspended solids or in solution. Pollutants transported as suspended solids include soil sediments and heavy metals. In addition, some chemical compounds such as fertilizers and pesticides, which are adsorbed to the soil, may be carried along with suspended sediments in runoff. Pollutants transported in solution include nutrients, pesticides, mineral salts, and disease organisms.

The form of pollutant transport determines the ultimate "sink" or receiving body as well as the types of controls that are likely to be effective. Leaching primarily carries compounds in solution. Thus, nutrients (particularly nitrates), pesticides, and other soluble chemicals are the dominant agricultural sources of ground-water contamination, and sediments and adsorbed compounds are important additional sources of surface-water contamination. Pollutants transported as sediments or adsorbed to sediments can be controlled by reducing erosion, whereas pollutants transported in solution can be controlled by reducing the availability and/or solubility of the compounds.

## Impacts of Agricultural Pollution

The generation of residuals and ultimate transport to receiving water bodies is of concern for two reasons. One concern revolves around the onsite effects on agricultural productivity. Erosion and loss of nutrients reduce soil productivity and increase costs of production. Likewise, losses of pesticides reduce their effectiveness in combating pests, resulting in lower yields and increasing costs.

There have been several attempts to quantify the onsite effects of soil erosion. For example, the U.S. Department of Agriculture estimated that sheet and rill erosion occurring over the past 30 years on land planted only to corn resulted in soil damage costs of nearly $700 million. Total economic productivity losses from eroding soils in the United States have been estimated at about $1 billion per year (Ribaudo, 1986). In the short run, the primary onsite costs associated with erosion are borne by the landowner via reduced yields, increased costs, and lower land values. In the long run, society as a whole may be concerned about the intergenerational implications of resource depletion.

Another general area of concern about agricultural pollution arises from the externalities, or offsite damages, caused. These effects are external to agricultural production in that the damages are incurred by other users of surface waters (rivers, lakes, estuaries) or ground-water aquifers.

*Surface Water Impacts.* Agricultural pollution of surface-water bodies takes three general forms: (1) sedimentation arising from soil erosion; (2) eutrophication, or nutrient enrichment by nitrogen and phosphorus; and (3) contamination from toxic chemicals such as herbicides and insecticides or from disease organisms.

Soil particles cause instream impacts both while suspended in water and after they have settled out. Instream impacts include damages to aquatic organisms, water-based recreation, water-storage facilities, and navigation. Sediment damages aquatic organisms by destroying spawning areas, food sources, and habitat as well as directly damaging fish, crustaceans, and other aquatic wildlife. Water-based recreation activities, including fishing, boating, swimming, and waterfowl hunting, are adversely affected by sediment. Fish numbers and composition change, fishing success declines, weed growth and siltation hampers boating and swimming, and habitat changes reduce food supplies and cover for waterfowl. Finally siltation of channels, lakes, and reservoirs reduces water-storage capacities and limits navigation, thus requiring increased dredging or the construction of additional waterways.

Offstream impacts of sediment include increased flood damages, siltation of water conveyance facilities, and raised water-treatment costs. Sediment contributes to flood damages by increasing the frequency and depth of flooding due to aggradation of streambeds, by expanding the volume of the water/soil mixture, and by exacerbating the damage caused by sediment deposited by the flood waters (Clark et al., 1985). Sedimentation of drainage ditches and irrigation canals significantly raises the annual maintenance dredging costs. In addition, the costs of treating water for municipal and industrial uses increase because sedimentation basins must be built, chemical coagulants added, and filters cleaned more frequently.

Nutrients, pesticides, and other contaminants create both instream and offstream water quality impacts through complex and indirect chemical and biological interactions rather than the relatively simple physical processes associated with sedimentation. Eutrophication is the excessive nutrient enrichment of a body of water so that rates of biological productivity are stimulated (Clark et al., 1985). Although eutrophication is part of the normal aging process of a water body, it is substantially accelerated by enhanced concentrations of nutrients in runoff. The impact of a specific nutrient depends upon the biological availability of the particular form and whether that particular nutrient is the limiting factor. Phosphorus is most commonly the factor limiting growth in surface-water bodies.

Nutrient enrichment stimulates rapid growth of aquatic micro- and macrophytes, which in turn affects aquatic habitats. Changes in plant species and distribution affect food supply and cover, which in turn may affect the number and types of fish. Oftentimes game fish such as trout, bass, or perch are displaced by "rough" fish such as gar, carp, or shad. Increased growth of surface macrophytes also interferes with fishing, boating, and swimming. Algal blooms and decomposing organic matter in a eutrophic water body can cause undesirable changes in water color, taste, and smell (Clark et al., 1985). Some types of algae are toxic and their blooms can make the fish within a water body toxic. Shellfish are particularly affected by blooms of toxic algae such as the "red tides" of dinoflagellates. Furthermore, the decomposition of algae and other vegetation can combine with other biological oxygen demand (BOD) loadings to deplete oxygen levels in the water, seriously harming all forms of animal organisms and occasionally causing massive fish kills.

Excess nutrients also cause serious offstream impacts. Nitrogen and phosphorus can directly affect drinking-water supplies when a nutrient is in a toxic form or combines to form toxic compounds, and can indirectly affect supplies by stimulating algal growth, which hampers water purification. Toxic levels of nutrients are rare, although high nitrite concentrations can cause methemoglobinemia in infants. The most serious offstream impacts revolve around the costs of removing algae from drinking water. Algae clogs filters and often requires the use of additional chemicals to purify the water.

The third type of agricultural pollution affecting surface-water bodies is contamination by toxic chemicals or disease organisms. The potential damage associated with a particular compound depends upon its toxicity, solubility, and persistence. In general, the more toxic, soluble, and persistent a compound the greater the potential damage.

The effects of toxic chemicals can be loosely classified as acute effects, which produce an immediate and violent response such as death; and chronic effects, which persist at low levels or may not appear for a long period of time (Clark et al., 1985). Concentrations of toxic chemicals are normally too dilute to produce acute effects. However, storm events or spills can trigger pulses of contaminants that cause massive fish kills. Data from the U.S. Environmental Protection Agency (EPA) (1981), based on reported fish kills in the United States for which the causes were known, indicate that between 1961 and 1980 an average of 1.8 million fish were killed annually by agricultural pesticides, nutrients, or drainage from livestock areas. Two-thirds—an average of 1.2 million fish—were attributed to pesticide contamination.

Chronic effects such as impaired respiration, reproduction, or locomotion are more common. Pesticides with low water solubilities and high fat solubilities, such as organochlorines, can bioaccumulate in the fatty tissues of animals that ingest them. Shellfish have been reported to bioaccumulate pesticides up to 70,000 times the concentration in the surrounding water (Butler, 1966). Concentrations of pesticides in animal tissues can also "biomagnify" or become increasingly concentrated as they are passed up the food chain. A well-known example is DDT, which became concentrated at very high levels in fish-eating ospreys and eagles, causing them to lay thin-shelled eggs that could not hatch (Clark et al., 1985). Pesticides can also indirectly affect aquatic species by reducing food supplies or destroying natural habitat.

Toxic compounds also affect offstream uses of water including drinking water, irrigation, and industrial uses. Pesticide concentrations in drinking water are rarely high enough to cause acute effects; however, there is great uncertainty and concern about chronic effects such as cancer, miscarriage, and mutations. Pesticides are difficult and expensive to detect and remove from drinking water supplies. Home water filtration systems that use activated carbon, distillation, or ion exchange are effective in removing most chemicals from drinking water. However, these systems cost from $500 to $800 to install and annual maintenance costs range from $100 to $350 (Nielsen and Lee, 1987). Pesticides can also create unintended side effects in irrigation water, such as toxic levels of herbicides, which damage crops.

Mineral salts also cause serious offstream impacts. In drinking water, they create health, taste, and corrosion problems. Industrial uses of water are also impacted by corrosion problems, and certain chemical uses are incompatible with high concentrations of dissolved salts. Saline irrigation water is a particular problem. High salt concentrations are toxic to many agricultural crops, and salt concentrations in irrigated soils can build up over time, reducing productivity. Annual salinity damages in the Colorado River system were estimated to range between $75 million and $104 million in 1980, and are predicted to increase to $165 million by the year 2000 (U.S. Department of the Interior and U.S. Department of Agriculture, 1983). Similarly, annual salinity damages in the Murray-Darling River system in Australia have been estimated at A$115 million (about US$100 million) (Murray-Darling Basin Ministerial Council, 1988).

It is extremely difficult and in some cases impossible to estimate the costs associated with all of the instream and offstream impacts caused by agricultural nonpoint pollutants in surface waters. Clark et al. (1985) undertook a comprehensive attempt at quantifying the annual damages caused by nonpoint pollution in the United States. In purely physical terms, they estimated that nonpoint sources dominate point sources, contributing approximately 73 percent of total biochemical-oxygen-demand loads, 99 percent of suspended solids, 83 percent of dissolved solids, 82 percent of nitrogen, 84 percent of phosphorus, and 98 percent of bacteria loads in surface waterways of the United States. Christensen and Ribaudo (1987), in an update of the economic damage estimates made by Clark et al. (1985), estimated total damages that can be quantified at $7.1 billion annually, $2.6 billion of which is attributed to agricultural cropland. Clark et al. (1985) noted that nonquantifiable biological effects resulting from degradation of aquatic habitats might well outweigh any of those that were quantified and that the ranges on the estimates are quite wide.

*Ground-Water Impacts.* Agricultural pollution can also cause serious ground-water contamination problems. Ground-water contamination can arise from both point and nonpoint-sources (Canter et al., 1987). Agricultural nonpoint-source pollutants include nutrients (particularly nitrates), pesticides, mineral salts, heavy metals, and disease pathogens. Agricultural point sources are relatively rare, although agricultural contamination entering ground water via abandoned wells, pesticide spills, or disposal areas may constitute point sources.

Potential ground-water contamination depends upon the pollutant transport and fate in the subsurface environment. The central issue is whether the contaminants will move with the water phase through the unsaturated and saturated zones. Pollutant transport and fate is a complex process that is dependent upon hydrodynamic, abiotic, and biotic processes (Canter et al., 1987).

Ground-water contamination effects are quite similar to offstream impacts of nutrient, pesticide, and mineral salt contamination of surface waters. These contaminations create serious health concerns in drinking water, cause corrosion and chemical reaction problems in domestic and industrial water uses, and can affect the productivity of irrigated lands.

There are no adequate data available on a national or international scale to estimate the extent of ground-water contamination or to assess the impacts of this contamination. It is extremely difficult and expensive to test for contamination, and even more difficult and expensive to ascertain the potential damages associated with various concentrations and mixtures of contaminants. Nielsen and Lee (1987) estimated that first-time monitoring costs for the 50 million people in the United States that depend on ground water would range from $1.0 billion to $2.3 billion. However, more than 60 pesticides have been detected in ground water in 30 states, many at concentrations believed to cause serious chronic health effects (Zinn, 1988). These contamination incidents, although relatively isolated, along with the general level of uncertainty surrounding the extent and potential effects of contamination, have created a great deal of concern over the safety of ground-water supplies and an increase in governmental activity aimed at ground-water quality protection. The EPA is currently testing for 125 pesticides in a nationwide sample of 1,300 drinking-water wells.

## Economics of Prevention, Mitigation, and Treatment of Agricultural Pollution

Agricultural pollution clearly can cause damage to both surface and ground water, and in fact has done so. Conceptually, it is useful to think of these damages as the basis of a demand function for cleaner water (pollution damage mitigation). This composite demand function includes derived demands arising from quality effects on intermediate uses of water (e.g., irrigation, industrial uses, and commercial fishing) and quality effects on final demands for water, such as drinking and recreation. Derived demands for water quality arise from the productivity value of improved water quality in the production process. Thus, the demand for improved water quality is dependent upon the nature of the production process, the value of the product being produced, the costs of other inputs to the process, and the price of improved water quality. For example, the demand for less saline irrigation water is dependent upon the effect of salinity on crop growth, the value of the crop, the cost of substitute inputs such as land or increased quantities of water, and the price of higher quality irrigation water.

Final demands arise from the utility gains associated with improved water quality. For example, recreation use value of water is increased if improved water quality reduces the potential health risks and improves aesthetic aspects of swimming, boating, or other recreational activity. Final demands for improved water quality are dependent upon population, income levels, and the prices of alternative goods. Thus, we would expect the demand for recreation (improved water quality) to increase as population, income, and prices of alternative sources of entertainment increase.

The other half of the conceptual equation is the supply of improved water quality (damage mitigation). Improved water quality, like any other good, costs money to produce. The supply curve reflects the marginal cost of additional improvements in water quality. Water quality can be improved by reducing loadings, delivery rates, or transport rates or by treating the water prior to reuse. Conceptually, the overall supply curve is a composite of the marginal costs of these various processes for producing improved water quality.

The intersection of the demand and supply curves reflects the optimal level of damage mitigation. At this intersection, the marginal value of improved water quality just equals the marginal cost of additional mitigation. Obviously, the optimal level of damage mitigation will vary as the demand and/or the supply curves shift in response to changes in the various underlying parameters.

This conceptual model is quite useful in identifying underlying demand and supply forces; however, there are a number of aspects of the demand and supply of improved water quality that complicate this basic analysis. First, the optimal or efficient solution is dependent upon a particular set of property rights. Bishop and Heberlein (1979) showed that the payment a user would be willing to accept to part with clean water would probably be greater than what he would be willing to pay to acquire a new supply of clean water. The initial allocation of property rights therefore will influence estimates of the demand and supply of water quality improvement. An additional problem is that historically property rights in water quality have not been clearly defined. This issue will be addressed later.

A second complication is that the causes and effects of water pollution are generally separated temporally and spatially. This renders a static framework inadequate for addressing the marginal costs and benefits and greatly complicates the possibility of matching "buyers" and "sellers" in order to carry out the necessary transactions. The irreversibility of damages is also an important temporal concern. Irreversible effects rule out treatment as an option, and the focus normally shifts to prevention via highly reliable mechanisms such as banning chemical use.

A third complicating factor is that many water quality-based goods are public goods or what Randall (1987) would call "nonexclusive" goods. Because it is impossible to collect payments for the provision of nonexclusive goods, they cannot be offered in private markets. Nonexclusivity introduces a number of issues including how to determine the socially optimal level of the good to provide, how to provide it, and how to pay for it.

Finally, the overall lack of information about water quality damages and the costs of water quality improvement introduces tremendous uncertainty. This uncertainty limits the willingness of private individuals to participate in "market transactions" and introduces a safety-first perspective as the public strives to achieve an acceptable level of reliability (Milon and Boggess, 1988). Thus, as uncertainty increases there is a tendency to focus on prevention rather than treatment and to employ more reliable control mechanisms.

The complexity of the demand for and the supply of improved water quality suggests that a private market institution is inadequate for solving many water quality problems. As a result, numerous other approaches have been, and probably will continue to be, used to deal with particular problems. These options include education, technical assistance, cost sharing, cross-compliance, effluent taxes, tradable discharge permits, regulation, and direct contracts such as public purchase.

Because people respond to private incentives, the key is to determine an institutional framework that provides the incentives necessary to achieve the desired level of damage mitigation in an economically efficient manner and that results in the desired distribution of benefits and costs. This is obviously a very difficult task to which we now turn our attention.

## INSTITUTIONAL CONTEXT

Water quality is a problem for agriculture because of competing rights to those attributes of water that create utility. When farms are the polluting source it means that farmers have exercised a right to employ water to enhance plant growth, carry needed chemicals to the plant, and to carry off residuals. Although the latter function may be unintended, it is a use nonetheless and it imposes limits on other users. The polluting farmer may be exercising a legitimate right to use the ground or surface source but in the process is limiting the options available to others. Those experiencing reduction in water access may well press their concerns and promote changes in water quality policy. Policy, then, is the consequence of competing claims—a setting of the balance at some point representing the relative "power" of the competitors. Changes in water quality policy entail redefinition of property rights to water— a change in ownership reflecting relative capacity of competitors to impose cost on others. Change requires conflict—a difference of opinion on water use; in policy, as in physics, a body at rest tends to remain at rest.

"Reasonable use" is the prevailing doctrine for rights to both ground and surface sources of water. There are variations, and volumes of case law, but basically a farmer or anyone else has reasonable access to water under or abutting his or her land. Reasonableness is a moving target, a product of competing claims and the value or intensity of those claims. A farmer whose irrigation or pesticide application deprives a nearby subdivision of adequate or acceptable drinking water will create conflict. If conflict happens often, with enough people, rule changes may be expected. Those harmed gain access to legal processes by which ownership is defined. "To own is to coerce, to create costs for others. It is to be able to choose without the consent of others when your acts impinge on others" (Schmid, 1988, p. 14). Rights to water and other resources are not absolute but a consequence of political and economic bargaining within a defined institutional structure.

### Levels of Government

Policy changes (redefinitions of ownership) for water quality come at all levels of government. In the United States, local governments have been particularly active in protecting ground-water supplies. Because the basic strategy for avoiding future contamination is to physically separate potential polluters from ground-water recharge zones, local governments have both authority and tradition for regulating land-use patterns. Specific local land-use actions targeted at ground-water protection have generally come within a state ground-water program. Location of waste disposal sites, regulation of underground storage tanks, and general source reduction efforts tend to be state level initiatives. Nearly all states in the United States have some sort of ground-water protection program. Thirty-six states have pesticide regulations (Crutchfield, 1988).

The particular program emerging in any state is a function of the severity, urgency, and visibility of the ground-water problem and the general political setting in that state. Acceptable actions in one setting may be totally inappropriate in another. Differences in culture, history, and basic values help determine policy differences among nations or regions. Willingness of citizens to bear the risk of future contamination is influenced by the general economic situation. In a poor or high-growth region, returns from development can weigh heavily against alleged need for protection. Where perceived returns from pesticides and fertilizers are high, controls in the interest of avoiding possible future problems will be difficult to accomplish. A recent assessment by the U.S. National Research Council (1986) acknowledges state differences with respect to ground-water situations, but urges all states to establish a defensible data system for supply and quality characteristics to assure that appropriate action can be defined and taken.

National water quality programs in the United States have emphasized protecting public drinking water supplies and regulations on potential contaminants. Agricultural pesticides are given special attention in those regulations and are likely candidates for even closer scrutiny in the future (Carriker, 1988). Provisions of the Soil and Water Resources Conservation Act of 1977 and, more recently, the conservation provisions of the 1985 Food Security Act increase the scrutiny of agriculture as a polluter of ground and surface waters. In 1986, the U.S. Department of Agriculture (USDA) formally adopted regulations to reduce agriculture's contribution to nonpoint and ground-water contamination problems. A recent cooperative agreement between the Soil Conservation Service and Federal Extension, both in USDA, focuses on educational programming regarding agriculture's contribution to water pollution. The 1987 Clean Water Act mandates state action to reduce nonpoint contamination sources, with little direction as to how to do this or who should pay for it (Braden, 1988).

Whatever the level of government involved, the basic purpose of these programs is to reconcile the interests and rights of those creating a potential hazard with those who may bear the consequence of dirty water. Neither set of rights is absolute, and expectations are under constant adjustment as information is assembled by competing water users. When polluter and pollutee are geographically close, local governments may best be able to establish rules of action that will avoid relying on common law court action in every case. States must act when problems cross local boundaries or are so poorly defined that there is real doubt as to whose rights or actions are really involved within a state. National action is essential for problems that cross state boundaries or for compelling immediate threats to public safety that require national responses. Pollution of rivers and harbors seems to require federal action to assemble competing water-use claims.

Nonpoint sources are by nature diffuse and often poorly defined, therefore they are often a focus for federal action. Beneficiaries of abatement are also broadly distributed. It is probably unreasonable to expect an agricultural jurisdiction to enact abatement measures sufficient to produce adequate water quality benefits for downstream users in other jurisdictions.

## Economics and Institutional Design

Reducing agricultural pollution of both ground and surface waters has major economic implications. Pollution is an expensive problem, but abatement can be expensive as well. Economists can help define the efficiency questions of marginal cost and marginal returns to abatement or pollution. At some level of abatement, the cost of an additional increment of purity exceeds the gain from that increment. There are few absolutes in the political economy. The ubiquitous law of diminishing returns applies to investment in clean water as to other unquestioned societal "goods." We can make a logical defense of incentive approaches that force the polluter to bear the full cost of the polluting action, thus creating a new cost curve for the related product or service. We can encourage quasi-market arrangements that enable competitors for water services to bid for water rights.

Economics is a useful, even essential, discipline for clarifying the conditions that lead to environmental degradation and the likely performance of ways to alter polluter behavior. Effective policy requires specific attention to incentives that face both polluter and pollutee. Despite all of this, economics and economists have emerged as the "bad guys" in pollution debates, and a sharp dichotomy is asserted between economics and environment. Not so. Economics as a discipline is confused with certain ramifications of selected markets, as if all economists are apologists for all markets with whatever environmental impacts. There are important distinctions between economics and business. Market-defined economic efficiency is *not* the inviolate normative goal of all resource allocation processes. Opportunity cost and marginality are important concepts to clarify the consequence of actions to reduce pollution, but it does not necessarily follow that water should be used to generate the highest possible monetary return per increment. By the same token, other agricultural scientists—those in physical and biological fields— must avoid the temptation to be apologists for farmers, as if anything a farmer does with or to water is defensible.

The most useful function for economics and economists in policy attempts to reduce agricultural water pollution is to measure or clarify distributional implications of alternative means for allocating water rights. Monetary returns to water in various uses is part of the picture, but policy decisionmakers need better information about who pays and who gains (in a broad sense) from policy options designed to reconcile competing claims for clean water. "Efficient" distribution of water to the highest monetary bidder is but one allocation scheme. Each pollution abatement option implies distribution of abatement cost and an initial distribution of water rights. "Who must come to whom" is an important attribute distinguishing policy options. Choices for dealing with surface-water pollution will be different from those for ground-water problems.

*Regulations.* The regulatory approach to pollution abatement implies that the right to use water in ways that diminish its utility to others is transferred from water user to a public acting on behalf of other water users. Obligation replaces privilege. The assumption is that inconvenience to the polluter is more than offset by improvements to health and safety of other water users, with overall net benefit. Reasonableness of a water quality regulation depends on clear evidence that limiting the water rights for a former user will in fact enable an improvement in water quality and that public health and safety are at risk. Regulation must not be arbitrary and must be uniformly applied.

Most experience with environmental regulation applies to specific point source contaminants, such as underground storage tanks, waste disposal sites, and toxic substances, that may enter the water at some time. Nonpoint agricultural sources are less susceptible to regulation because the economic and technical link between the transfer of property rights and desired change in water quality is difficult to establish. Further, acceptable nonpoint regulations are difficult to implement because those who gain are often separated in time and distance from those whose water use is apparently creating the problem. Mandatory management practices may be imposed in a well-defined watershed (Davenport, 1988), although most river systems require more imaginative arrangements by which those who benefit from a new regulation may compensate those who are hurt by that rule change (Park and Shabman, 1982). Land-use regulation (zoning) may be used to limit accepted uses to those that will protect water quality.

Economic analysis of existing or proposed regulations must address the monetary impact of the transfer as income forgone when opportunities for the water user are adjusted. If a citrus grower in southwest Florida loses the right to apply fertilizer with irrigation water, an alternative technology must be used involving a measurable economic consequence. Impacts will vary among users when an administrative standard is applied. There are also enforcement costs, perhaps including a water quality monitoring system and legal costs in bringing polluters to justice. In Connecticut, for example, a farmer may be required to provide an alternative water source if well contamination can be attributed to a specific farm. Proposition 65 in California may require food processors to warn consumers of health risks associated with certain farm chemicals (Phipps, 1988). These are costly regulations to administer.

From an efficiency standpoint, costs of acquiring a given change in water quality through regulations may be compared to costs of alternative methods. Policymakers will also want to know who pays that cost—large or small farms, citrus or dairy, south or north.

*Taxes and Other Monetary Incentives.* An alternative to regulation is to charge or subsidize those water-using actions that generate costs or benefits for others. The idea is that augmented self-interest *within* an existing distribution of property rights will entail social utility as well. Braden (1988) identified the primary options as fees on polluting inputs, fees on outputs, cross-compliance, and abatement subsidies. Iowa has imposed a tax of 75 cents per ton on fertilizer, with proceeds used to fund quality monitoring and research on sustainable agriculture. Sweden uses a fertilizer tax for a similar purpose. The amounts are arbitrary, not defensible measures of the social cost of fertilizer use. But the principle is established—the right to use fertilizer entails an obligation to help cope with the full consequence of the use. It is conceivable that increased cost of that input will reduce application rates, depending on returns involved.

The administrative challenge of constructing a fee schedule that is tied to real social cost is practically insurmountable. Although there is little real experience with tax schemes, Seitz et al. (1979) used a linear programming model of hypothetical farms representing western Illinois agriculture to conclude that a soil loss tax would be "more efficient" than a regulation in reducing erosion.

Cross-compliance methods provide a different kind of inducement for those private choices preferred for their social consequence. Eligibility for certain types of public assistance could be contingent upon making land-use decisions that protect water quality. Decisions remain with land users, but they must consider a set of administered "prices" on the use options that include the broader impacts. In the United States, focus on water quality decisions could be added fairly easily to the conservation cross-compliance provisions of the 1985 Food Security Act. Protection of ground-water recharge zones and reduction of nonpoint runoff could also lend themselves to cross-compliance techniques.

Subsidy approaches, closely related to outright acquisition, seek to induce quality protection through positive incentives. Landowners may be eligible for an interest rate subsidy or credit for quality protecting actions, or an administered price advantage for minimum tillage or low production systems that make limited use of purchased inputs.

Analysis of monetary incentive approaches must examine the extent to which those incentives are adequate to induce or acquire needed behavioral change by water users. Is there producer surplus involved where water quality improvements could actually be induced at lower cost or consumer surplus where willingness of the general public to buy water quality enhancement is greater than the price charged or offered to farmers? Assumptions about initial distribution of property rights obviously differ between regulatory and incentive approaches to water quality improvement and could affect the result when choices made by individual managers are the key ingredients of success. Relative bargaining position, "who must come to whom," could be important. A farmer may be more responsive to attempts to deprive him of an option he already has (cross-compliance) than attempts to "bribe" him to do something different (subsidy). Cross-compliance is fruitless when the target land users are not eligible for the benefit programs to begin with. Part of the price of water quality enhancement may be reduced performance of the program used as the compliance inducement. A disaster relief program is supposed to help farmers in times of dire need. Lost eligibility because of a water quality goal could leave a farmer in the depths of crisis. "Good riddance," perhaps, but the intent and political rationale of the original program have been thwarted. Further, correspondence between distributions of pollution and program participation will influence performance of compliance measures.

Beyond the efficiency question—how much quality improvement at what price (including administrative cost)—there are important distributional implications here as well. Farmers being taxed or losing eligibility for current programs are clearly paying a larger portion of the clean water bill than those being enticed by positive inducements. Water rights are transferred from farmers to the public in cross-compliance cases, whereas they stay with the farmer in subsidy cases. Determining which distribution is "fair" is problematic—equity in policy matters is a moving target. But those distributional consequences must be defined, and economists are the ones to do it.

*Acquisition.* An alternative to simply taking (regulation) or inducing transfer (tax or subsidy) of rights to clean water is for a public to buy those rights. Acquisition may be for full or partial rights to the land uses that affect water quality. Once acquired, those rights may be exercised by a public manager to assure water quality. Perhaps the best way to assure adequate ground-water recharge areas is to buy the critical land and permit only those uses consistent with safe recharge. Less than full rights could be purchased with a negative easement or another instrument that provides the desired land-use restrictions while remaining rights stay on the local tax rolls. The Land and Water Conservation Fund has been used to acquire land for wildlife habitat in the United States; it could also be used for critical recharge zones or very erosive lands near rivers.

Transfer of development rights (TDR) could be adapted to water quality objectives. Essentially, those whose land may be sold for high value development must also acquire a development right from an owner whose land is to be protected for recharge. Dade County, Florida, and Southampton Township on Long Island, New York, have used TDR for water quality purposes.

The Conservation Reserve Program (CRP) of the 1985 Food Security Act provides the United States a means for leasing certain land-use rights from farmers to reduce soil erosion. This approach could be extended to important ground-water recharge areas, and has been used for filter strips to reduce nonpoint pollution of rivers, streams, and lakes (Carriker, 1988). There is also discussion of extending CRP to saline cropland that may pollute nearby water (Aillery, 1988).

Acquisition is a more straightforward policy approach than the others. Taxpayers compensate the farmer or other landowner for rights transferred at a level that presumably captures the value of any forgone opportunities. Government could always employ the power of eminent domain if critical land could not be bought in an "arms-length" transaction, with a fair price established administratively. Timeliness is particularly important in this approach. Acquisition of open land must anticipate the possibility of future ground or surface-water quality problems, not wait until development is imminent and land values have escalated. Distributional aspects favor the owner of critical land. Rights actually transferred, with appropriate indication in the deed, could not be taxed by the local government, adding to the overall administrative cost involved.

*Research and Education.* Timely transfer of accurate and usable information can affect behavior. Education may not transfer property rights or substantively alter the opportunity sets of polluters or pollutees in competition for the services of water, but it helps them clarify their options and their places in the policy process. Many people *do* acknowledge responsibility for the well-being of their friends and neighbors. A sense of obligation may be transferred with the knowledge that one's actions substantially affect other people. Land stewardship remains the bulwark of soil conservation policy. In the face of compelling evidence that most soil conservation practices contribute little net monetary return to farmers, many farmers continue to invest in conservation. There is nothing "uneconomic" about that. Real people know better than some academics that the utility functions of people are tightly intertwined.

As with other policy options, research and education may be analyzed for their performance characteristics. How much water quality improvement can be bought with studies and educational programs that enhance understanding of the sources, consequences, and institutional context of water pollution? We have little available evidence. Education is a major part of the ground-water quality programs in most areas. On a global scale, education has been a major component of development efforts supporting sustainable production systems (World Commission on Environment and Development, 1987). The United States has recently attempted to develop a national extension program in ground-water quality policy, but performance of that component of an overall policy program would be difficult to specify.

*Policy Mix.* Various strategies have been employed to affect the water-use opportunities for farmers in ways that will improve or protect water choices of others. Any strategy will probably employ a combination of restrictions, bribes, threats, pleadings, and promises to get the attention of the water user whose actions are crucial to water quality. No single set of instruments works for all circumstances or all occasions. In the final analysis, good policy is acceptable policy, and standards of acceptability vary with demographics, problem urgency, information, and even the persuasiveness of a few individuals.

There is no "correct" approach from an economic standpoint. Economists disagree about as much as any group on how to deal with the agricultural pollution issue (or any other policy issue). The generalization that "economists will give more weight to . . . remedies that mimic market processes, environmentalists to finding equitable ones from political processes. . . . [T]his predisposes economists to recommend tax and subsidy and environmentalists to favor regulation" (Crosson and Phipps, 1986, p. 282) is hard to swallow. There is no such dichotomy, and no reason to limit economists' options. In the first place, economics is a discipline—an analytical and conceptual apparatus for organizing information for choice. "Environmentalist" characterizes people of any intellectual persuasion who happen to be interested in a particular set of issues. An economist working for the government budgeting office may draw a quite different inference from a given data set than one with the same scientific training and integrity working for an environmental organization or the agency in charge of environmental programs. One is an environmentalist, the other less so. Both of them vote, pay taxes, participate in markets, and support causes. Both understand economic performance and have observed impact at some measured consequence to participants. *All* policy prescriptions are value based, implying who should pay, whose options are expanded, and whose options are confined to achieve observable change. Economists should not allow their discipline to limit their contributions to dealing with water pollution or other social problems. Efficiency concepts, including market failure, are useful to clarify problems but lack prescriptive power of their own.

## FUTURE DIRECTIONS

There are several water quality issues that social scientists interested in agriculture will be dealing with in coming years. To a considerable extent, the list of options is shaped by larger forces in the political economy. These are predictions, not statements of preference; their order here does not imply priority.

## Water Quality Consequences of Alternative Production Technologies

The adoption of alternative production technologies has the potential to reduce agriculture's impact on water quality by changing the quantities, composition, and/or timing of agricultural wasteflows. Biotechnology, in particular, has the potential to provide agriculture with inputs that have fewer byproducts with negative effects on the environment and human health (Offutt et al., 1988). The rate of development and adoption of technologies, and the nature of those technologies, depend on the incentives provided by the marketplace as well as by the institutional environment. Environmental regulation of existing inputs will accelerate the development of more benign technologies.

Tauer (1988) recently appraised current and emerging technologies in agriculture to determine which technologies may have significant impacts on water quality and to identify areas where additional economic research is warranted. Two comprehensive U.S. agricultural technology assessment efforts (Lu, 1983; U.S. Congress, 1986) provided the basis for Tauer's appraisal. These assessments identified the likely impacts of the technology on productivity, resource use, and the environment. From these impacts, Tauer identified water and irrigation management as the technology with the highest priority for economic research. Biological nitrogen fixation, plant pest control strategies, minimum tillage, multiple cropping, and animal growth hormones followed in order as priorities.

Tauer followed up his ranking by reviewing the economic literature to determine the extent to which economic research has been conducted on each of the priority technologies. He identified significant economic research gaps in the areas of the economic value of biological nitrogen fixation; the water quality impact of emerging biotechnology pest control mechanisms and the impact of this technology on the structure of farms and the input supply industry; the farm structure impact of minimum tillage; and the impacts of animal growth hormones. Tauer also recommended that technology forecasting and assessment be considered as important as commodity forecasting in providing critical information to decisionmakers.

Despite the fact that much research has been completed on both the farm management and structural issues of irrigation, there remains a significant gap in our knowledge base. Additional research is needed on the relationship between water and irrigation management and water quality impacts.

## Understanding Acceptable Risk:
## Cost versus Benefits of Reducing Pollution

The term "acceptable risk" suggests a process by which the trade-offs between the costs and benefits of reducing or preventing water contamination are discussed in a rational fashion. In reality, the very concept is highly controversial. Some environmentalists argue that acknowledging certain levels of contamination as economically acceptable fails to appropriately stigmatize polluting behavior. They argue for zero-tolerance or zero-discharge types of regulations. On the other hand, some agricultural interests argue that there is no justification for imposing costly controls when the benefits are so highly uncertain.

Unfortunately, discussions in the middle ground are also dominated by the lack of information about the trade-offs involved. Serious knowledge gaps exist in at least four key areas. First, our ability to detect and measure chemical concentrations far exceeds our understanding of their significance. Second, the effects of low-dose, extended exposure toxicities are very difficult to evaluate, particularly when the resultant health problems are characterized by long latency periods. Third, the toxicities of mixtures of chemicals and the synergistic effects of combined chemical exposures greatly complicate evaluation of the potential health impacts. Finally, information is scarce on the cost and efficacy of alternative control strategies, particularly given the site-specific nature of many contamination problems.

Two additional characteristics of the general populations' perceptions of risk also complicate the discussion of trade-offs. First, people are generally much more tolerant of and willing to undertake "natural" risks as opposed to "unnatural," or man-made, risks (Lawrence, 1976). In a similar vein, they are more tolerant of and willing to take voluntary risks than involuntary risks (Starr, 1972). Chemical contamination problems are generally characterized as imposing involuntary, unnatural risks.

Reliability theory (Heiner, 1983) suggests that when faced with high levels of uncertainty, people will select actions that provide a high degree of reliability. This suggests that the uncertainty surrounding the trade-offs involved in determining levels of acceptable risk limits the willingness of private individuals to participate in market transactions and introduces a safety-first perspective as the public strives to achieve an acceptable level of reliability. This also suggests that as our knowledge base concerning chemical contamination grows, the general public will be increasingly willing to evaluate cost/benefit trade-offs when establishing levels of acceptable risk.

## Need for Further Disciplinary Work

The economics of water use in agriculture and its relationship to water quality consists of three major components: (1) the demand for water (quantity and quality), (2) the supply of water (quantity and quality), and (3) institutions for allocating water (quantity and quality) and for resolving disputes. Major gaps in our knowledge base exist for each of these components.

Our biggest disciplinary challenge in demand is how to value nonmarket goods. At one extreme is the problem of how to value a human life or the costs of reduced health. At the other is the problem of determining the value of an increase in recreational fishing success rates or some other marginal change in optional activities. Both present difficult conceptual and methodological issues. Further research and development of contingent valuation, experimental economics, and opportunity costs, as well as exploration of new and innovative valuation techniques are needed.

Water quality supply is characterized by tremendous uncertainty. The lack of information and complexity of the supply situation presents major challenges. The costs of testing and monitoring to determine the current supply situation are exorbitant, which makes it difficult to assess even the status quo. In addition, the spatial and temporal variability of water quality problems often dictates that water quality improvement techniques have to be site specific. Our challenge is to find cost-effective ways of assessing water quality supply relationships in order to determine cost/benefit trade-offs and to prioritize water quality solutions.

Greater disciplinary investment also is needed in the design and analysis of water management institutions. Institutions establish the context for individual and collective choice in water use. Improved understanding of behavioral responses to the complex incentives that influence action will require greater investments in social psychology and related social science disciplines. Without undertaking this important interdisciplinary work, the likelihood of institutional development based on some understanding of anticipated performance is remote indeed. We must improve on the general trial and error approach. It is simply too costly. Economists must improve methods for measuring both the efficiency and distributional performance of existing water institutions, and combine those results with accurate behavioral predictions in developing new water quality institutions.

## The Changing Politics of Agriculture in the United States

Political scientist William Browne has characterized agricultural politics as "meandering" and "fragmented" (Browne, 1988b, p. 136). There is a certain aimlessness implied by that statement that may be a disservice to those who are actually gaining control. Traditional elements of the agricultural policy power cluster have less control of the agenda than they have had in the past. This is not a sudden change, although certain legislative actions seem to consolidate and formalize incremental adjustments over time. Rather, it is the inevitable consequence of a whole complex of economic and demographic changes in the United States (Browne, 1988a; Tweeten, 1979). The question of immediate interest concerns the impact on agricultural water quality issues of the future. The focus is on U.S. policy; similar inference may be drawn for other nations as well.

*Natural Resource Issues in Food Policy.* In the United States, the 1985 Food Security Act is a landmark legislative acknowledgment that resource quality and food production are parts of the same process (Ogg, 1988). There is just no way that resource issues can be kept out of the agricultural policy debates. Benbrook (1988) felt that successful farm legislation must incorporate natural resource components. Basically, the word is out: agriculture has damaged the land and water, making it less available for other people. Agriculture has contributed good things, too, of course, but damage is undeniable. Manifestation of that fact in the policy process varies importantly from one level of government to another.

   Government agencies know how to survive in a changing environment. This survival instinct is an important aspect of the adaptive capability of our policy process. When the on-farm consequence of soil erosion seems to lack sufficient urgency to sustain programs, the Soil Conservation Service alertly raises the priority of off-farm water quality impacts of erosion. The Environmental Protection Agency has discovered agriculture and is working on a colloquial style to improve its communications with USDA professionals. The Food and Drug Administration is paying more attention to agriculture as well. The professional cadre that does the work of governance— in agencies, research foundations, interest groups, and congressional committees—flows easily among those components of the agricultural policy power cluster. They are well-educated, articulate, "white collar" types who can readily accept the linkage between farm production and water quality. Many try to retain empathy with people and problems back home, but they basically are part of the homogeneous professional governing establishment.

   Bureaucracy is an essential component of any organized society; similar patterns evolve in most countries. Each area of policy has its small group of skilled influential professionals who accomplish the work of government. They draft the legislation, prepare the testimony, advise the decisionmakers, even deliver the necessary support. They know each other, meet frequently, and, although there will be important differences in priority, generally agree on the basic outcomes of the process. Among this group, the water quality problems of agriculture are accepted facts. The agricultural and environmental staff specialists have far more in common than at difference, and frequently exchange roles just to prove it. In government, then, the natural resource/agriculture linkage is readily accepted.

There is far less consensus out in the countryside. "Environmentalist" is still a dirty word for many commercial agriculture groups in the rural towns and state capitals around the United States. And agriculture is viewed as unresponsive and insensitive by many in natural resource groups or agencies. Debates can be strident, agreements few. That is where policy changes really have impact—where one person loses rights and another gains. Those transfers are simply not felt as keenly at the national level. Many farm and producer groups doubt the validity of environmental concerns and pass them off as the ravings of ill-informed zealots who "have never made a payroll." There is a fortress mentality as farm groups erect various defenses to fend off the irresponsible do-gooders challenging their livelihood. They cannot hold these concerns back for long, of course, and there will be resource quality actions in state and local policies, but they will not come easily.

The land grant universities are to some extent caught in the middle. The changing political economy of each state creates new needs and problems to be analyzed. The resource consequences of advanced-technology agriculture are among them. Scientists, faculty, and college administrators must respond to remain relevant to the most compelling challenges of the times, yet agricultural support is essential for their very survival. As public funding of land grant universities diminishes, colleges of agriculture are increasingly dependent on outside funding. But there is no obvious funding source for treating the resource quality problems from farming. By its very nature, water quality enhancement lacks the well-organized self-interest that tends to generate research grants to universities. Funding for new crop varieties, new pesticides, or new farm equipment is more likely to generate measurable return for the grantor. To the extent that soft money influences research priority, and it does, land grants will find themselves in an even tighter spot. The greatest hazard is that we become fragmented and meandering ourselves, squabbling along disciplinary and departmental lines over what our obligations really are. Articulate leadership for the overall mission of the land grant university has never been more important.

*Polluter Pays.* An inevitable result of the changing mix of rural population, more diverse agricultural politics, and evidence of agricultural pollution will be greater shifting of responsibility for abatement to the farmer. The mix of policy will favor mandatory controls over education and subsidy. Farmers are simply going to have fewer resource use options than they have had in the past. This change results less from anything the farmer has done than from the changing situation around him. It is not that farmers are less concerned about resources than they used to be, or that production technologies have become more damaging, but that more people are aware of agricultural pollution and will expect the farmer to do things differently.

## CONCLUSIONS: THE ROLE FOR RESOURCE ECONOMISTS

Our greatest challenge is to clarify the consequences of the physical and biological reality that farming affects water quality. We need to continue measuring the economic losses attributed to dirty water and the cost of alternative abatement strategies. Economists must give particular attention to distributional characteristics of the institutional devices used to "get the farmer's attention." A water quality standard imposed on all users evenly imposes very different impacts on different users. An understanding of basic property rights and other institutions within a given economic system is essential for effective work.

The same scrutiny must be given to water quality impacts of agriculture in developing countries. U.S. policies have encouraged or at least permitted agricultural practices that have literally destroyed productive resources in other countries. Environmental problems can be a major source of social conflict in the development process. Resource stability and political stability interact (World Commission on Environment and Development, 1987). Economists have the crucial role in examining the overall economic consequences of agricultural development.

Economists can also help articulate "the commons" in water quality—the gains to society beyond the immediate financial interests of water users. Security and a general sense of well-being require a safe, clean supply of water. Resource economists must be the renaissance social scientists, responding to the eclecticism that defines our subdiscipline. The burden is great indeed.

## NOTE

This chapter is Florida Experiment Station Journal Series No. R-00026. Review comments by John Braden, University of Ilinois; Linda Lee, University of Connecticut; and Donald Rosenthal, U.S. Department of Interior are gratefully acknowledged.

## REFERENCES

Aillery, M. 1988. "Water Quality and the Conservation Reserve Program: Implications of Targeting Saline Croplands." In *Nonpoint Pollution: 1988— Policy Economy, Management and Appropriate Technology*, ed. V. Novotny, pp. 261–270. Bethesda, MD: American Water Resources Association.

Batie, S. 1988. "Agriculture as the Problem: The Case of Groundwater." *Choices* 3(3):4–7.

Benbrook, C. 1988. "The Environment in the 1990 Farm Bill." *Journal of Soil and Water Conservation* 43(6):440–443.

Bishop, R. C., and T. A. Heberlein. 1979. "Measuring the Values of Extra Market Goods: Are Indirect Measures Biased?" *American Journal of Agricultural Economics* 61:926–930.

Braden, J. 1988. "Nonpoint Pollution Policies and Politics: The Role of Economic Incentives." In *Nonpoint Pollution: 1988—Policy, Economy, Management, and Appropriate Technology*, ed. V. Novotny, pp. 57–66. Bethesda, MD: American Water Resources Association.

Browne, W. 1988a. *Private Interests, Public Policy and American Agriculture.* Lawrence, KS: University of Kansas Press.

———. 1988b. "The Fragmented and Meandering Politics of Agriculture." In *U.S. Agriculture in a Global Setting, an Agenda for the Future*, ed. A. Tutwiler, pp. 136–153. Washington, DC: Resources for the Future.

Butler, P. A. 1966. "Pesticides in the Marine Environment." *Journal of Applied Ecology 3* (Supplement):253–259.

Canter, L. W., R. C. Knox, and D. M. Fairchild. 1987. *Ground Water Quality Protection.* Chelsea, MI: Lewis Publishers, Inc.

Carriker, R. 1988. "Water Issues: How We Got Here and What Others Are Doing." In *Water Quality and Soil Conservation: Conflict of Rights Issues*, Special Report 394, pp. 21–31. Columbia, MO: Missouri Agricultural Experiment Station.

Christensen, D. A., and M. O. Ribaudo. 1987. "How to Slow a 175-Tons-a-Second Landslide." In *Our American Land, 1987 Yearbook of Agriculture*, pp. 185–194. Washington, DC: U.S. Department of Agriculture.

Clark, E. H. II, J. A. Haverkamp, and W. Chapman. 1985. *Eroding Soils, The Off-Farm Impacts.* Washington, DC: The Conservation Foundation.

Crosson, P. R., and T. T. Phipps. 1986. "Lessons for Policy Analysis." In *Agriculture and the Environment*, pp. 276–295. Washington, DC: Resources for the Future.

Crutchfield, S. 1988. "Effects on U.S. Water Resources of Agricultural Chemicals and Run-off: Magnitude, Extent, and Economic Consequences." In *Nonpoint Pollution: 1988—Quality, Economy, Management, and Appropriate Technology*, ed. V. Novotny, pp. 39–48. Bethesda, MD: American Water Resources Association.

Davenport, T. 1988. "Nonpoint Source Regulation—A Watershed Approach." In *Nonpoint Pollution: 1988—Policy, Economy, Management, and Appropriate Technology*, ed. V. Novotny, pp. 117–122. Bethesda, MD: American Water Resources Association.

Day, J. C., and G. L. Horner. 1987. *U.S. Irrigation: Extent and Economic Importance.* Agricultural Information Bulletin No. 523. Washington, DC: U.S. Department of Agriculture, Economic Research Service.

Georgescu-Roegen, N. 1972. "Process Analysis and the Neoclassical Theory of Production." *American Journal of Agricultural Economics* 54:279–294.

Guldin, R. W. 1988. *An Analysis of the Water Situation in the United States, 1989–2040: A Technical Document Supporting the 1989 RPA Assessment.* Washington, DC: U.S. Department of Agriculture, Forest Service.

Heiner, R. A. 1983. "The Origin of Predictable Behavior." *American Economic Review* 73(4):560–595.

Lawrence, W. 1976. *Of Acceptable Risk: Science and the Determination of Safety.* Los Altos, CA: William Kaufman, Inc.

Lu, Y. 1983. *Emerging Technologies in Agricultural Production.* Washington, DC: U.S. Department of Agriculture, Cooperative State Research Service.

Milon, W. J., and W. G. Boggess. 1988. "The Implications of Reliability Theory for Environmental Design and Decision Making." *American Journal of Agricultural Economics* 70(5):1107–1112.

Murray-Darling Basin Ministerial Council. 1988. *Draft Salinity and Drainage Strategy.* Discussion Paper No. 1, Canberra, Australia.

National Research Council. 1986. *Groundwater Quality Protection: State and Local Strategies.* Washington, DC: National Academy Press.

Nielsen, E. G., and L. K. Lee. 1987. *The Magnitude and Costs of Groundwater Contamination from Agricultural Chemicals: A National Perspective.* Agr. Econ. Rept. No. 576. Washington, DC: U.S. Department of Agriculture, Economic Research Service.

Offutt, S., F. Kuchler, and J. McClelland. 1988. "Genetic Engineering: The Value of Science Under Surplus," *Forum for Applied Research and Public Policy* 3(2):104–112.

Ogg, C. 1988. *The Conservation Title of the Food Security Act of 1985.* Washington, DC: U.S. Department of Agriculture, Economic Research Service.

Park, W., and L. Shabman. 1982. "Distributional Constraints on Acceptance of Nonpoint Pollution Controls." *American Journal of Agricultural Economics* 64(3):455–462.

Phipps, T. 1988. "Some Rays of Hope for Agriculture and the Environment." In *U.S. Agriculture in a Global Setting, an Agenda for the Future*, ed. A. Tutwiler, pp. 186–202. Washington, DC: Resources for the Future.

Randall, A. 1987. *Resource Economics: An Economic Approach to Natural Resource and Environmental Policy.* 2nd Edition. New York: John Wiley & Son.

Ribaudo, M. 1986. *Reducing Soil Erosion: Offsite Benefits.* Agr. Econ. Rept. No. 561. Washington, DC: U.S. Department of Agriculture, Economic Research Service.

Schmid, A. A. 1988. "The Idea of Property: A Way to Think About Soil and Water Issues." In *Water Quality and Soil Conservation: Conflict of Rights Issues*, Special Report 394, pp. 14–20. Columbia, MO: Missouri Agricultural Experiment Station.

Seitz, W., C. Osteen, and M. Nelson. 1979. "Economic Impacts of Policies to Control Erosion and Sedimentation in Illinois and Other Corn Belt States." In *Best Management Practices for Agriculture and Silviculture*, pp. 373–382. Ann Arbor, MI: Ann Arbor Science Publishers.

Starr, C. 1972. "Benefit-Cost Studies in Sociotechnical Systems." In *Perspectives in*

*Risk Benefit Decision Making.* Washington, DC: National Academy of Engineering, Committee on Public Engineering Policy.

Tauer, L. W. 1988. *The Assessment of Economic Impacts of Current and Emerging Agricultural Technologies That Affect Water Quality,* A.E. Res. 88–14. Ithaca, NY: Cornell University, Department of Agricultural Economics.

Tweeten, L. 1979. *Foundation of Farm Policy.* Lincoln, NE: University of Nebraska.

U.S. Congress. 1986. *Technology, Public Policy, and the Changing Structure of American Agriculture,* Office of Technology Assessment, OTA-F-285. Washington, DC: U.S. Government Printing Office.

U.S. Department of the Interior and U.S. Department of Agriculture. 1983. Final Environmental Statement, Colorado River Water Quality Improvement Program. Washington, DC.

U.S. Environmental Protection Agency. 1981. *Fish Kills by Source of Pollution, 1961–1980,* EPA-440/4-79-024. Washington, DC: U.S. Government Printing Office.

Wischmeier, W. H., and D. D. Smith. 1978. *Predicting Rainfall-Erosion Losses: A Guide to Conservation Planning,* Agr. Handbook No. 537. Washington, DC: U.S. Department of Agriculture.

World Commission on Environment and Development. 1987. *Our Common Future.* New York, NY: Oxford Press.

World Resources Institute. 1988. *World Resources—1988–89.* New York: Basic Books, United Nations Environmental Programme.

Yaron, D. 1986. "Economic Aspects of Irrigation with Saline Water." In *Irrigation Management in Developing Countries,* eds. Kenneth C. Nobe and R. K. Sampath. Boulder, CO: Westview Press.

Young, R. A., and G. L. Horner. 1986. "Irrigated Agriculture and Mineralized Water." *The National Center For Food and Agricultural Policy: Annual Policy Review 1986,* pp. 77–113. Washington, DC: Resources for the Future.

Zinn, J. A. 1988. *Ground Water Issues in the U.S. Department of Agriculture—An Institutional Perspective,* 88-322 ENR. Washington, DC: Library of Congress, Congressional Research Service.

# TWO

# Incentive Policies for Control of Agricultural Water Pollution

KATHLEEN SEGERSON

Water pollution from agriculture can take several forms, including surface-water pollution from runoff of soil, pesticides, fertilizer, or manure, and ground-water pollution from leaching of pesticides and fertilizer. A goal of environmental policy is to correct the misallocation of resources that results when these sources of pollution are uncontrolled, or, in economic terms, to internalize the negative externality generated by them.

Incentive policies for internalizing externalities attempt to improve the allocation of resources indirectly by providing economic incentives for polluters (farmers) to reduce pollution.[1] These are in contrast to regulatory policies, which force the polluter (by law or regulation) to comply with certain restrictions on the level of pollution or polluting activities. Incentive policies can be separated into two groups: (1) those that use ex ante mechanisms for inducing pollution control, and (2) those that use ex post mechanisms. Ex ante mechanisms are applied at the time the polluter undertakes the activity that could potentially lead to pollution. These include taxes on inputs or outputs and subsidies for changes in production processes. Alternatively, ex post mechanisms are applied only if and when pollution is detected. These include rules for assigning liability for pollution damages. Although these mechanisms are not actually applied unless a pollution problem occurs, the prospect of liability for damages can still create an indirect incentive for the polluter to change his behavior to reduce the possibility of having to pay damages in the future.

This chapter discusses the use of incentive policies to control agricultural sources of water pollution. It provides an overview of the types of incentive policies that could be used (rather than a review of those that actually have been used) and discusses their advantages and disadvantages. The ex ante mechanisms are discussed first, followed by a discussion of ex post mechanisms. In both cases, the discussion begins with an overview of general issues relating to the use of incentives and then turns to the specific question of their use to control water pollution from agriculture. A concluding section summarizes and presents a proposal for the use of incentive policies in this context.

39

## EX ANTE INCENTIVE MECHANISMS

### Overview of Incentive versus Regulatory Approaches

As noted above, the main difference between incentive and regulatory approaches to pollution control is that incentive policies attempt to control the polluter's behavior indirectly, whereas regulation controls it directly by limiting or prohibiting certain activities. With ex ante incentives, the indirect control or effect works through the price system. The prices the polluter faces are changed in a way that induces a desired change in behavior. For example, changes in the price of a pesticide (through taxes or subsidies) can change the amount of the pesticide that a farmer chooses to apply. The actual change in behavior is voluntary in the sense that the polluter voluntarily chooses to change his/her use of an input in response to a change in its price. In fact, the policy is designed so that it is in the polluter's self-interest to respond in the desired way. This is in contrast to the regulatory approach, under which the change in behavior is mandatory.

Most of the previous discussions of incentive policies for pollution control have focused on point sources of pollution, where the point of emission is easily identifiable (e.g., Anderson et al., 1977; Nichols, 1984; Schelling, 1983; OECD, 1976). In this context the most commonly discussed incentive policies are taxes on emissions[2] and subsidies for reductions in emissions.[3] There is a large body of theoretical literature comparing the efficiency effects of emission taxes or subsidies to those of a regulatory approach to environmental control.[4] Many economists believe that the incentive approach (in particular, an emission tax) is preferred to regulation on the basis of economic efficiency.[5] Some of the reasons for this conclusion are discussed briefly here. More detailed treatments appear in Nichols (1984) and Schelling (1983).

If all firms are identical, then it can easily be shown that the efficient level of pollution per firm can be achieved by either uniform emission standards (direct regulation) or the imposition of a uniform tax per unit of emission, where the tax rate is equal to marginal damages caused by emissions when they are at the efficient level. Clearly, the regulatory approach achieves efficiency by simply mandating that firms emit no more than the efficient level. The tax approach, on the other hand, achieves efficiency by putting a price on an otherwise unpriced input (emissions or use of the environment) to force users of the input to consider the costs their use imposes on the rest of society.[6]

Although both of these approaches are equally efficient in terms of pollution per firm, if firms can enter or leave the polluting industry in response to changes in profitability, then in terms of total pollution (aggregated over all firms) the tax policy is efficient and the standards approach is not.[7] The total amount of pollution depends upon emissions per firm and the number of polluting firms. The number of firms in the industry is determined by the decisions of individual firms to either enter or exit the industry. In terms of economic efficiency, a polluting firm should enter the industry only if the total social benefits from its operation exceed the total social costs, including environmental costs. In making its entry/exit decision, however, the firm instead compares total private benefits (the revenue it would receive from selling its output) to total private costs (the costs of its inputs). Under the tax approach, the firm is forced to pay the social costs of all of its inputs including the environmental input; therefore, the firm's private costs coincide with social costs, and its decision regarding whether or not to stay in the industry is efficient. With the regulatory approach, however, although the firm pays the costs necessary to comply with the regulation, it does not pay for the remaining emissions. Thus, the cost of the environmental input that it continues to use after compliance with the regulation is not included in the firm's private costs. As a result, social costs are not equal to private costs and the firm's decision regarding entry/exit is not efficient. Too many firms enter the polluting industry and the total amount of pollution exceeds the efficient level.

Emission taxes have a theoretical advantage over emission standards even on a per firm basis when the costs of pollution abatement vary across firms. As long as the benefits of abatement are the same for all firms, a uniform emission tax applied to all firms will still yield efficiency. The idea behind the tax approach is to place a price on the environmental input equal to the marginal damages or costs associated with use of the input, or equivalently the marginal benefits from not using the input. As long as those damages (i.e., the benefits of abatement) are the same across all firms, each firm should face the same price (tax) for emissions. Thus, a single tax rate can be used to induce efficiency for all firms. In order for standards to be efficient, however, a different standard would have to be set for each firm. With differing abatement costs, the efficient level of abatement per firm will vary across firms and thus efficiency can be achieved under this approach only by having standards that also vary across firms. This argument has been used in favor of emission taxes over standards when abatement costs are not identical for all firms.[8]

The above arguments apply when the regulatory approach to control takes the form of setting a maximum allowable level of emissions by a firm. In practice, regulation often instead requires the use of certain pollution-control technologies or changes in production processes. Incentive policies have another advantage over regulation when the regulations take this form. Emission taxes give the firm the flexibility to achieve the desired reduction in pollution in the least-cost way. Thus, they are more cost-effective than regulation if the regulation imposes use of a process or technology that is not least-cost for all firms. This advantage seems particularly relevant to the case of agricultural pollution, where regulation might take the form of mandating the use of certain "best management practices" that might not be cost-effective for all farmers. In addition, the emission tax creates an incentive for technological innovation in pollution control because any cost savings resulting from innovation would directly benefit the firm. A regulatory scheme mandating the use of certain pollution-control equipment would provide no incentive for innovation.

The results described thus far have all been derived in the context of perfect certainty, assuming that both the regulatory or tax-setting agency and the firm have complete information about the costs and benefits of abatement. Introducing uncertainty can change the results. In particular, even if all firms are identical, the efficiency effects of emission taxes (price controls) and regulatory standards (quantity controls) are no longer equivalent—even on a per firm basis—when there is uncertainty about the marginal cost of abatement. The seminal work in this area by Weitzman (1974) was followed by many other studies (e.g., Adar and Griffin, 1976; Fishelson, 1976; Yohe, 1976). The basic conclusion is that the preferred approach depends upon the nature of the uncertainty and the properties (such as slope and curvature) of the marginal benefit and marginal cost curves. Thus, although emission taxes may be more efficient than regulatory controls in a world of perfect certainty, the same may not be true under the (realistic) assumption that the marginal costs of abatement are uncertain.

Finally, in addition to any efficiency differences that exist between the two approaches, payment for residual emissions under the tax approach provides a source of revenue that is not generated by the regulatory approach. This revenue could be used to compensate victims suffering damages from residual emissions or to subsidize investment in pollution-control equipment or processes. In practice, this could be an important advantage of the tax approach. In fact, most emission taxes that have been used in practice have been used for revenue-raising purposes (Hahn, 1989).

## Tax versus Subsidy Incentive Policies (Carrot versus Stick)

The above overview suggests that under some circumstances there may be at least a theoretical justification for the use of incentive policies over a regulatory approach to environmental control. However, the discussion was based primarily on emission taxes as the specific form of incentive policy used. An alternative incentive approach is the use of subsidies for reductions in emissions. This approach is often ignored in the theoretical literature on incentives (for reasons discussed below). However, for our purposes it is useful to consider the subsidy option explicitly. Our ultimate interest here is in the application of some general concepts to the specific case of water pollution from agriculture. Historically (at least in the United States) attempts to modify farmer behavior have used a "carrot" (subsidy) approach rather than a "stick" (tax) approach. For example, farmers have been paid to reduce output and to convert erodible land to low-erosion uses. If the concerns that led to the use of this approach to agricultural policy continue, then subsidy policies for controlling agricultural pollution may be more likely than tax policies. For this reason, we consider next the theoretical similarities and differences between the carrot and the stick approaches.

It can easily be shown that, in terms of the incentives created for individual firms to change their behavior at the margin, the tax and the subsidy approaches are identical. In other words, the efficient level of pollution abatement per firm can be achieved by either: (1) imposing a tax per unit of emissions equal to the marginal damages caused by pollution (or, equivalently, the marginal benefits from pollution abatement); or (2) providing a subsidy per unit of reduction in emissions also equal to the marginal damages from pollution. Either approach puts a price on emissions (use of the environmental input) equal to marginal damages. The tax approach imposes a price directly by making the firm pay explicitly for each unit of emissions. The subsidy approach makes the firm pay indirectly by forgoing the subsidy for each unit of emissions. In either case, the cost of emissions (either out of pocket or through loss of the subsidy) is the same.[9] Thus, in terms of marginal incentive effects, the two policies are equivalent.[10]

The obvious difference between the two approaches is that under the tax approach the firm makes a payment to the government whereas the reverse is true under the subsidy approach. As noted above, the revenue raised by an emission tax could be used for victim compensation or to offset pollution control costs. An emission-reduction subsidy, on the other hand, would require government outlays. This could be an important limiting factor in the future use of the subsidy approach, even in sectors such as agriculture, where it has historically been popular.

In addition, the implications for output prices differ. If the output sector is competitive, any change in producer costs through taxes or subsidies would in the long run be passed along to consumers. Under the tax approach, product prices would be expected to increase, whereas the subsidy approach would likely lead to (relative) reductions in product prices. The difference is that consumers pay directly under the tax approach and indirectly (through higher taxes or reductions in other governmental services) under the subsidy approach. Depending on how the additional revenue necessary for the subsidy is raised, the two approaches could result in differing distributional effects.

The difference in the direction of the flow of funds can also affect the firm's profitability[11] and thus the equilibrium size of the industry. It is this difference that has led many economists to conclude that the tax approach is preferred to the subsidy approach. By making some firms that would otherwise be unprofitable now profitable, the subsidy approach can lead to excessive entry into the industry. Thus, a firm's entry/exit decision would not be based on a comparison of the total social costs and benefits of its operation, as required for efficiency. Instead, it would compare its private benefits, including the subsidy, to its private costs. The marginal firm would stay in operation just to take advantage of the subsidy. Thus, if the industry is competitive, the subsidy approach will lead to an industry size that would exceed the efficient size. This would not be true under the tax approach (see discussion above). Thus, on the basis of long-run efficiency (i.e., industry size), many prefer the tax approach.

Implicit in the above discussion of the differing effects of taxes and subsidies on output prices and industry size is an assumption that the subsidy would be available only to firms actually in operation. In other words, if a firm leaves the industry, it would lose its subsidy. Likewise, any firm entering the industry would be eligible for the subsidy. Thus, the subsidy is conditional on engaging in the polluting activity. In the terminology of Holderness (1989), the subsidy applies to an "open class." It is this aspect of the subsidy policy that creates the long-run inefficiency.

It is possible, however, to design a subsidy policy that would not lead to excessive entry and thus long-run inefficiency. This could be done by having the subsidy apply to a "closed class," such as a fixed set of land parcels or the set of firms in the industry at a given time (perhaps the time the subsidy is imposed).[12] If the subsidy were granted to specific parcels of land, then the value of the subsidy would simply be capitalized into the value of the land.[13] There would be no possibility of entry into the set of eligible parcels (because this set would be fixed), and thus no excessive entry in response to the subsidy. Likewise, output prices would not be affected by the subsidy because increased land prices would offset any benefits from the subsidy. Alternatively, if the right to the subsidy were granted to a specific set of firms, then the subsidy would become an asset that could be bought and sold. Firms wishing to leave the industry could sell their right to the subsidy and those wishing to enter would have to purchase the right from an eligible firm. Again, the availability of the subsidy would not distort the entry/exit decision of any individual firm because there is no net loss to the exiting firm nor net gain to the entering firm. Likewise, output prices would be unaffected because the subsidy would not represent a reduction in the cost of doing business. Thus, by making the subsidy available only to a closed class of firms or parcels of land, the long-run inefficiency often created by subsidies can be eliminated.

Even if the subsidy approach is not inefficient in the long run, some might still argue for the tax approach over the subsidy on the grounds of the implied allocation of property rights under the two approaches. The tax approach implicitly gives the property rights to the environmental input to society as a whole because it requires firms that want to use the input to "buy" it from the public through payment of the tax. The subsidy approach, on the other hand, implicitly gives those rights to the firm, because if the public wants a cleaner environment it must "buy" it from the firms through payment of the subsidy.

Many feel that the allocation of property rights under the tax approach is preferable to that under the subsidy. In addition, the tax approach is consistent with the "polluter pays" principle advocated by the OECD (1975), whereas the subsidy approach is not.

However, the subsidy approach may seem less objectionable if viewed as a means of providing compensation for a government "taking." When the U.S. government takes private land for public purposes under its power of eminent domain, the Constitution requires that the government provide "just compensation" for the loss to the private landowner. Any government action that reduces the private value of an individual's land can also be viewed as a taking (Epstein, 1985), where the taking is partial rather than full because the private value of the land is reduced but not eliminated (as it is under eminent domain). Although there is no constitutional requirement for compensation for partial takings, it might be argued that consistency requires that full and partial takings be treated similarly, as the difference between the two is simply a matter of degree.[14] If this is true, then the compensation granted for full takings should be extended to partial takings as well. The subsidy approach provides such compensation. When viewed in this light, it might seem less objectionable than it would otherwise.

## Tax-Based Incentive Policies for Agricultural Water Pollution

Having discussed some general issues regarding the use of incentive policies for pollution control, we turn now to the specific case of water pollution from agriculture and the role that incentives might play in reducing it. As noted above, most of the literature on incentive policies focuses on point sources of pollution. However, most cases of water pollution from agriculture are examples of nonpoint pollution, where the pollution points are dispersed.[15] Both runoff to surface water and leaching to ground water come from entire fields rather than specific locations such as the end of a pipe or a smokestack. This implies that monitoring emissions is extremely difficult, if not impossible. As a result, emission taxes per se cannot be readily applied to these forms of agricultural pollution (Griffin and Bromley, 1982). Nonetheless, alternative incentive policies that serve as proxies for an emission tax can be used. We consider next some specific incentive policies that could be used in the case of agricultural pollution as proxies for an emission tax. We then turn to policies that would serve as proxies for an emission-reduction subsidy. Although theoretically tax and subsidy policies provide equivalent marginal incentives for pollution control, we consider them separately because in practice they are viewed quite differently (for the reasons discussed above).

*Taxes on Output.* If agricultural activities cause water pollution, one way to reduce that pollution is to reduce the level of the activity. For example, reductions in the number of acres planted to environmentally damaging crops would, ceteris paribus, reduce runoff and leaching and thus reduce water pollution. Policies that encourage reductions in these crops would then be a means of controlling agricultural pollution. One such policy is a tax on output, particularly for those crops with the greatest potential for generating pollution.

Although output taxes have been commonly discussed as a means of controlling negative production externalities, they suffer from several drawbacks, particularly in the case of agricultural pollution. The first stems from the fact that the misallocation of resources is not from the production of the output per se but rather from the way in which the output is produced. For example, if the same amount of output could be produced with fewer pesticides, then the total amount of pollution generated would (ceteris paribus) be reduced. Output taxes provide an incentive for reduced production, but they do not provide an incentive for the firm to change to a less-polluting production process. Thus, they are less efficient than policies that directly change the firm's production process.

In the context of agricultural pollution, output taxes have an second disadvantage. If the tax is not fully capitalized into land values, then product prices will rise as a result of the tax. Most agricultural products (except, for example, tobacco) are used to produce food or clothing. Output taxes on these products would therefore be viewed as taxes on food and clothing, goods that are considered to be necessities. Such taxes are usually "regressive," with the burden of the tax falling proportionately more on lower income families.

*Taxes on Soil Erosion.* Although emissions of agricultural pollutants cannot generally be observed because of their nonpoint nature, soil erosion might be viewed as a proxy for emissions of certain types of pollutants, such as sediment, pesticides, and fertilizers. When soil erosion cannot be measured directly, it can be estimated using models that incorporate farm characteristics and management practices (Griffin and Bromley, 1982). A tax on estimated soil loss would then provide farmers with an incentive to change their management practices to reduce erosion and thereby reduce the transport of pollutants to nearby lakes and streams.

Although a tax on soil loss would directly influence the farmer's choice of production process, it also has some disadvantages. First, soil erosion is not always a good proxy for pollution potential (Ribaudo, 1986). If land with a high erosion rate is relatively flat and located far from lakes and streams, then it will not necessarily contribute substantially to offsite pollution. Thus, it may be more efficient to target incentives to pollution potential rather than simply soil erosion.

Second, even if incentives were targeted to erosion that is likely to cause offsite damages, this would address only surface-water problems from agriculture and not ground-water contamination. Because ground-water contamination stems from leaching rather than runoff, policies designed to control runoff would be ineffective in controlling ground-water pollution. In fact, such policies might actually aggravate ground-water problems. For example, reducing pesticide or fertilizer runoff can leave larger quantities available for leaching. In addition, management practices designed to reduce soil erosion, such as reduced tillage, can require increased use of pesticides and thus increase the potential for ground-water contamination.[16] In this sense, there may be a trade-off between surface- and ground-water pollution. Taxes on soil erosion could control one, but possibly at the expense of the other.

*Taxes on Ambient Concentrations of Pollutants.* A third incentive policy, which is related to taxes on soil erosion but addresses the targeting issue, is a tax based on ambient concentrations of pollutants in nearby waterways. This essentially would be a tax on reductions in surface-water quality. The efficiency implications of such a mechanism have been explored by Segerson (1988). A main advantage of this approach is that it allows the desired water quality goal to be achieved in a cost-effective manner. Those farmers for whom changes in management practices would have little effect on water quality will not seek to alter their production processes (as this would involve costs but little benefit in terms of reduced taxation), whereas farmers whose behavior substantially affects water quality would be induced to take steps to reduce pollution. Moreover, those farmers for whom changes would be effective would have the flexibility to reduce pollution using techniques that are least-cost given their specific site characteristics. This might be through reduced runoff or, alternatively, through reduction in pesticide or fertilizer use. Finally, although it requires monitoring of water quality, a tax on ambient concentrations does not require that either runoff or farming practices be monitored.

Although this policy approach has several' advantages in terms of efficiently meeting a desired water quality goal, it also has several disadvantages. First, as with the tax on soil loss, it addresses surface-water problems but not ground-water problems, and again the control of surface-water pollution using this approach could be at the expense of increased ground-water contamination. Second, when several farmers contribute pollutants to the same waterway, there will still be only a single measure of water quality for that waterway.[17] With tax rates based on this single measure, the tax payments of one farmer will in general depend not only on his behavior but also on the behavior of other farmers contributing to the waterway. Although this creates an incentive for individual farmers to exert pressure on others who do not take steps to reduce ambient concentrations, it also makes the individual farmer's tax payments dependent to some extent on factors that are outside his/her control. This has no efficiency effects, but it may raise legal and equity issues.

*Taxes on Purchased Inputs.* A final tax-based incentive policy that could be used to reduce agricultural water pollution is a tax on inputs that contribute to pollution, such as pesticides or fertilizers. These taxes would increase the prices of these inputs, with the extent of the increase determined by the elasticities of supply and demand in the input markets and the market structure. The price increases create an incentive for reductions in use of the inputs and thus reductions in water pollution from that use.

The advantage of this approach is that it provides direct (rather than indirect) incentives for reductions in use of environmentally damaging inputs. If chemical use per se is the problem, then controlling it directly is the most efficient approach. In addition, it addresses sources of both surface- and ground-water pollution. Finally, it would be easier to implement administratively than would a tax on soil loss or water quality because it is easier to record sales of pesticides or fertilizers than it is to monitor (or estimate) soil loss or water quality.

A tax on inputs can also provide an incentive for changes in the application methods used for those inputs. In some cases, water pollution may depend not only on the quantity of the input used but also on the timing and the care taken in application. If pesticides or fertilizers became more expensive, farmers will have an increased incentive to use application methods that prevent the pesticides or fertilizers from being displaced from the point of application. This should contribute to an improvement in both surface- and ground-water quality.

A disadvantage of the use of input taxes is that they are not tailored to the site-specific pollution characteristics of different farms. Thus, a uniform tax will cause too little reduction of use in highly sensitive areas and too much in areas with low pollution potential. In addition, this approach can be used only for purchased inputs. Inputs that are not purchased, such as manure fertilizer, cannot be controlled in this way. For these reasons, an input tax policy may be less efficient than a water quality-based tax.

Although in theory input taxes should improve water quality, in practice their effectiveness depends upon the supply and demand elasticities for those inputs.[18] Empirical analysis suggests that high tax rates would have only modest effects on use (e.g., Kumm (Chapter 4) and Dubgaard (Chapter 5), this volume). Thus, very high tax rates may be needed to induce significant environmental improvements. The effect on land values could be significant (Dubgaard (Chapter 5), this volume).

## Subsidy-Based Incentive Policies
## for Agricultural Water Pollution

The four tax-based incentive policies discussed above represent a range of approaches that could be used to reduce water pollution from agriculture. As noted previously, at least in the United States the tax approach has not been applied much to agriculture, primarily due to concerns about its adverse effects on the farming sector. Instead, when incentive policies have been used (for example, for supply control), they have been subsidy-based policies. We consider next some subsidy approaches that can be (and have been) used. These approaches parallel the tax-based approaches, and the advantages/ disadvantages of each are similar (provided the subsidy is granted to a closed class). However, with subsidy policies the payment vehicle is often less direct. Whereas the tax approach would generally involve direct tax payments by the farmer to the government, the subsidy approach could involve indirect benefits that farmers would receive for desired changes in behavior rather than direct subsidy payments. Alternatively, the subsidy could take the form of cost sharing, in which the government offers to pay some portion of the cost associated with the change in behavior. Packaging the subsidy in either of these ways can make it more politically attractive than it would be otherwise.

*Reductions in Output.* As noted previously, on a per firm basis the same reduction in output could be achieved by either a tax on the output produced or a subsidy for reductions in the amount produced. Thus, either could be used to reduce agricultural sources of water pollution by simply reducing the activities that generate it. Although both the tax and the subsidy approach have the drawback of targeting output rather than pollution, the subsidy approach does not have the direct adverse effect on land values and/or food prices that the tax approach could have.

Subsidies for reductions in output have been used extensively in the United States. In general, these have been designed for supply control and income enhancement rather than pollution control. However, the existing programs for supply control (such as the acreage reduction program) could be targeted toward environmentally damaging crops. "Payment" for the reduction would then take the form of eligibility for other commodity program benefits.

An example of an output-based subsidy program in the United States is the Conservation Reserve Program, which pays farmers to take highly erodible land out of production. The payment is a subsidy for the reduction in planted acreage where such a reduction is likely to result in a significant decrease in soil erosion.[19] Although the unit of measurement is acreage rather than output, this policy can be viewed as a discrete form of an output tax designed to reduce soil erosion by reducing production on erodible land. To the extent that soil erosion is correlated with offsite water pollution, it provides an incentive for improvements in water quality. However, water quality goals could be achieved more efficiently if the program were targeted toward lands with significant pollution potential rather than just significant soil erosion.[20]

*Reductions in Soil Erosion.* As an alternative to a tax on soil loss, farmers could be paid for reductions in soil loss or, equivalently, for improvements in soil conservation. As a means of achieving water quality goals, this policy suffers from the same drawbacks as the tax—namely, that soil erosion may not be a good proxy for water pollution and that surface water may be improved at the expense of increased ground-water contamination.

An example of the type of subsidy policy that could be used is the concept of cross-compliance. Under cross-compliance, farmers would be eligible for agricultural commodity program benefits only if their land met certain soil conservation standards. In essence, farmers would be paid (in the form of eligibility for commodity program benefits) for improvements in soil conservation or reductions in soil loss. The effectiveness of this subsidy policy depends, however, on the potential benefits of the commodity programs (Reichelderfer (Chapter 6), this volume). Thus, external changes in the attractiveness of participation in commodity programs could reduce the efficacy of cross-compliance.

*Reductions in Ambient Concentrations of Pollutants.* The tax on ambient concentrations of pollutants or reductions in water quality could alternatively have been specified as a subsidy for water quality improvements. Although the subsidy version of this policy would still suffer from the potential trade-off between ground- and surface-water quality, it might be less objectionable than the tax approach when several farmers contribute pollutants to a single waterway. Because the basis for payments (water quality) depends on the behavior of all contributing farmers, the payments for an individual farmer would depend in part on factors outside his/her control. This might be viewed as less objectionable if the payment is being made to the farmer (as with the subsidy approach) rather than by the farmer (as with the tax).

*Reductions in Input Use.* Instead of taxing purchased inputs that contribute to water pollution, such as pesticides and fertilizers, farmers could alternatively be subsidized for reductions in the use of these inputs. Unlike the tax approach, however, use of an explicit subsidy would require identification of a baseline to use in measuring reductions. Thus, the direct subsidy approach would have the same drawbacks as an input tax (such as not targeting problem areas and applying only to purchased inputs) and in addition would be more difficult to administer.

It is possible, however, to have an indirect subsidy for reduced input use, similar to the indirect subsidy for soil conservation created by cross-compliance. For example, eligibility for certain benefits could be tied to reductions in pesticide use. The state of Connecticut has used an interesting variation of this approach to encourage the use of integrated pest management.

When ground-water contamination is discovered, state legislation requires that the responsible parties provide alternative sources of drinking water. However, farmers have recently been granted a statutory exemption from this provision for cases in which the contamination is from pesticide use, provided the farmer uses integrated pest management and keeps appropriate records. The exemption from future payments is in essence a promise of a future subsidy to farmers for current reductions in pesticide use. Although the payment vehicle is indirect (and in this case even stochastic), it still should provide an incentive for farmers to reduce their current use.

## Use of "Best Management Practices"

A final subsidy policy (for which a tax counterpart was not discussed) is the use of subsidies or cost-sharing programs to encourage the use of "best management practices" (BMPs). This approach attempts to change farmer behavior by offering to pay to the farmer part of the cost of that change.[21]

Because most BMPs are designed to reduce soil erosion, this policy approach suffers from the same drawbacks as other policies that target soil conservation rather than improvements in water quality, In addition, in most applications of this approach, the offered cost-sharing payment is less than 100 percent of the cost to the farmer. Thus, the farmer has an incentive to accept the offer and undertake the change only when it would generate sufficient private benefits to justify the private (uncovered) costs. If the private benefits are small, then this voluntary policy will not be effective in inducing the desired changes in farmer behavior.

This overview of alternative incentive-based policies that could be used for control of agricultural water pollution indicates that no single ex ante policy instrument is ideal. This stems from the nonpoint nature of agricultural pollution. In cases of point pollution, the emission tax (or subsidy, if granted to a closed class) gives a first-best outcome in terms of efficiency. Here, however, the proxies for an emission tax/subsidy all have drawbacks. These include a possible trade-off between ground- and surface-water quality or the lack of appropriate targeting.

Since no single ex ante policy can guarantee an efficient outcome, it may be possible to improve efficiency through the use of an ex post incentive mechanism. The consideration of ex post mechanisms seems particularly appropriate when the ex ante instruments do not adequately protect ground-water quality because ex post measures can be applied much more easily to contamination of ground water than to surface-water pollution. The following section discusses the use of ex post mechanisms to control ground-water pollution from agriculture.

## EX POST INCENTIVE MECHANISMS

### Overview of Liability-Based Incentive Policies

Ex post incentive mechanisms work by holding responsible parties liable for any damages that result from their activities. Although the mechanism is not activated until damages occur, the knowledge that the firm will be held liable for damages when (and if) they occur should provide an incentive for the firm to change its behavior ex ante to reduce the probability or magnitude of damages. Thus, even though the liability rule is only implemented ex post, it has incentive effects ex ante.

Although in theory liability rules could be structured to provide correct ex ante incentives, it should be noted that in practice there are a number of factors that limit the incentive effects of these rules. For example, for some types of pollution the responsible party may not be identifiable due to long time lags before damages are discovered and uncertainty over causation. Even when identified, the responsible party may not always be able to compensate victims fully due to limited assets. Finally, for cases of dispersed damages, it is possible that no individual has an incentive to bring suit even though in the aggregate the legal costs would be justified. All of these factors tend to diminish the incentive effects created by the existence of a liability rule.[22] Nonetheless, there is evidence (Opaluch and Grigalunas, 1984) that liability rules do provide incentives for potentially responsible parties to take care to reduce expected damages.

The incentive effects created by liability depend upon the structure of the rule used and the nature of the injury-causing activity. Shavell (1980) showed that for cases of unilateral accidents (where only the injurer can take steps to reduce expected damages) a strict liability rule leads to efficiency. Under strict liability, the responsible party is held liable whenever his/her actions can be shown to be the cause of the damages. Thus, liability is not contingent on the nature of those actions. The alternative to strict liability is a negligence rule, which assigns liability only if the actions that caused the damages were negligent in the sense of not conforming to a due standard of care. The negligence rule is not efficient in the long run if polluting firms can enter or exit the industry (Polinsky, 1980).

The intuition behind these results can be found in the previous discussion of emission taxes versus regulation. In terms of ex ante decisions, strict liability acts like a tax on the polluting activity, with the magnitude of the tax equal to the expected damages caused by the activity. It is thus similar to an emission tax and shares the efficiency properties of that tax. A negligence rule, on the other hand, is similar to a regulatory standard (equal to the due standard of care). Although it induces the correct amount of prevention in the short run, in the long run firms do not face the full social costs of their actions and thus make inefficient entry/exit decisions. This suggests that strict liability is preferred to negligence for unilateral accidents in which long-run incentives are important.

## The Role of Liability in Controlling Agricultural Water Pollution

Ground-water contamination from agriculture is an example of a unilateral "accident" because only the farmer can take steps to reduce the probability or magnitude of contamination—i.e., the victim is unable to prevent contamination.[23] Thus, imposing strict liability on farmers for damages resulting from their operations would provide the proper incentive for them to reduce polluting activities. Liability could be imposed either statutorily (for example, treating farmers the same as any other responsible party in legislation explicitly assigning liability for pollution damages) or through common law (as implemented by the courts).

There has, however, been some reluctance to impose liability on farmers for pollution damages resulting from "normal" farming activities. This reluctance is exemplified by "right-to-farm" laws that have been enacted in some states. The reluctance seems particularly strong when victims are viewed as "coming to the nuisance," as when housing developments spring up next to an existing farm and the developers and purchasers are well aware of the existence (and likely effects) of the neighboring farm. In fact, there is some economic justification for not imposing liability in this case if locating the development in another place would be less costly than moving the farm or having it cease operation.

The right-to-farm argument seems more reasonable in the context of nuisances such as unpleasant manure odors than damages from water pollution. There is little a farmer can do (at reasonable expense) to prevent certain odors, and the existence of the odors is readily apparent to anyone purchasing neighboring property. Contamination of water supplies, on the other hand, may not be readily apparent (or even existent) at the time of purchase. In addition, faced with the proper incentives, farmers could take steps to reduce pollution. Thus, it seems inappropriate to use right-to-farm grounds to argue against imposing liability on farmers for damages due to water pollution.

Nonetheless, several explicit exemptions for farmers from liability for ground-water contamination have been granted in the United States. One is Connecticut's Potable Water Law, noted above, which exempts qualifying farmers from liability for the costs of providing alternative drinking water when contamination is due to the use of pesticides. The Comprehensive Environmental Response, Compensation and Liability Act (CERCLA) also grants farmers an exemption from liability for damages resulting from agricultural applications of pesticides. These exemptions seem to reflect more the political power of the farm lobby than any logical distinction between farmers and other polluters.

It can be shown, however, that in the case of pesticides (or any other purchased input), exempting farmers from liability for the resulting contamination of ground water should not cause any loss of incentives for reductions in use. When all responsible parties are targeted for liability, the exemption granted to farmers is tantamount to holding the manufacturer liable because generally the manufacturer is the only remaining potentially responsible party. Although shifting liability to the manufacturer clearly changes the allocation of risk,[24] the quantity of pesticides used will be the same with or without the shifting (Segerson, 1989). At the time input decisions are made, expected future liability acts such as a tax on pesticide use and the effect of that tax on the quantity produced/consumed are independent of whether the tax is nominally borne by the user (farmer) or the producer (manufacturer). In either case, the cost of pesticide use borne by the users will reflect both production costs and expected liability payments. Thus, imposing liability on the manufacturer is equivalent (in terms of ex ante incentives) to imposing it on the farmer.

Although the proper incentives for the use of a purchased input can be attained without any farmer liability for damages, the same is not true for inputs that are not purchased or damages that depend not only on the quantity of an input used but also on the application procedure. This suggests that an exemption from liability should not apply to contamination from nonpurchased inputs such as manure fertilizer. In addition, to the extent that contamination from pesticide use depends upon the timing and method of application (as well as the total quantity used), an exemption for pesticide contamination will reduce farmers' incentives to improve water quality.[25]


## CONCLUSIONS AND A POLICY PROPOSAL

There is considerable theoretical literature supporting the belief by many economists that incentive policies for environmental control are preferred on efficiency grounds to regulatory policies, at least under perfect certainty. For point sources of pollution, the preferred incentive policy is an emissions tax. This is generally preferred to an emissions-reduction subsidy either because it is viewed as being more efficient in the long run (where firms can enter or exit the industry) or because it implies a preferred distribution of initial property rights. However, if the subsidy is granted to a closed class so that eligibility is not contingent upon continued operation of the polluting activity, the long-run inefficiency of the subsidy can be eliminated. In addition, if the subsidy is viewed as "compensation" for a government "taking" similar to that granted for eminent domain takings, then the distribution of property rights implied by it may be considered less objectionable.

These general concepts relating to the use of incentive policies for pollution control can be applied to the specific case of water pollution from agriculture. Because agricultural pollution is an example of nonpoint pollution, the standard emissions tax or emissions-reduction subsidy cannot be applied directly. However, several proxies for these policies exist. Proxies for an emissions tax include taxes on output, soil erosion, ambient concentrations of pollutants (reductions in water quality), and input use. Proxies for an emissions-reduction subsidy parallel the tax proxies, although in some cases a disadvantage of the tax approach (for example, in terms of perceived inequities) is not necessarily shared by the corresponding subsidy.

Although in the case of point pollution an emissions tax yields a first-best outcome, for agricultural nonpoint pollution none of the proxies for an emissions tax (or subsidy) can achieve this same result. Each has some drawback in terms of efficiency. For example, output-based policies do not provide the efficient incentives for changes in the farmer's production process such as changes in the input mix. Policies based on changes in soil erosion or surface-water quality do not adequately address contamination of ground water, and in some cases might aggravate it. In addition, because soil erosion is not always a good proxy for potential water pollution, soil erosion controls (or cost-sharing policies to encourage use of certain best management practices) may not be cost-effective. Finally, taxes on polluting inputs such as pesticides provide incentives for reduction in use but, if applied uniformly, they do not target highly sensitive areas. In addition, empirical analysis suggests that even fairly high tax rates would have only modest effects on use.

The above policies are examples of ex ante incentive mechanisms. They are applied to farmer decisions at the time those decisions are made. In contrast, ex post mechanisms (liability rules) can also be used to provide incentives for pollution control. Although these mechanisms do not become operative until pollution damages occur, the prospect of facing future liability provides an incentive for taking preventive actions today.

The use of liability as a control policy is most applicable to ground-water contamination. Ground-water contamination is an example of a unilateral problem; thus efficient incentives result from the imposition of strict liability on farmers for any damages resulting from their operations. However, in the case of purchased inputs, exempting farmers from liability would still lead to efficient levels of use provided liability was shifted back to the manufacturer of the pesticide. Because the liability acts ex ante like a tax on pesticide use, imposing it on the manufacturer is equivalent (in terms of the effect on the level of use) to imposing it on the farmer. However, exempting farmers from liability would eliminate the incentives for reductions in the use of polluting inputs that are not purchased.

No single incentive mechanism (either ex ante or ex post) is capable of producing a first-best outcome for both ground- and surface-water pollution. It is therefore likely that the best policy approach will involve use of several instruments to control agricultural pollution, based on both incentives and regulation. Choice of the specific instruments to be used will require a balancing of multiple objectives, relating to efficiency, distributional implications, budgetary effects, and administrative ease (low transactions costs). A policy package that attempts to balance these concerns will be imperfect in terms of any single criterion, and it should not be judged in that way. Instead, it must be evaluated as a compromise solution to an environmental problem that defies easy solution.

With this in mind, this chapter concludes by outlining a policy package that seems to represent a possible compromise. This is not a perfect package, nor necessarily even the best package. At this time, empirical work on alternative policies is too limited to allow such a claim to be made confidently. Rather it is an example of how several policy instruments might be combined to address nonpoint agricultural water pollution, recognizing the need to balance multiple objectives.

The proposed package is comprised of three parts. The first is a set of taxes on environmentally damaging agricultural inputs such as pesticides and fertilizers. Such taxes would raise the prices of these inputs to reflect the social costs that can result from their use. This would thus provide some incentive for decreased use, although the effect may be modest. The burden of the taxes is likely to be shared among pesticide and fertilizer producers, consumers of agricultural products, and owners of agricultural land. In addition, these taxes would be relatively easy to administer—excise taxes on other goods are common. Finally, even if the effect on water quality were modest, the taxes would provide a source of revenue that could be used to promote improvements in water quality (as suggested below). If the revenue is targeted for water quality improvements, the taxes may be more politically acceptable than if the money were simply used for general purposes.

The second component of the policy package would be a set of mandatory regulations controlling soil erosion. Because erosion is difficult to monitor, incentive policies such as taxes or subsidies based on actual reductions in erosion would involve high transaction costs. However, soil conservation plans can be developed and implemented. These plans can be designed on a site-specific basis with water quality goals in mind. Regulation of soil erosion through mandatory implementation of these plans would ensure that both soil conservation and water quality goals would be met more effectively. In addition, that effectiveness would not be tied to the attractiveness of other government programs, as is true with approaches such as cross-compliance.

Reductions in soil erosion would generate benefits for the landowner (through improvements in land quality) as well as potential offsite water quality improvements. Thus, the "burden" on the farmer from mandatory soil erosion control would be partially offset by increases in land values due to increased land quality. The burden could be further reduced by cost-sharing provisions designed to cover a portion of the costs of implementation. Of course, cost sharing must be financed by government revenues and these revenue requirements may be substantial if all farmers are eligible. One possible source for cost-sharing funds is the revenue generated by the pesticide and fertilizer taxes proposed above.

As noted previously, a drawback of policies targeted to soil erosion is that they may improve surface-water quality at the expense of ground-water quality. To the extent that the input taxes reduce pesticide and fertilizer use, they would provide some protection for ground-water resources. However, this seems unlikely to be sufficient. Explicit regulation of the use of these chemicals seems imperative, particularly given the asymmetric information about the potential hazards associated with their use. However, if these substances are allowed to be used (even in a restricted way), the possibility of ground-water contamination remains. If farmers face liability for the resulting damages, they will have an incentive to try to reduce the likelihood (or the severity) of that contamination. In addition, explicit liability would provide a source of funds that could be used to compensate victims of ground-water contamination. Thus, the third component of the proposed policy package would be a set of regulations governing agricultural chemical use and an explicit imposition of at least partial (strict) liability for farmers for ground-water contamination resulting from that use.

Because liability is only actually imposed ex post, there is great uncertainty about what an individual farmer's future obligations might be. This risk would be difficult for small farmers to absorb. In addition, it is possible that, at the time of contamination, the farmer may be judgment proof. Anticipation of this possibility would dilute the incentives created by liability. In addition, funds would not be available for victim compensation. A means of addressing both of these problems is the establishment of an insurance fund for farmer liability. Under such a fund, farmers could purchase "pollution liability" insurance similar to insurance that has in the past been available to other types of firms. If such insurance is not offered by private insurers, it could be publicly provided. However, to maintain the incentive for farmers to minimize contamination risks—i.e., to avoid a "moral hazard" problem—eligibility for such insurance should be limited to those farmers who demonstrate that they have taken steps to minimize those risks.

In summary, the proposed policy package would have three components: (1) a set of input taxes designed to reduce pesticide and fertilizer use and raise revenue; (2) mandatory regulation of soil erosion targeted toward water quality, which could be coupled with cost-sharing provisions financed by the input taxes; and (3) regulation of pesticide and fertilizer use and explicit (possibly partial) farmer liability for remaining ground-water contamination, with the possibility of purchasing pollution liability insurance. Although such a package is imperfect in some ways, it provides an example of how a variety of policy instruments, based on both incentives and regulation, could be combined in an attempt to balance the many concerns involved in policy design. No single policy instrument is ideal, but a package that combines a number of instruments in this way seems to be the most promising approach to controlling agricultural sources of water pollution.

## NOTES

The author would like to thank Ronald C. Griffin and John B. Braden for very useful comments on an earlier version of this paper.

1. See Schelling (1983) for an overview of the incentive approach to pollution control.

2. Emissions include not only emissions of standard pollutants but also other negative externalities such as noise.

3. Marketable emission permits are an alternative approach that combines the incentive and regulatory approaches. See Baumol and Oates (1988) for a discussion of this approach.

4. See Shortle and Dunn (1986) for an interesting comparison of the incentive versus regulatory approaches in the case of agricultural pollution.

5. Although economists usually argue for incentives on the basis of efficiency, Frey et al. (1985) have recently suggested that the preference for taxes over regulation expressed by many economists is in fact based more on factors such as job type, political ideology, and country of residence.

6. It should be noted, however, that since production decisions are based on relative rather than absolute prices, the effectiveness of the incentive approach depends on the magnitude of the tax (or subsidy) relative to other prices. Thus, the level of the tax must be adjusted to any changes in other prices that occur. If an adjustment is not made, the effectiveness of the tax in inducing efficient pollution control will be diminished. See Chapters 3 and 6.

7. This result requires that marginal damages be (approximately) constant over the range of emissions of the firm. See Baumol and Oates (1988) and the references cited therein for further discussion.

8. If marginal benefits of abatement also vary across firms, then a uniform tax would no longer yield efficiency, that is, the efficient tax rate would also have to vary across firms. However, the tax approach would still have the advantage of inducing the efficient industry size if marginal damages are constant for any individual firm.

9. In fact, the per unit subsidy can simply be viewed as a lump-sum subsidy payment coupled with a per unit tax.

10. They may not be equivalent administratively, however. In particular, administration of the subsidy requires identification of a baseline from which reductions are to be measured; this is not required for the tax.

11. This is a likely explanation for the use of subsidies over taxes or regulation in the agricultural sector, where concerns over profitability exist.

12. An example of the use of such a closed-class subsidy in the United States is the Conservation Reserve Program, in which eligibility is restricted to land qualifying as "highly erodible". Subsidies applying to all agricultural land in production at a certain time would also be closed-class, provided land going out of production would not lose its eligibility.

13. See Shoemaker (1989) for evidence that the benefits of the Conservation Reserve Program have been capitalized into land values.

14. Miceli and Segerson (1989) present a framework for analyzing the economic efficiency of compensation in which full and partial takings are treated as identical in structure and differ only in terms of the extent of the reduction in the private value of the land.

15. Some forms of water pollution from agriculture, such as runoff from manure storage facilities or pollution from accidental spills of pesticides or fertilizer, are examples of point rather than nonpoint pollution.

16. This could also reduce surface-water quality if the vehicle for transport of chemicals to waterways is water rather than soil runoff.

17. In this sense, this mechanism implicitly treats surface water-pollution as a common property problem. See Quiggin (1988) for an application of this concept to salinity problems.

18. Because production decisions are based on relative rather than absolute prices, the effectiveness of the tax also depends upon output prices. For example, if the increased costs resulting from the tax were offset by increased product prices (through, for example, increased commodity support prices), the effectiveness of the tax in reducing use would be diminished.

19. To qualify for the program, the land must be converted to a low-erosion use such as grassland or forestry.

20. Ervin and Dicks (1988) discuss the efficiency of such programs for achieving environmental improvement.

21. A similar policy that encourages changes in farmer behavior by offsetting some of the associated costs is the provision of technical assistance to farmers. See Chapter 6 for a discussion of incentives provided by technical assistance in the United States.

22. Imperfections in the legal system have led some to conclude that liability rules should be coupled with regulatory policies to ensure proper incentives. See, for example, Shavell (1984) and Johnson and Ulen (1986).

23. In some cases the victims can take steps to prevent damages once contamination has been discovered. For example, they can purchase bottled water or filtration units. In fact, Raucher (1986) suggested that in some cases this may be the most cost-effective control approach. However, this possibility does not change the conclusions drawn here because the liability that the farmer faces could simply be for the costs of providing clean drinking water.

24. It shifts risk from the farmer to the manufacturer. If the manufacturer

is better able to spread risks, then this shift will result in efficient risk sharing.

25. Increased pesticide prices due to manufacturer liability will provide some incentive for farmers to take care in applying pesticides to improve efficacy. However, the increased price will not be targeted to the site-specific characteristics of an individual farm or individual farming practices. Thus, a moral hazard problem will remain.

## REFERENCES

Adar, Zvi, and James M. Griffin. 1976. "Uncertainty and the Choice of Pollution Control Instruments." *Journal of Environmental Economics and Management* 3:178–188.

Anderson, Frederick R., Allen V. Kneese, Phillip D. Reed, Serge Taylor, and Russell B. Stevenson. 1977. *Environmental Improvement Through Economic Incentives.* Baltimore: Johns Hopkins University Press.

Baumol, William J., and Wallace E. Oates. 1988. *The Theory of Environmental Policy.* Cambridge and New York: Cambridge University Press.

Epstein, Richard. 1985. Takings: *Private Property and the Power of Eminent Domain.* Cambridge, MA: Harvard University Press.

Ervin, David E., and Michael R. Dicks. 1988. "Cropland Diversion for Conservation and Environmental Improvement: An Economic Welfare Analysis." *Land Economics* 64:256–268.

Fishelson, Gideon. 1976. "Emissions Control Policies Under Uncertainty." *Journal of Environmental Economics and Management* 3:189–197.

Frey, Bruno S., Friedrich Schneider, and Werner W. Pommerehne. 1985. "Economists' Opinions on Environmental Policy Instruments: Analysis of a Survey." *Journal of Environmental Economics and Management* 12:62–71.

Griffin, Ronald C., and Daniel W. Bromley. 1982. "Agricultural Runoff as a Nonpoint Externality: A Theoretical Development." *American Journal of Agricultural Economics* 64:547–552.

Hahn, Robert W. 1989. "Economic Prescriptions for Environmental Problems: How the Patient Followed the Doctor's Orders." *Journal of Economic Perspectives* 3:95–114.

Holderness, Clifford G. 1989. "The Assignment of Rights, Entry Effects and the Allocation of Resources." *Journal of Legal Studies* 18:181–189.

Johnson, Gary V., and Thomas S. Ulen. 1986. "Designing Public Policy Toward Hazardous Wastes: The Role of Administrative Regulations and Legal Liability Rules." *American Journal of Agricultural Economics* 68:1266–1271.

Miceli, Thomas J., and Kathleen Segerson. 1989. "Compensation for Full and Partial Takings: Who Should Pay What to Whom?" Working paper, Department of Economics, University of Connecticut, Storrs.

Nichols, Albert L. 1984. *Targeting Economic Incentive for Environmental Protection.* Cambridge, MA, and London: The MIT Press.

Opaluch, James J., and Thomas A. Grigalunas. 1984. "Controlling Stochastic Pollution Events Through Liability Rules: Some Evidence from OCS Leasing." *Rand Journal of Economics* 15:142–151.

Organization for Economic Co-operation and Development. 1975. *The Polluter Pays Principle: Definition, Analysis, Implementation.* Paris, France.

———. 1976. *Pollution Charges: An Assessment.* Report to the Secretariat. Paris, France.

Polinsky, A. Mitchell. 1980. "Strict Liability vs. Negligence in a Market Setting." *American Economic Review* 70:363–367.

Quiggin, John. 1988. "Murray River Salinity: An Illustrative Model." *American Journal of Agricultural Economics* 70:635–645.

Raucher, Robert L. 1986. "The Benefits and Costs of Policies Related to Groundwater Contamination." *Land Economics* 62:33–45.

Ribaudo, Marc O. 1986. "Consideration of Offsite Impacts in Targeting Soil Conservation Programs." *Land Economics* 62:402–411.

Schelling, Thomas C., ed. 1983. *Incentives for Environmental Protection.* Cambridge, MA, and London: The MIT Press.

Segerson, Kathleen. 1988. "Uncertainty and Incentives for Nonpoint Pollution Control." *Journal of Environmental Economics and Management* 15:87–98.

———. 1989. "Liability for Groundwater Contamination from Pesticides." Working paper, Department of Economics, University of Connecticut, Storrs.

Shavell, Steven. 1980. "Strict Liability Versus Negligence." *Journal of Legal Studies* 9:1–25.

———. 1984. "A Model of the Optimal Use of Liability and Safety Regulation." *Rand Journal of Economics* 15:271–280.

Shoemaker, Robbin. 1989. "Agricultural Land Values and Rents Under the Conservation Reserve Program." *Land Economics* 65:131–137.

Shortle, James S., and James W. Dunn. 1986. "The Relative Efficiency of Agricultural Source Water Pollution Control Policies." *American Journal of Agricultural Economics* 68:668–677.

Weitzman, Martin L. 1974. "Prices vs. Quantities." *The Review of Economic Studies* 41:477–491.

Yohe, Gary. 1976. "Substitution and the Control of Pollution: A Comparison of Effluent Charges and Quantity Standards under Uncertainty." *Journal of Environmental Economics and Management* 3:312–323.

# THREE

# Control of Agricultural Pollution by Regulation

GLEN D. ANDERSON
ANN E. DE BOSSU
PETER J. KUCH

Regulation has been the favored and generally effective strategy for controlling point-source water pollution in the United States; in Europe, point-source pollution has been effectively reduced using economic incentives (Anderson et al., 1977; Tietenberg, 1984). How either approach might be applied to the more intractable problem of nonpoint-source pollution, particularly that of agriculture, are issues worth exploring. This chapter focuses on the current and potential use of regulation to mitigate agricultural pollution.

Compared with other commercial and industrial activities, agriculture has been subject to relatively little regulation. Regulation may, however, be a legitimate response to the spotty results of voluntary approaches, the public's perceptions about "bribing" farmers not to pollute, and political aversion to the high levels of input taxes required to change farmer behavior. Notwithstanding the antiregulatory ethos that has taken root in some countries, regulation may be an economically sound aspect of nonpoint-source pollution control.

Almost all developed countries favor regulatory approaches for controlling the manufacture and use of pesticides as well as managing animal wastes. Regulations concerning the application of fertilizers are similarly well established, and several countries have set limits on toxic components of manufactured fertilizers. Information on sedimentation control efforts outside the United States is not readily available. U.S. programs at the state and national levels have employed mostly voluntary approaches such as education and cost-sharing; at the local level, zoning and other land-use regulations have been used primarily.

This chapter examines the economic theory underlying environmental regulation and compares the efficiency of incentive and regulatory approaches for controlling agricultural pollution. It also surveys patterns of current agricultural regulation that have emerged around the world. In particular, such questions as the following will be examined:

1. Are regulatory approaches appropriate tools for addressing agricultural pollution?
2. Under what circumstances are regulatory approaches preferable to voluntary or incentive-based approaches?

3. What are the impediments to more extensive use of regulation for dealing with agricultural nonpoint sources of pollution?
4. How is regulation of agriculture likely to evolve in the United States and other countries?

The chapter is divided into five sections. The following section presents the economic theory underlying firm behavior regarding production and abatement decisions and the effect that regulatory approaches such as quotas, bans, and use restrictions are expected to have on firm behavior. The next section then focuses on issues directly related to the regulation of agricultural pollution, including the nature of the problem, environmental quality objectives, selection and evaluation of regulatory approaches, and compliance and enforcement. A survey of regulatory approaches used in the United States and Europe is presented next, followed by a comparison of regulatory and incentive programs. The chapter concludes with a brief discussion of future directions that regulatory approaches might take.

## AN OVERVIEW OF REGULATION

This section provides an overview of regulatory approaches and examines their expected impacts on firm behavior using a simplified profit maximization framework.

### Options for Improving Water Quality

Government has several conceptual options for encouraging or compelling firms to modify their discharges into ground and surface water. Broadly speaking, these options can be divided into incentive approaches and regulatory approaches. Incentive approaches involve the use of taxes or subsidies on outputs, inputs, technology, or pollution. The objective of these approaches is to alter the relative prices and costs faced by firms and encourage entrepreneurs to revise their production and/or abatement decisions in a way that promotes environmental quality. Regulations rely on the use of performance standards or direct controls on outputs, inputs, or technology. This chapter examines the regulatory options.

*Performance Standards.* A performance standard is usually defined in terms of an established maximum discharge rate per unit of time. It is typically expressed in physical units that are understandable to the regulated firm, and allows the regulatory agency to monitor compliance. If it is prohibitively expensive to monitor discharges, performance standards could be defined in terms of minimum levels of environmental quality (or maximum pollutant levels) in ground and surface waters. However, ambient water quality standards engender a whole new set of implementation and compliance monitoring problems for a regulator that are not likely to be easier or less expensive to deal with than effluent standards.

*Design Standards.* A performance standard allows the firm some flexibility in modifying its production and abatement decisions. A design or technical standard, however, constrains firms to use a specific technology or select from a limited number of best management practices (BMPs). Design standards can be established for either production or abatement technology and have been used widely to address randomly occurring environmental problems such as accidental releases of hazardous wastes from storage tanks and disposal facilities.

*Quotas and Use Restrictions.* Quotas may be imposed on output levels or on the quantity of inputs used in production. They can be specified for any time period ranging from an hour to a year, or for specialized intervals such as a season. Use restrictions typically refer to prohibitions or reductions in the use of a technology or input over a given time period.

*Licensing and Registration.* Licenses may be required for the use or sale of certain types of substances, equipment, technologies, or for applicators of chemicals. Generally, their goal is to moderate the use of chemicals in production activities. Licensing may also provide a way to disseminate information about environmental and health safety practices through training prerequisites. Registration is often required for the manufacture of certain chemicals. The registrant is usually required to conduct or pay for assessments of the potential environmental or health effects and provide a justification for the chemical's uses and use rates. Once granted, product registration represents a set of defined, enforceable property rights, which may be exchanged in market transactions. Licensing and registration may increase the costs of inputs or limit the mix of inputs or technologies that can be used in production.

*Activity Permits and Management Plans.* An activity permit is a legal document that enables a firm to engage in certain activities provided it complies with requirements established by the regulator. These requirements may include adherence to performance and design standards or other regulatory controls. Activity permits are usually tailored to specific site conditions. Management plans are similar to permits except they tend to focus more heavily on the selection of technologies and the use of design standards rather than the imposition of performance standards. Although they can be viewed as voluntary, management plans are often made requisite by regulatory agencies.

## The Effects of Regulations on Firms

The likely effects of regulations on a firm's welfare and production decisions can be illustrated in a simple model. The firm's objective is to choose a combination of inputs that maximizes profits, subject to a production constraint. In order to achieve this objective, firms will utilize additional units of inputs provided the value of the marginal product of the input exceeds its cost. Note that there is an implicit assumption that the firm has selected the optimal production technology as well as the optimal mix of inputs.

The absence of an environmental constraint implies that firms have property rights to the assimilative capacity of ground and surface water. To analyze the effect of a regulation that limits these rights, the profit maximization framework outlined above must first be modified.

If a performance standard is imposed on a firm, an additional constraint will be placed on profit maximization. It is assumed that a firm's discharges are a function of the levels of inputs and abatement and the type of technology used to produce output. The firm's problem is to select inputs, abatement level, and technology to maximize profits given that the firm must comply with the performance standard. Because technology usually cannot be viewed as a continuous choice variable, the profit-maximizing solution is obtained in two steps. First, the firm determines the mix of inputs and abatement level that maximizes profits for alternative technologies. Second, the firm selects the technology that yields the maximum level of profits while simultaneously meeting the performance standard.

A firm will increase its use of an input up to the point where the value of its marginal product is just equal to the sum of its factor price plus the shadow price of discharges times the marginal increase in discharges associated with an increase in the input. In effect, the sum of the input price and marginal cost of discharges can be viewed as the social marginal cost of the input under conditions of perfect information. The result is a Pareto-optimal allocation of resources under which the firm internalizes the externality costs into its production function, thereby equating marginal social benefits of resource use with marginal social costs. A firm will invest in abatement up to the point where the marginal benefits of abatement (shadow price of discharges times the marginal decrease in discharges due to abatement) is just equal to the sum of the marginal cost of abatement plus the value of the marginal physical product of abatement (i.e., the reduction in product output due to abatement measures). These costs represent the opportunity cost of abatement expressed in terms of reduced profits. For example, if sedimentation damages can be traced to a specific farm operation, that farmer may in theory comply with a performance standard by adopting erosion control measures up to the point where the marginal benefit of avoided discharge penalties equals the marginal cost of erosion control plus the value of reduced crop output due to erosion control.

It is clear that the firm has some discretion in complying with the performance standard: it may alter its technology, change the input mix, or invest in abatement. (In reality the selection of any of these alternatives usually entails changes in one or both of the others.) If not initially in compliance with the performance standard, the firm will encounter costs to comply. As Archibald (1988) pointed out, the effect of compliance upon output will depend on the availability and cost of abatement. If discharge levels are proportionately related to output, and abatement technology is not available, the firm will reduce its use of inputs. This in turn reduces output, so that the value of the marginal product of an input equals its cost plus the marginal cost of discharges. Where abatement is possible, it is likely to increase costs to the firm as higher priced inputs are substituted into the production process. In the long run, the result will be decreased productivity in the agricultural sector and/or a reallocation of resources.

For a design standard, the firm does not face a discharge constraint but is limited in its selection of production technologies or may be compelled to use a particular abatement technology. If the firm must switch its production technology to comply with the design standard, it will reduce its use of inputs; for a particular level of use, the marginal physical product of an input under the required technology will be less than the marginal physical product of the input absent the design standard. Although the design standard is imposed on the choice of technologies, it nevertheless affects the firm's selection of inputs and/or the efficiency of input use. If a firm is required to utilize a specific abatement technology, it will be costly to the firm because of its reduced opportunity set. A design standard for abatement will lead to a change in the input mix if the firm modifies its production technology to mitigate the negative effects that abatement has on output.

Both quotas and use restrictions have effects similar to a design standard imposed on production technology in that they limit the firm's opportunity set. For example, if a quota is placed on a particular input, the firm no longer has discretion to select the optimal level of that input in order to maximize profits (unless it would be optimal to use less than the quota amount).

Licensing and registration may also affect the firm's discretion in selecting technologies or inputs. In addition, these regulations may also increase the costs of certain inputs and labor services. For these types of regulations (design standards, quotas, use restrictions, licensing, and registration), the firm does not face a discharge constraint. Instead, the regulator expects that the regulation—by compelling the firm to modify its production activities—will lead to a reduction in discharges to acceptable levels.

Activity permits and management plans can have a wide range of impacts on firm behavior. A permit may simply require a firm to use a certain technology (design standard) or it may impose a combination of regulatory controls. In the United States, permits for point discharges into surface waters may specify performance standards for each discharge pipe. Permits for hazardous waste disposal may require facilities to comply with numerous design standards. Management plans, even when tailored to a farm operation, typically entail constraints on selection of technologies and inputs, which performance standards do not, but there are no legal or other impediments to combining performance standards and direct controls. In all cases, we would expect permits and management plans to have effects on firms that are similar to those of the regulations discussed above.

This discussion has presented a simplified static model of firm production decisions. In actuality agricultural production is characterized by input and output dynamics that affect intra- and interseasonal productivity (Antle, 1988). Although a thorough discussion of these dynamics is beyond the scope of this chapter, we should caution that analysis of the effects of regulation is greatly complicated by the dynamic nature of agricultural production and the uncertainty attached to most production decisions. When farmers are induced by regulation to account for externalities generated by their operations, they must relate their decisions to a joint production function in which both output and externalities depend on prior input levels, prior production decisions, and stochastic events. Just as the effects of externalities are interdependent across a range of time periods, so also are their control measures. The abatement decision described previously, in which the farmer strives to equate the marginal benefits of discharge payments avoided to the marginal costs of abatement plus the value of the marginal physical product of abatement, compresses the temporal separation between intermediate production activities and crop output, whose value, outside of contractual arrangements, cannot be foreseen by the farmer. Thus abatement decisions may be more relevant to future production decisions.

The abatement decision framed above overlooks another factor that should be considered in a dynamic model of production: the change in input quality over time (Archibald, 1988). A decline in marginal physical product may be attributed not only to control measures but to loss of soil productivity due to erosion, decreased pesticide effectiveness due to increasing pest resistance, or decreased water quality due to intensive irrigation. These costs are usually undervalued by farmers, particularly if they relate to "common pool" resources such as pest resistance or water quality. Farmers may compensate for their effect on production by substituting other inputs at higher private and/or social costs. Although the intended effect of a regulation is to reduce levels of externalities, input substitution may actually increase levels as new pesticides or fertilizers are brought into use. A production function that incorporates externalities should reflect a related set of social costs—the opportunity costs of resources used to develop new technologies or inputs to compensate for declining input quality.

The dynamic nature of agricultural production and the often latent nature of its externalities greatly compound the administrative and informational costs of pollution control measures, both incentive and regulatory. Baumol and Oates (1975) discussed at length the difficulties of setting standards and charges at optimal levels in either a direct or iterative manner: determination of marginal net benefits/damages, administrative flexibility, and time lags and uncertainty surrounding the effects of the control measures. Applying control measures to agricultural production amplifies each of these problems. It is often difficult to define the degree of damages, due to input substitution or long-term effects; appropriate adjustment of taxes or standards to induce desired environmental quality is made more difficult by stochastic influences on production of externalities; and time lags and variability surrounding externalities obscure the effects of control measures. These problems limit effective use of both incentive and regulatory approaches.

## REGULATING AGRICULTURE

This section discusses the design, implementation, and evaluation of an agricultural regulatory program, and how regulations may be used to control agricultural discharges to surface and ground water.

### Developing Agricultural Regulatory Programs

The development of agricultural regulations involves four interrelated issues:

1. The nature of agricultural pollution problems
2. The range of solutions available to deal with agricultural problems
3. The evaluation of alternatives
4. Achieving and enforcing compliance

*Types of Agricultural Pollution.* There are three major agricultural pollution problems of concern: sedimentation, nutrients, and pesticides. Sedimentation is a surface-water problem that annually results in billions of dollars of damages due to increased turbidity, impacts on vegetation and fish, and increased costs of dredging navigable streams and reservoirs behind dams. Nutrients pose both surface- and ground-water problems. The major sources of nutrients are animal wastes and fertilizer residuals. Pesticides may also contaminate both ground and surface waters, although most of the emerging concern is about chemicals leaching into ground water.

The nature of agricultural discharges is quite different from those of most point discharges. With the exception of discharges from concentrated animal operations, most agricultural pollution is viewed as a nonpoint problem because of the diffuse nature of discharges. Nonpoint agricultural discharges are difficult to monitor because they occur over a wide area and because they vary from day to day, depending on weather conditions and the frequency and timing of applications of pesticides and fertilizers.

Agricultural pollution is also different from other discharges to surface waters in that discharges are normally not made directly to the water body but begin as residuals in soils before they ultimately reach water. Thus, even if discharges could be monitored at the edge of the river or stream, all of the discharges could not be attributed to the nearest farm. The fact that discharges (and particularly sediment) are transported over land also suggests that there will be considerable time lags between the implementation of a regulation and observable improvements in water quality. Similar lags can be expected for pesticide and nitrate contamination of ground water, although these phenomena are only beginning to be understood.

*Addressing Agricultural Discharges.* The options for regulating agricultural pollution are more limited than for other environmental discharges because fewer opportunities for abatement exist. Usually, abatement in the context of point sources of pollution refers to treatment or alteration of a waste stream to mitigate its harmful effects before it enters a stream or river. It is difficult to abate agricultural discharges because of the diffuse nature of the discharges. The primary exceptions are the abatement of concentrated animal wastes and the use of buffers or filter strips to control sedimentation or at least influence the rate of runoff (or release of chemical residues into surface waters). Thus, the regulator must rely more heavily on approaches that affect the farmer's production decisions.

The prospects of using performance standards to address agricultural pollution are also somewhat limited in comparison to other water pollution problems. The major problems with performance standards for agriculture are the difficulty of identifying sources, monitoring compliance to the standard, and farmers' resistance to burdens imposed by changes in production practices needed to achieve a desired level of performance. The problem of controlling sedimentation serves as a useful illustration of the limitations of performance standards. Ideally, a performance standard for sedimentation would be defined in terms of the mass of soil crossing a property line or entering a water body. The costs of monitoring these discharges are probably prohibitive, assuming such monitoring is technically feasible. Also, sediments may move from one farmer's field to another's so it is difficult to assign responsibility for measured discharges.

An alternative performance standard for sedimentation would be to limit erosion and measure a farm's performance in terms of the estimated rate of soil loss. At present, we do not have great confidence in the ability of measurement tools such as the universal soil loss equation or the wind erosion equation to predict soil losses (Batie, 1983). These tools provide measures of soil removal but do not describe the ultimate fate of displaced soil, whether to other field areas or to water bodies. Even if improvements allow us to more accurately estimate soil loss rates, there still remain the problems of determining how each soil loss standard translates into offsite effects and then selecting the appropriate standard. For either type of performance standard, we still need to determine how discharges relate to water quality and ultimately to benefits.

A third option would be to define a water quality standard and monitor sedimentation in the surface water. The use of such ambient water quality standards would mitigate the monitoring problems but would require the regulator to allocate discharge rates and responsibility for noncompliance among numerous dischargers. In all instances, a performance standard will require farmers to determine what changes are necessary in production practices to insure compliance. Generally, this information is not readily available to farmers and would be costly for them to acquire. Also, land and the microclimate vary considerably across farms—two farmers implementing the same practices might achieve very different discharge rates.

Given these limitations, we would expect most agricultural regulatory programs to emphasize design standards and direct controls rather than performance standards. In fact, there appear to be few agricultural regulations that employ performance standards.

*Evaluating the Alternatives.* There are myriad approaches an agency might use to evaluate alternative regulations. A key constraint that affects the choice of evaluation methods is the statement of statutory intent regarding the objectives of the regulation. Regulators may be required to consider only alternatives that meet a prescribed goal, or they may be given considerable discretion because of a general goals statement such as "protect human health and the environment." Regulators also may be required to use or may be prohibited from using specific economic criteria such as the net benefits or cost-effectiveness criteria, as discussed below.

An agency could use the net benefits criterion to evaluate and possibly select among alternatives. If the net benefits criterion is used to select the regulation, the regulator avoids the problem of setting an environmental goal. However, depending on the magnitude of the relative benefits and costs, it could be efficient to take no action rather than implement a regulatory program. This may be unacceptable in the political arena or to the general public. Nevertheless, even if there is an environmental goal or the regulator is required to consider only options that result in environmental improvements, the net benefits approach can still be used to rank alternatives that meet the environmental criterion, assuming one can define more than one way of satisfying the criterion.

The major problem with the use of the net benefits criterion to evaluate agricultural regulations is our limited ability to accurately predict the environmental results (or estimate the benefits of environmental improvement). The first problem is the difficulty of understanding how discharges are affected by the regulation and then relating those changes in discharges to environmental quality. As noted in the discussion of agricultural pollution, there are stochastic factors that affect discharges as well as lags between discharges and resulting changes in environmental quality that complicate the estimation of environmental results. A second problem is the difficulty of valuing changes in environmental quality. The three types of agricultural discharges (sediment, nutrients, and pesticides) engender a range of environmental and health effects. Many of these effects are difficult to quantify or express in monetary terms. Thus, the net benefits approach has serious drawbacks as a method for evaluating agricultural regulations.

Another, more ubiquitous, evaluation approach—cost-effectiveness—avoids the problem of valuing the benefits of the regulation. The regulator establishes a qualitative or quantitative environmental goal and then evaluates alternatives that meet the goal according to their cost-effectiveness. The major drawback of this analysis is that it is useful only for comparing alternatives that achieve the same environmental results. The regulator will encounter difficulties in determining whether an agricultural regulation will achieve an environmental objective because of the problems of predicting how the regulation affects agricultural discharges and ultimately water quality. If the environmental results of alternative regulatory approaches are uncertain, the agency cannot conduct a credible analysis of the relative cost-effectiveness of the options.

There are other criteria that the regulator can use to assess agricultural regulations. These include economic impacts on farmers, administrative costs, environmental results, enforceability, flexibility to local conditions, and equity to farmers. Later in this chapter these criteria are considered in comparing agricultural regulatory and incentive approaches.

*Developing a Compliance Strategy.*   The final element of regulatory development is the implementation of the regulation. It is interesting to note that the supporting economic analyses of regulations typically assume that everyone in the regulated community will comply. Yet, like any innovation, there is likely to be a lag in compliance because of the costs and time required to disseminate information about the regulation and the time and expenditures required by firms to comply with the regulation. There may also be individuals within the regulated community who would not comply with the regulation unless compelled to do so. For this latter group, noncompliance is usually attributed to the fact that the costs of compliance exceed the expected costs of noncompliance, largely due to the probabilistic nature of detection and conviction and the limited severity of fines and other sanctions.

One element of an agency's compliance strategy is to make sure firms have information concerning their responsibilities under the regulation. A second element is compliance monitoring and detection of violations. There are many ways that regulatory noncompliance might be detected by an agency. The primary method is the site inspection. Site inspections may be conducted at regular intervals or in response to tips and other allegations of noncompliance. Other options include self-monitoring (and mandatory recordkeeping), ambient monitoring, and aerial surveillance methods. The appropriate method depends primarily on the type of regulation involved and the resources available to conduct monitoring activities. Another important consideration in selecting the monitoring method is the evidentiary requirements for imposing sanctions on violators.

For agricultural regulations, there are significant problems in trying to monitor discharges or ambient water quality. Both surface- and ground-water discharges are troublesome to monitor because of their diffuse nature and complex fate and transport properties. If contamination is detected at a location remote from the source, it may be difficult to determine and prove that a given farm is responsible.

The third element is to determine how the agency will encourage or enforce compliance with the regulation. The primary goal of enforcement is to bring all firms into compliance with the regulation. To accomplish this goal, an enforcement program generally relies on the use and threatened use of sanctions. Sanctions provide a linkage between incentives and regulations: they must be hinged on regulatory standards and they create ex ante incentives to comply. They can range from warnings or notices of noncompliance for first offenses to stiff civil or criminal penalties.

There are four basic attributes of sanctions: (1) they deter noncompliance specifically or generally; (2) they provide for retribution (less important with environmental noncompliance); (3) they may allow for removal of recalcitrants from the regulated community (e.g., bar firms that violate permits from surface mining) or at least temporarily suspend the firm's activities; and (4) they provide for restitution. Specific deterrence refers to the ability of a sanction to bring a violator into compliance, whereas general deterrence refers to the ability of sanctions imposed on one violator to affect the behavior of other firms or individuals. Restitution can be of two forms. The sanction may recover the dollar value of damages imposed on individuals or on the environment or they may recover the benefits enjoyed by the firm during the period of noncompliance. Conceivably, the size of the required restitution need not be tied to either of these amounts.

It is difficult to predict what level of agency effort will be required to implement a compliance strategy for a given agricultural regulation or to anticipate the level of noncompliance and the need for strong sanctions. As a result, compliance programs are often developed after a regulation is in effect—after the regulated community has had an opportunity to learn about its responsibilities and the agency can assess the likely rate of compliance. If the regulation is complicated, requires major expenditures by farmers, or is perceived to be unenforceable, the rate of initial compliance will likely be low.


## CURRENT AGRICULTURAL/ENVIRONMENTAL REGULATIONS

This section presents an overview of the regulatory approaches currently employed by a number of developed countries. These approaches are summarized in the tables in the appendix to this chapter.


### A Survey of Current Regulations

The regulation of agricultural nonpoint sources of pollution varies not only from country to country, but often from region to region within countries. Detailed information is not readily available for many regulatory programs, particularly in European countries. For this reason, in the following discussion U.S. programs may be overrepresented relative to those of other countries.

*Pesticide Regulations.* There are three general aspects of pesticide pollution that are amenable to control. The first relates to their manufacture and market availability—regulations concerning this aspect affect chemical manufacturers, firms that market pesticides, and retail dealers. In theory, enforcement should be straightforward because the regulated community is comprised of a relatively small number of firms that are readily identifiable and experienced in complying with regulations. The second area of control pertains to restrictions on pesticide use affecting farmers and commercial applicators directly. Regulations in this area have the closest connection to environmental quality but face major obstacles in enforcement. The third area of control concerns the manner in which pesticides are applied, including pesticide handling and equipment.

Most developed countries appear to have some form of pesticide registration. In those programs for which we have detailed information, the applicant must bear the cost of providing relevant data and the burden of obtaining approval, implying that registration is not a right but a privilege that may be revoked.

In the Netherlands, registration is considered by a committee representing four government ministries, each responsible for a different aspect of pesticide review: the Ministry of Housing, Physical Planning and Environment analyzes manufacturers' data regarding pesticide behavior in soil and water; the Ministry of Health examines pesticide toxicity; the Ministry of Agriculture and Fisheries reviews data on pesticide chemistry; and the Ministry of Social Affairs is concerned with issues of worker safety. After assessing their leachability, the committee classifies pesticides into one of two groups, "black" or "white," which differ in the use restrictions placed on them. The most notable aspect of the Netherlands program is the finite life of registration, a characteristic described as "sunsetting": although a registration period of up to ten years is statutorily permitted, most pesticides are assigned a two- or three-year registration period. This limitation is intended to facilitate the removal of chemicals from the market should health or environmental hazards be revealed at a later time. If such issues should arise, the burden of defending registration renewal would fall squarely on the registrants' shoulders.

West Germany's pesticide registration program is directed by the federal agricultural research institute, to which manufacturers must provide analytical data. The institute is entitled to review data and methodology for up to six months; requests for supplementary data must be answered by applicants within two weeks to avoid a recommencement of the six-month period. Data requirements have been expanded considerably by law since 1987 and now include behavior in air, ground-water contamination risk, and waste disposal. In addition, manufacturers must report annual amounts sold. As part of the review process, the institute requires applicants to conduct environmental fate studies according to set guidelines. The review itself is conducted by a committee representing three federal agencies: the agricultural research institute, the health agency, and the environmental protection agency. As in the Netherlands, compounds are classified according to leachability into one of three groups with different use restrictions. A further condition has been placed at the retail level—as of January 1988 all pesticide sales are required to be conducted by trained salespeople.

Sweden's pesticide registration program contains several unique elements affecting initial registration, renewal, and sales. In addition to providing information on effectiveness at normal usage rates, manufacturers are required to test for efficacy at lower application rates. Renewal of registration is not automatic—upon expiration, applicants bear the responsibility of demonstrating that continued registration is justified. In contrast to the requirement for trained salespeople in some countries, training for purchasers is obligatory in Sweden—farmers must complete a three-day course before they are permitted to buy pesticides.

In the United States, federal pesticide registration is administered by the Environmental Protection Agency under the Federal Insecticide, Fungicide and Rodenticide Act (FIFRA). FIFRA extends to the EPA a two-fold objective: to consider whether and under what circumstances a pesticide might have "unreasonable adverse effects," and to weigh these risks against the benefits of the pesticide's use. Based on the applicant's submitted data on toxicological characteristics, environmental impacts, and perceived benefits, a pesticide may be granted either general or restricted use registration. Restricted use registration applies to compounds that may pose unacceptable risks of user injury or environmental damage. Use of such pesticides requires certification, which indicates a knowledge of pest control practices and the proper handling and disposal of pesticides and their containers. Pesticide registration results in a label specifying conditions for its proper use and any other restrictions that may exist; in essence, the label defines what constitutes legal use of the product. Once a pesticide has been registered, its registration may be suspended or cancelled if subsequent information indicates that it poses unacceptable risks to human health or the environment. These risks again are balanced against benefits derived from the use of the pesticide, That is, the effect that its withdrawal would have on agricultural production and prices and thus on societal welfare. Pesticides thought to pose imminent hazard are subject to "emergency suspension." This involves immediate cessation of sale and use, as well as compensation for users, distributors, and manufacturers holding stocks of the "suspended" product.

Pesticide registration under FIFRA has become enmeshed in a number of substantive and administrative dilemmas. Debate about risks and benefits of pesticides founders on unresolved questions of long-term health effects and environmental fate, and is further complicated by questions concerning the aggregate impact of these chemicals and comparative risks of substitute pesticides. Due to the time required for review, few pesticides presently in use have undergone thorough analysis. Although registrations are supposed to be reviewed every five years, the burden of determining adequacy of support data and unreasonable risk still rests with government. Effectively, registration becomes a permanent property right once it has been granted.

Several U.S. states have established their own registration programs for pesticides sold within the state. Two of these, California and Nebraska, illustrate the different forms such programs might take.

California has a pesticide registration program that imposes more restrictive conditions than those attached to federal registration. With passage of the Pesticide Contamination Prevention Act in 1985, registrants were required to provide documentation to the state's Department of Food and Agriculture of the effects that agricultural compounds have on ground water. Any pesticide that appears in ground water and poses a threat to human health, according to statewide monitoring, will have its registration cancelled. A number of regulations also affect the sale of pesticides. Dealers must be licensed and keep records of the type and quantities of chemicals sold to individual farmers. In addition at least one trained salesperson must be present at each sales outlet.

By contrast, the orientation of Nebraska's pesticide registration program is toward protecting the farmer as consumer rather than promoting health or environmental safety—a relic of past problems with product standards. The state's Department of Agriculture reviews product labels and verifies that application conditions and performance claims are warranted. Standards for environmental impact are not included in the review process.

Great Britain is in the process of developing a new pesticide registration program under its 1986 Food and Environment Protection Act. Committees representing six ministries will review pesticide data and approve registration; these ministries will be those of Environment, Agriculture, Employment, Social Services, the Scots Office, and the Welsh Office. Registration will come under one of three categories: (1) full approval, with a 10-year registration period that is renewable but subject to review at any time; (2) provisional, limited to a single year or season but renewable after that period; and (3) experimental.

Where ground water is of critical importance as a drinking water source, regulations protecting wells and other sensitive areas can be the most direct means of safeguarding water quality.

The Netherlands has had well protection zones since 1970. Three zones are circumscribed around each well based on distance and travel time for ground water, the more conservative criterion being operative. The first zone is marked by a 50-day travel time or a distance of 30 meters from the well; the second zone is bounded by a 10-year travel time or a distance of 300 meters. No pesticides may be applied in either of these zones. The boundary of the third zone is the distance ground water would travel in 25 years or 1,200 meters from the well; only the less leachable "white list" pesticides may be used in this zone. In addition to well protection zones, a 1986 law gives provinces the authority to designate soil and ground-water protection areas, restricting use of substances that might harm endemic organisms, disrupt their biological cycles, or contaminate soil or water. Because control of this program is found at the provincial level, there appears to be much variation in its implementation.

Well protection regulations have existed in West Germany for about 10 years. Wellheads are circumscribed by four zones. The boundary of the first is 10 meters from the wellhead; pesticides and manure application are prohibited here. The second extends from 10 meters to the distance ground water travels in 50 days; nonleaching pesticides of low persistence may be used in this zone, although farming is prohibited. The third zone is the area from the second zone up to 2 kilometers from the wellhead; leachable pesticides of low or moderate persistence may be used in this zone. The fourth zone extends from the end of the previous zone to the outside edge of the well catchment area; highly leachable and persistent pesticides are banned in this area. Unlike the Netherlands program, the West German program is administered by each state ("Länd"). This delegation of authority may help to explain the fact that approximately half of public ground-water resources are not protected by the program (Welling, 1988).

Aside from federal pesticide registration, nonpoint-source pollution is viewed in the United States as a problem properly belonging in each state's domain. In practice, states often delegate much authority in this area to local government. In Florida, state permits for surface-water use are issued by water management districts. A great deal of discretion lies with individual districts as to the type of pollutants that may be controlled, given available resources. State permits are of two types: a Management and Storage of Surface Waters (MSSW) permit and a consumptive use permit. An MSSW permit must be obtained for activities such as highway construction that may affect water quality. It requires applicants to present plans indicating what best management practices will be instituted to control surface runoff. A "grandfather" clause exempts existing farm operations from obtaining an MSSW permit, although altering current land or water use eliminates this exemption. The consumptive use permit is required for routine use of water and enables the district to better manage its water resources. Unlike an MSSW permit, which has no expiration, a consumptive use permit is renewable. If, upon renewal, the district stipulates a condition such as a structural change that alters an applicant's current water use, the applicant will have to obtain an MSSW permit, which requires control of nonpoint-source pollution. The consumptive use permit can thus be an indirect means of overcoming MSSW permit exemptions allowed for agricultural activities.

Unlike some districts in the state, Florida's St. Johns River Water Management District uses the permit system to control pesticide contamination. Permits are contingent on management plans that may draw upon a broad range of practices, including integrated pest management, with specific instructions for pesticide use; structural elements such as buffer zones and vegetative cover on embankments; and fertilizer management plans that account for all nutrient sources. Where a risk exists that runoff may enter a body of surface water, the permit may prescribe the use of pesticides with a short half-life. Management plans for MSSW permits must specify which pesticides the applicant will use, and the district monitors the applicant only for those compounds. Another feature of the permit system is that permittees bear much of the cost of monitoring. Quarterly monitoring reports include chemical analysis by state-approved laboratories, although, due to the expense of such tests, testing for pesticides is limited to periods following actual application. Weekly monitoring may be undertaken when short-lived pesticides are in use to ensure that they adequately control pest problems. The expense of monitoring, particularly for pesticides, has prompted farmers in the St. Johns District to pool their resources in paying for laboratory and other services required for compliance to permit conditions; uniform performance standards are attached to permits, thereby reducing individual transaction costs. Ground-water monitoring is a provision being introduced into permits— as with surface water, ground-water monitoring will be based on performance standards, which are being developed by the district. Violations of permit conditions carry penalties of up to $10,000 per day for each violation. Although by state law agricultural operations may be exempted from severe sanctions, the permittee must present a persuasive case to be granted such an exemption.

Other measures have been adopted in several countries to regulate the application of pesticides. West Germany has recently mandated that new spraying equipment be approved by the federal government. Testing of equipment, presently a little-used voluntary service, can be mandated by individual states ("Länder"). A more stringent approach is being adopted by Sweden, which plans to introduce compulsory testing of all farm machinery. Aerial spraying of pesticides is banned by Sweden and restricted by several other countries including Greece; such restrictions are still in the planning stage in Great Britain. Great Britain is also planning to implement certification of pesticide salespeople and applicators. Sweden's 1984 Act of Agricultural Land Management bans the use of pesticides on nonarable land such as unplowed areas near fences and the edges of fields, as well as ditchbanks and roadsides.

In the United States, regulations affecting application are issued largely at the state or local level. California has several types of licenses or permits related to pesticide use. Before being granted a permit to use restricted pesticides or other materials, a farmer must become a certified private applicator. Actual use must be preceded by a notice of intent to apply the substance, specifying the time and site of application. This allows the California Department of Agriculture to verify that the substance has been approved for the intended use and that conditions for use are properly indicated. Licenses must be held by pest control operators and pest control advisors; the latter often work as salespeople for pesticide dealers or provide consultative services for farmers. Licenses entail 40 hours of classwork and must be renewed every two years. In Nebraska, wells used for chemigation must have valves to prevent chemicals from backing up into ground water. Ensuring compliance with this regulation is difficult, however.

*Pesticide Controls.* Of the three types of agricultural pollution, pesticides present the strongest case for regulation. The primary reason is the magnitude of harm that may result from pesticide contamination. Damage to the environment or human health may be catastrophic or may occur over a longer time period, adding an intertemporal aspect to the social cost. This is of major concern because the carcinogenic and mutagenic properties of most pesticides is unknown. Another argument for regulation of pesticides (although it does not appear to be a major factor in current regulations) is the "common pool" characteristic of pest resistance—unfettered use of pesticides shortens their useful life as an increasing number of pest generations are exposed and develop a resistance to the chemicals. No individual farmer has an incentive to reduce pesticide use because overuse by a neighbor may just as effectively reduce the resistance of their shared pest population.

As indicated in the preceding section, pesticide regulations are ubiquitous.

Nearly all developed countries appear to have established registration programs, several impose additional controls on farmers' use of pesticides if ground water is potentially threatened, and a few countries require licenses and training of pesticide applicators.

Registering the large number of pesticides in use seems a necessary and appropriate undertaking of government in its role as a gatherer and disseminator of information. However, registration can serve only a limited function in controlling agricultural pollution, acting not as a gate that allows "safe" chemicals to pass through, but one that merely bars the most potentially hazardous from access to the environment. With regard to manufacturers, the registration process should be evaluated at two stages: the efficacy of the initial evaluation and the procedures that ensue at the end of the registration period.

Most countries appear to have stringent toxicologic and environmental standards for evaluating pesticides, although the extent is unclear (most likely due to the limited available information for this chapter). If, as in the United States, assessments must consider benefits of use, risks to applicators, food residues, and external offsite impacts, then the evaluation process becomes vastly more problematic. Relevant chemical and analytical data must be provided by registrants, who presumably can gather this information at lower cost than could government.

Virtually all registration programs place the burden on manufacturers and other applicants to petition for initial registration, implying that they do not have an unbounded property right to place pesticides on the market. In many countries, however, this implication does not appear to hold at the point of expiration. If the expiration of registration has no discernible consequences for the registrant, particularly regarding the continued marketing of the pesticide, then the property right may shift de facto to the registrant. Such is the case in the United States, which, mainly because of administrative entanglement, effectively grants registration in perpetuity. By contrast, upon expiration Swedish registrants must present a strong case that continued marketing of individual pesticides is warranted. The Netherlands appears to tread a middle path, granting registrations of short duration to allow chemicals to be withdrawn from the market if hazards come to light; this approach may be the least costly in social terms given that limited resources may permit only reactive measures by government. However, the frayed ends of registration expiration/renewal in some countries point to an inherently flawed program. A critical element that seems to be missing from the programs surveyed is an assessment of relative risks rather than simply absolute risks—evaluating individual pesticides outside the context of substitutes and aggregate effects does not adequately portray risks that may exist. Available information about Sweden's program suggests that it requires such an evaluation to justify continued market availability; if so, it may place an inordinate burden upon registrants. Providing it has sufficient information, government is the agent best suited to conducting a comprehensive assessment of pesticide groups, which reasonably should occur when registration is initially considered.

A second but critical aspect of pesticide registration relates to "proper use" by applicators. Because pesticides are poisonous, registration sanctioning their use is vitally linked to specific methods of application. The difficulty of enforcing these provisions is a major flaw in most programs, which depend heavily upon compliance with product labeling. Promising approaches include mandatory training, licensing, or certification of applicators. California provides a noteworthy model in its requirement that farmers obtain permits to use pesticides, much as pharmaceuticals require a prescription. Regulations affecting pesticide use are also found outside registration programs, for instance, equipment and applicator training. This training is more likely to be related to safety concerns, although proper application rates may be included in such training.

The use restrictions described above that apply to individual pesticides are in some countries supplemented by use restrictions that apply to location. The effectiveness of such restrictions varies according to their specificity and level of implementation. In the Netherlands, wellhead protection criteria are established and enforced by the national government; it is possible that relatively homogeneous geographic and hydrogeologic conditions exist in this small country so that a uniform standard does not impose inequitable costs among farmers. Uniform standards may not be appropriate in a country with as large and varied a landscape as West Germany, however. Although the wellhead zones are set by the federal government, they are implemented (or, as often as not, not implemented) by the Länder. Even though there may be a recognized need for restrictions, local authorities may be reluctant to enforce standards that cannot be tailored to suit local conditions and may put the local agricultural economy at a competitive disadvantage relative to other areas. The problem of enforcement is compounded if it appears that the only party incurring risk due to contamination is the farmer himself. Local governments may have an interest in setting differentiated use restrictions for site-specific conditions; their familiarity with local resources might enable them to gather information at a lower cost than national government. In that case national government might best serve as a facilitator of local regulators, providing sufficient resources and enforcement authority to establish and implement local rules.

A problem that may not be sufficiently considered in pesticide regulation is the trade-off that exists between contamination of ground and surface waters. A number of European countries have sought to protect ground water with restrictions on the leachability of pesticides, but chemical residues that are not broken down in soil may ultimately endanger surface water as they are washed off. Conversely, U.S. programs that focus on erosion control may contribute to the decline of surface-water quality; for example, conservation tillage, a low-cost measure to reduce erosion, can entail increased pesticide use and greater surface runoff.

*Sedimentation Regulations.* Little information is available concerning sedimentation control measures outside the United States. Australia appears to have some regulations prohibiting the cultivation of highly erodible soils and restricting cultivation near watercourses. In the United States, sedimentation control has long been a central feature of voluntary programs directed at agricultural activities. Several states, including Iowa, Illinois, and Ohio, have gone beyond the voluntary approach to pass laws requiring that soil erosion be limited to specified soil-loss tolerances (T-values). With the conservation provisions of the 1985 Farm Bill, federal action against soil erosion has taken on a semiregulatory cast: by linking compliance with eligibility for farm program benefits ("cross-compliance"), the provisions do not mandate conservation measures, but they leave few options for farmers whose operations depend on program benefits. The conservation compliance provision requires farmers to prepare and implement conservation plans for cropping activities on highly erodible soils that are not placed in a conservation reserve in order to maintain eligibility for all farm program benefits, including price and income supports, crop insurance, farm loan programs, and other commodity-related payments. Plans must be completed by January 1, 1990, and fully implemented by January 1, 1995, in consultation with local soil conservation services. A "sodbuster" provision concerns highly erodible soils that have not been cropped between 1981 and 1985. Farmers who plow such land without an approved conservation plan forfeit eligibility to all farm program benefits. A similar "swampbuster" provision applies to wetland areas converted to cropland after 1985—cropping of such areas is prohibited subject to loss of program benefits.

Pennsylvania faces sedimentation problems, which are not adequately addressed by the conservation compliance program. This state has a permit system aimed mainly at controlling erosion due to nonagricultural activities such as mining and construction. Agricultural activities do not escape regulation, however. Operations exceeding 25 acres are required to follow erosion and sedimentation control plans; failure to do so can lead to criminal prosecution by the state. These plans specify structural BMPs such as berms or retention basins, which the farmer must put in place, subject to fines of up to $10,000 per day. The structural emphasis of the plans reduces the costs of monitoring and enforcement because violations can be documented simply by photographs. The state may delegate authority for permitting and enforcement to individual counties; at that level of implementation, program effectiveness depends heavily on the willingness of local representatives to enforce plans. A recent study indicated that although approximately 85 percent of agricultural sites studied had been assigned erosion and sedimentation control plans, implementation of the plans was often inadequate or incomplete. Even among counties granted equal levels of authority by the state, implementation can vary significantly.

A rigorous enforcement approach has been used in Bucks County, Pennsylvania. Violations there bring not a warning notice but prompt action by local officials. In dealing with agricultural violations, authorities may use a cooperative approach to bring the operation into compliance. Ultimately, however, violators may be brought before an administrative forum where the ruling of the local conservation district chairman is legally binding.

Florida's Water Management District permits, described previously, are used by some districts primarily to control sedimentation. This is the case in the South Florida Water Management District, where MSSW permits prescribe BMPs that are predominantly structural. Construction of BMPs must be certified by registered engineers, and responsibility for maintenance must be assigned before construction begins. Monitoring costs are shifted onto permittees via conditions attached to permits: bimonthly or semiannual reports produced by state-approved laboratories are required. The district has begun to verify the accuracy of these reports by testing duplicate samples. Allocation of the district's resources appears to emphasize prevention rather than prosecution of violations—oversight is focused upon the initial period of a new MSSW permit to ensure proper implementation. The district has a surveillance program that enables it to confirm adherence to permit conditions and evaluate their effectiveness in meeting water quality goals; however, this program is not used to routinely monitor agricultural operations (Rosenthal, 1988).

*Sediment Controls.* Erosion/sedimentation control has been subject to little regulation primarily because its effects were commonly seen as onsite, related mainly to individual production functions. If the concept of productivity is expanded beyond the farmer's concern with profit maximization, regulation would be justified. Soil productivity has consistently been undervalued by farmers compared to its social value because of the higher premium society places on long-term agricultural productivity and the lower discount rate it applies to investments that conserve soil. Increased cognizance of the offsite effects of sedimentation and the inadequacy of voluntary measures has strengthened the rationale for regulation.

A key issue that must be considered in implementing erosion control is what level of control might be achieved at reasonable cost, given a marginal cost curve that rises steeply with incremental gains in erosion control. The conservation provisions of the 1985 U.S. Farm Bill entail costs to the farmer at the lower end of the cost curve, because they target highly erodible soils. This approach is not strictly regulatory, as compliance affects only those who wish to receive farm program benefits. Erosion control rather than water quality has been the top priority of the U.S. Department of Agriculture's

National Conservation Program, a concern that was reflected in the 1985 Farm Bill (U.S. Department of Agriculture, 1988). As a result, farmers have been encouraged to take up low-cost erosion control measures, such as conservation tillage, which entail greater use of pesticides. Other regions have found that conservation compliance measures were not sufficient in meeting their sedimentation problems. The states of Pennsylvania and Florida have permit or permit-like systems that are implemented at local levels. Due to the measurement problems involved in assessing erosion, these permit systems focus on the use of BMPs that are primarily structural and thus less costly to monitor, requiring visual rather than chemical monitoring. Even so, the will to regulate can be extremely variable, particularly at the local level. Although instituting BMPs offers a great deal of flexibility, substantial resources are required to devise and review plans, to undertake and maintain construction, and to assess and certify effectiveness of the practices.

*Nutrient Pollution.* There are three general areas susceptible to nutrient pollution control: the manufacture or generation of nutrients; the storage of nutrients, particularly animal wastes; and the disposal or application of nutrients.

Several countries have set limits on toxic components of manufactured feedstuffs and fertilizers, including Sweden, Denmark, and the Netherlands, which has set a limit on cadmium content of 30 parts per million in fertilizer.

Another type of regulation limits livestock numbers on farm operations based on an animals-to-land area ratio; the rationale is to avoid overstocking land beyond its capacity to assimilate animal wastes. Norway and the Netherlands have such rules, as does Denmark, where the limit is two livestock units per hectare. Individual Länder in West Germany have the authority to enact similar regulations under the Federal Waste Disposal Act, although only two have done so: North Rhine–Westphalia and Lower Saxony restrict the animal numbers according to the amount of waste generated, the limit being three fertilizer units per hectare, equivalent to 4.5 livestock units. Broader regulations apply to livestock operations in a number of countries. In France, a 1976 law set forth rules governing livestock operations. Reporting requirements apply to those with poultry operations between 5,000 and 20,000, or beef or pig operations of at least 50. These operations must be located at least 35 meters from waterways, 200 meters from bathing beaches, and 500 meters from fish farms. Additional requirements are imposed on larger operations—those with poultry populations exceeding 20,000, beef populations of at least 250, or pig populations of at least 450. Farmers must obtain permission before conducting operations of such size, providing environmental impact studies that indicate how ground water will be safeguarded and wastewater discharges handled.

Since passage of its 1969 Environmental Protection Act, Sweden also has required that farmers obtain permission for livestock operations exceeding 100 animal units (a unit being equivalent to 1 cow, 10 pigs, or 100 poultry). Operations of this size face regulations regarding the location and design of farm buildings and storage and disposal of animal wastes; however, there are indications that monitoring efforts are not adequate to ensure implementation of these rules.

The Netherlands strives for a comprehensive solution to the management of animal wastes. Its Fertilizer Act established a "manure bank" to accept and redistribute excess manure to areas in need of fertilizer. Farmers are required to maintain records on manure generated and used; there are also regulations affecting the composition of wastes and their transport, and manure dealers must obtain a permit. Denmark, which also requires that large-scale livestock operations obtain permission from government, allows less formal arrangements to be made among farmers to dispose of excess wastes. In the United States, livestock regulations are set by state or local authorities; permits are commonly required for waste disposal into waterways. In Wisconsin, permits are issued to feedlot owners, who must prepare manure management plans that include information on crop rotations and maps of areas where manure will be applied. The operation must follow plan specifications on the maximum quantity of manure that may be spread per acre and proper application under conditions of frozen soil or snow.

Storage of animal wastes and silage is regulated in several countries, and is a particular concern where manure spreading over frozen soil is banned. Switzerland requires adequate capacity for winter storage given the number of animals present. In Denmark a nine-month storage capacity is required for farms with over 30 livestock units. The Netherlands is developing mandatory specifications for animal waste and silage storage. In Sweden, storage capacity for 6 to 10 months is required.

Regulating the application of fertilizers and animal wastes is by far the most common approach to nutrient pollution control. Austria and West Germany prohibit or restrict the spreading of fertilizers in some water recharge areas; Finland bans such activity within 50 meters of a waterway. In several countries manure spreading is restricted either by total or nutrient volume. West Germany regulates the amount of waste that can be applied to land. The Netherlands makes a distinction between cropland and grassland in setting phosphate limits per hectare for manure—these limits will be reduced 20–30 percent by 1991 and will undergo a further reduction of 12–30 percent by 1995. Farmers are required to maintain records on the amount of manure that is produced and spread. In Denmark farmers may not spread waste that contains more than 200 grams of cadmium per hectare; there are also regulations governing the amount of nitrogen per hectare that is allowable, equivalent to 2.3 livestock units for dairy operations and 1.7 units for pig farms. Alongside limits on volume, there are usually timing requirements regarding seasonal application and incorporating waste sludge into soil once it has been spread. The Netherlands restricts spreading to the growing season and requires that wastes be plowed into the soil within 24 hours of application. A similar Danish law requires liquid manure to be incorporated within 24 hours unless it is applied to a crop or pasture and prohibits any application on uncropped soil following the fall crop; other manure must be incorporated within 12 hours. Similar time limits have been adopted by some West German and Austrian Länder. Denmark has also taken up several regulatory approaches to nutrient management, which appear to be unique in Europe. Farmers are required to prepare management plans designed to limit nitrate and phosphate pollution; it is difficult to estimate how effective such plans may be, however, because actual compliance is voluntary. To reduce leaching, Danish farmers must follow fall cropping with a cover crop or pasture planted on a specified proportion of their land—the required proportion increased from 45 percent of acreage in 1988 to 55 percent by 1989 and will increase to 65 percent by 1990. Sweden and Great Britain have regulations prohibiting the application of fertilizers to meadows that have not previously been fertilized, although this restriction appears to apply in Great Britain only to some protected areas.

The localized nature of ground-water pollution control in the United States is illustrated by Nebraska's 1987 Ground Water Protection Strategy as adapted by the state's Central Platte Natural Resource District. The keystone of the district's program is a set of fertilizer use restrictions directed at specific soil conditions and existing nitrate levels. Well sampling has allowed the program administrators to assign land within the district to one of three categories based on type of soil and average nitrate levels found in ground water. The first category includes areas with sandy soil in which ground-water nitrate levels have tested at 8–18 milligrams per liter; commercial use of fertilizers is prohibited in those areas during fall and winter. The second category covers heavier as well as sandy soils where nitrate levels of 18–24 milligrams per liter have been found; in addition to a ban on commercial use of fertilizers in fall and winter, usage is prohibited when temperatures fall below 50° F. Conditions and restrictions for the third category are still under development. Farmers are obliged to conform to use restrictions of their assigned category regardless of nitrate concentrations in their immediate vicinity because assignment is based on average nitrate levels within the area. Land assignments may be revised every three years based on the program's monitoring of 600 wells. This monitoring will supplement nitrate testing data required from farmers who apply fertilizers to their land. Before being permitted to use fertilizers, a farmer must undergo state certification as a fertilizer applicant, renewing this certification every four years with mandatory coursework.

*Nutrient Controls.* Nutrient pollution may be somewhat more amenable to the use of design standards and use restrictions than is sedimentation because it is less dispersed at its source—there is a clear relationship between specific inputs and resulting problems. There are primarily two aspects of nutrient pollution regulation: inhibiting the quantity of nutrients generated and timing their release to allow soil to assimilate them. It is not clear whether regulations designed to achieve the first goal can be adequately enforced, either because of limited enforcement resources or because of the dynamic nature of farm operations. Regulating the release of nutrients into the environment may be somewhat more feasible, particularly for storage requirements, as these are primarily structural and can be enforced with visual inspection. However, regulations governing timing and volume of application are not easily enforced without the use of performance standards. As described above, a new program in at least one region will apply performance standards to nutrient use. The severity of nitrate pollution in Nebraska and the dependence of the state upon ground-water reserves engendered the unusual plan adopted by Nebraska's Central Platte District, which uses specific ground-water quality data and soil criteria to restrict fertilizer use, much as wellhead protection programs do. A drawback of this approach is a "free-rider" problem—regardless of nitrate levels found on individual farms, farmers' fertilizer use will be restricted based on average levels in the region to which their land is assigned, thus undermining individual incentives to reduce fertilizer use. However, given the imperfect state of knowledge regarding transport properties of ground water, this approach may be reasonable.

Nutrient management cannot be viewed separately from erosion/sedimentation control because nutrients are transported along with surface runoff. Therefore, efforts in either area are bound to positively affect the other.

## REGULATIONS VERSUS INCENTIVES

The previous section surveyed regulatory approaches for controlling agricultural pollution. Regulatory approaches are used extensively to deal with pesticides and nutrients, and less so to control sedimentation. The advantages and disadvantages of regulations were highlighted, although the information on international programs that was readily available was extremely limited in providing even a superficial analysis of program effectiveness.

This section provides a comparison of regulatory and incentive approaches for controlling agricultural pollution. Given the intense competition for resources to devote to resolving environmental problems, and growing concerns about agriculture's contribution to ground- and surface-water degradation, it seems worthwhile to explore opportunities for addressing agricultural pollution cost-effectively. Economists have for many years argued for greater use of incentive approaches to address environmental problems, largely because of their presumed advantages in terms of economic efficiency.

This section will briefly review the conventional wisdom concerning regulations and incentives and then focus this debate on their relative merits in addressing agricultural problems.

## The Efficiency of Regulations and Incentives

For simplicity of analysis, it is often assumed that the costs of identifying and implementing an optimal tax $t^*$ or optimal standard $d^*$ are trivial. Firms are assumed to be similar in that the marginal cost of reducing discharges $MC$ is the same for all firms. For an undepletable externality, the optimal tax is that marginal tax rate that is just equal to the sum of the marginal damages incurred by consumers and other firms as a result of a firm's discharges (Baumol and Oates, 1975). Given full information, the regulator would be able to determine the level of discharges the firm generates if it faced $t^*$ rather than a standard. The corresponding discharge level $d^*$ would be defined as the optimal standard (Figure 3.1). The optimal tax and standard result in the same level of discharges (by construction) and the same abatement costs for the firm. However, for the tax scheme, the firm is required to pay compensation for the damages resulting from its discharges $d^*$, whereas these damages are internalized by consumers and firms affected by the discharges under the optimal standard (Figure 3.1). As economists have pointed out, the tax approach provides an incentive for firms to reduce discharges below $d^*$. For example, if the marginal cost curve shifts down to $MC'$, the firm would reduce its discharges to $d'$ and save an amount equal to the area of the triangle $CAB$ in Figure 3.1. The standard also provides an incentive to shift the $MC$ curve down to $MC'$ with the firm saving an amount equal to the triangle $ABE$, but there is no additional reduction in discharges. In effect, the marginal cost curve is kinked upward at the standard.

If there are two types of firms, differentiated according to their $MC$ curves, the optimal tax and a differential standard both achieve the same environmental result, albeit with very different effects on firms. Under the optimal tax, firms with $MC$ have discharges $d^*$, and firms with $MC'$ have discharges $d'$. Firms with a lower level of discharges have a relatively lower burden under the tax. For the optimal standard, firms with $MC$ are required to comply with standard $d^*$ whereas firms with $MC'$ must comply with a more stringent standard of $d'$ (note that the differential standard is required in order to minimize total cost of abatement). In the optimal standard case, firms that can more effectively reduce discharges bear a greater burden than those firms with marginal costs of $MC$ . The cost inequity (penalizing the more efficient firms) of differential standards can be rectified by switching to a uniform standard or by developing a compensation scheme whereby more efficient firms receive payments from less efficient firms for making a greater contribution to reductions in discharges. As illustrated in Figure 3.1, the

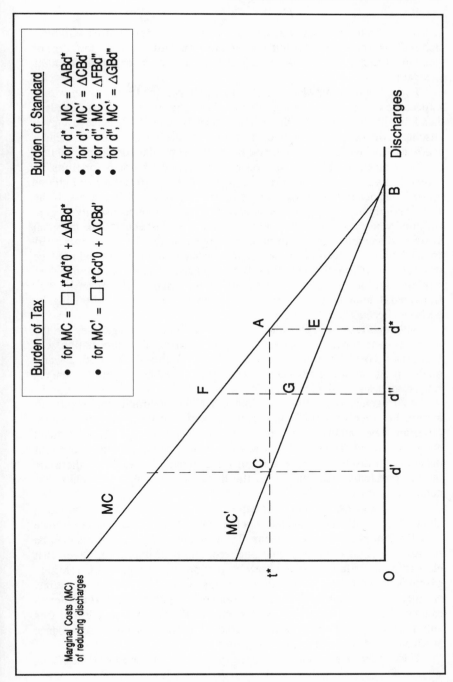

Figure 5.1 Taxes versus Standards

uniform standard $d''$ (assuming there are an equal number of firms with $MC$ and $MC'$) is less efficient than the differential standard in that the total cost of abatement under the uniform standard is greater than for the differential standard.

For a design standard as opposed to a performance standard, we would expect the marginal cost of abatement to be higher because firms have less flexibility in complying with the standard and may be unable to achieve a given discharge level at minimum cost. Thus, the design standard is clearly inefficient in comparison to either the performance standard or the optimal tax.

Subsidies and voluntary approaches imply lower burdens for firms. In effect, firms are vested with a right to freely discharge to surface and ground water, and society must bribe them to obtain reductions in discharges. If the firm is purely motivated by economic factors, it will reduce discharges up to the point where the marginal benefits to the firm are just equal to the marginal costs of abatement. For one form of subsidy where the firm is compensated for each unit of reduction below a certain benchmark, the firm would reduce discharges to $d*$ provided the subsidy rate $s$ is just equal to $t*$. Note that the cost of additional reductions below $d*$ to, for instance, $d''$ (given by the trapezoidal area $(FAd*d'')$ is greater than the increase in the subsidy $s \cdot (d* - d'')$.

Although taxes and subsidies are more efficient than regulations in the abstract, their superiority is less apparent when the full information/zero transaction cost assumption is relaxed. For agricultural pollution, a water quality program or policy—using incentives or regulatory controls—entails significant design and implementation costs.

If an agency is required to achieve a given environmental result, all approaches involve significant design costs and, at best, can deliver only uncertain water quality improvements. As previously noted, it is both difficult and costly to link discharge levels to water quality and production/abatement decisions to discharges regardless of the approach. In addition, there are unique problems associated with the different types of approaches that complicate program design.

For input taxes, the regulator will generally have imperfect information about the elasticity of demand that would enable it to set the tax rate or estimate how firms might respond to the tax. Typically, large marginal taxes may be required to elicit more than marginal reductions in input use. Given that elasticities are estimated for a narrow band of prices, the regulator is forced to extrapolate to effective prices far outside this range. For voluntary programs, an agency must understand the determinants of participation (in order to estimate the number of volunteers). For regulations, it is difficult to estimate ex ante what level of compliance will be achieved and how the rate of compliance is affected by different levels of enforcement effort.

Fluctuations in agricultural commodity markets can also exacerbate efforts to design pollution control programs. When market conditions are favorable, farmers may derive fewer benefits from voluntary programs and decide to bring marginal lands into production or alter production practices. Likewise, payment of input taxes may represent a low cost option to farmers if output markets are strong. Regulatory compliance rates may be affected by both weak and strong markets. In a strong market, the benefits of noncompliance coupled with uncertain detection and conviction may influence farmers' compliance decisions, and in a weak market farmers may be unable to afford the regulatory burden.

For those programs that provide farmers some discretion (taxes, subsidies, and performance standards), we need to recognize that it is costly for farmers to identify the combination of changes in production practices, input mix, and abatement that enables them to reduce discharges at minimum cost. A production/abatement strategy that seems appropriate to an agency may not be favored by farmers if it is costly to acquire information about the approach or if there are risks involved.

In general, incentive approaches are perceived to have lower implementation costs than regulations because they do not typically involve compliance monitoring and enforcement. However, if taxes are imposed on discharges or water quality, compliance monitoring costs can be significant. It should also be noted that there are methods such as cross-compliance requirements and recordkeeping that can reduce regulatory implementation costs. In addition, design standards and other direct controls are easier to enforce, although they are less flexible than performance standards.

## Matching the Approach to the Agricultural Problem

There are three types of problems for which regulations may be preferred to incentive approaches: ground-water contamination and pesticides, site-specific water quality problems, and multi-pollutant problems.

Pesticides, like other chemicals that engender human health effects, are typically viewed by the public as either safe or harmful. Farmers commonly consider a registered pesticide safe, and feel free to use it, complying with the manufacturer's application instructions. This view neglects the fact that the manner in which pesticides are used can greatly affect their potential for safety or harm—a pesticide's "safety" is inextricably linked to the quantity, timing, and method of its application. However, even if regulatory agencies were allowed to implement programs to reduce pesticide use at the margin, the problem of determining inframarginal effects of a vast number of chemicals with different response functions would be overwhelming.

Thus registration approach seems appropriate for dealing with hundreds of pesticides and their different formulations. Once an agency registers a chemical, it communicates to the public and to farmers that use is "safe."

Given our imperfect knowledge of the health effects and fate and transport properties of pesticides in ground water, it would be prohibitively costly to go beyond a determination of the safe threshold. The key drawback to using incentives to control pesticides is that the agency is expected to deter *all* use rather than achieve reductions. Admittedly, an agency could achieve the same result as a regulation by levying exorbitant taxes or offering large subsidies to farmers to quit using a given pesticide. If the tax or subsidy rate is set too low, market fluctuations or farmers' uncertainty about the relative costs of using and not using the pesticide might result in some use of the pesticide. Also, given the plethora of pesticides, it would be administratively costly to determine the appropriate charge for each pesticide.

Regulatory approaches—particularly use restrictions, permits, and management plans—are easier to tailor to local environmental conditions than taxes and subsidies, although information requirements may be substantial. Regulatory approaches do not provide price signals for technological development as well as incentives such as charges and taxes might. By the same token, the major problem with taxes and subsidies is that additional information is required to determine the tax or subsidy rate that will achieve the desired local environmental result. It may be difficult to administer a differential tax program as well. On balance, these factors may tilt the scales in favor of use restrictions, provided an agency can effectively enforce the use restriction.

Taxes and subsidies are also limited in their applicability if the agency must address more than one agricultural problem. A permit or management plan can be designed to address pesticide, sedimentation, and nutrient problems simultaneously whereas it would be difficult to design a tax that can accomplish similar results. Segerson (1988) suggested the use of a tax on ambient water quality combined with sanctions if the water quality goal is not achieved. However, such a tax scheme would impose considerable costs on farmers to determine their appropriate production/abatement decisions and to anticipate the actions of other polluters. Also, to reduce the free-rider problem, this tax scheme would require that farmers be jointly liable for exceeding the ambient pollution level. Such a strong liability rule is encountered in only one environmental program, the Superfund program in the United States.

## The Will to Control Agricultural Pollution

While economists weigh the appropriate use of regulations and incentives for mitigating pollution, in the real world a number of obstacles hinder extensive control of agricultural activities. Beyond the difficulties stemming from the diffuse nature of agricultural pollution, there are obstacles that spring from deeply rooted social and political convention and suggest a lack of "will" to regulate or use burdensome taxes.

Self-evident as it may be, it is important to note that agriculture's elemental role in the development of human society as well as the history of individual nations underlies its protected and even nostalgic status in most developed countries: to industrialized societies farming is viewed less as an economic activity than as a pristine way of life. Policies supporting the family farm exist in West Germany and Finland, where corporate entities are rarely allowed to purchase more than two hectares of land, and in the United States, which has a number of programs designed to assist the small farmer. European countries and the United States have implemented numerous programs to protect agricultural land from development. Farmers have been seen as stewards of the land whose entrepreneurial use of its resources was, for self-interest, tied to their proper maintenance; because damages were once assumed to be largely onsite, persuasion and education were viewed as the most reasonable methods of countering agricultural pollution. This bias in favor of a voluntary approach still prevails, often reinforced by a system of property rights that suggests the farmer has a "right" to use resources as he wishes. The political power of farmers in some countries is a strong deterrent to the enactment of regulations; those that do become law may not be stringently enforced due in part to local regulators whose sympathies might lie with those they regulate.

Another set of factors that has blunted the will to regulate or tax relates to the uncertainty that characterizes agricultural activities. Because of the competitive conditions and risk faced by individual farmers, government has often been reluctant to impose burdens that would in any way constrain profit maximization. There is a sense that the farmer is already heavily burdened by regulation and that additional restrictions would jeopardize operations that in any event tend to be financially vulnerable. In the United States there is a reluctance to establish regulations that might substantially reduce output and lower strategic commodity reserves, including measures that would make cropland, once taken out of production, difficult to put back into production. Flexibility in crop production is of particular concern in view of expectations that global climate warming will increase the frequency of droughts and consequently the risk of crop failures.

As discussed previously, the ability to implement regulations for agricultural nonpoint-source pollution is confounded by the diffuse and variable nature of the pollution: input use, weather conditions, hydrogeology, and chemical endurance pose a complex challenge to monitoring, detection, and enforcement efforts. The limitations are often technical as well as financial, due to the high costs of laboratory analysis and manpower requirements.

Given the lack of will to regulate and the expense and technical difficulties of adequate enforcement, it may be difficult to determine whether regulations will be any more effective than incentive approaches. However, it is worthwhile observing that tax approaches suffer from most of the same limitations as regulations and are consequently no more likely to be effective.

Incentives that involve subsidizing farmers to induce a change in behavior are popular with farm groups but are less popular with taxpayers who are becoming increasingly removed from rural areas and are increasing in political power vis-à-vis the farm constituency.

Finally, we need to recognize that the will to control problems is highly variable in agriculture. If agricultural activities threaten human health or vital resources, the will is much stronger, as we have seen with pesticides. Even though sedimentation and nutrient problems probably result in economic damages far greater than pesticides, there are many other sources of these contaminants besides agriculture and less concern about bringing them under control.

## FINAL THOUGHTS ON REGULATING AGRICULTURE

As the balance of political influence shifts away from agriculture and evidence mounts that most farmers are unwilling to extensively engage in voluntary conservation activities, regulatory solutions to agricultural pollution become more likely. (In the United States, astute people at the Department of Agriculture and in Congress are aware of this trend and are using the specter of environmental regulation to induce voluntary conservation among farmers.) Although tax approaches are potentially useful and more consistent with the "polluter pays" principle than other approaches, additional research on the elasticities of demand for inputs is needed to support tax schemes. Consideration should also be given to the relative effects that regulations and incentives might have on stimulating technological change.

Regardless of approach, there are some key research issues that need to be examined. We need to develop a better understanding of the profitability of alternative agricultural practices and the linkages between production decisions and discharges. Additional research is also required on the value of ground water and the value of health risks and other environmental damages associated with agricultural pollution.

The major expansion in regulations on agriculture is likely to be in two areas: agricultural contamination of ground water and pesticide residues in food.

### Agricultural Contamination of Ground Water

There is mounting evidence of the prevalence of ground-water contamination by agricultural chemicals, evidence that has generated support in the United States for targeting the most serious problems through the 1990 Farm Bill and other federal and state programs. Farm families are concerned about their health, and so there is a greater willingness to accept costly solutions to avoid or remedy contamination. Farmers may actually prefer regulation to voluntary approaches to avoid liability as well as free-rider problems.

## Pesticide Regulation

Public alarm over recent reports on the use of daminozide on apples has sparked renewed and intensified anxiety about the safety of the food supply in the United States. The U.S. public seems to have lost patience with the federal government's efforts to protect the integrity of the food supply and may insist that stronger measures be taken.

A prudent course for addressing sedimentation problems would emphasize permits or management plans. However, we need to go slow and form modest expectations regarding environmental improvement; we don't fully understand the cost implications of alternative practices or the lags between implementation and reductions in discharges. We also need to be cognizant of the joint production of sedimentation and nutrient concerns and of the potential for exacerbating agricultural chemical contamination of ground water while striving to reduce soil erosion.

## REFERENCES

Anderson, Frederick R., Allen V. Kneese, Phillip D. Reed, Serge Taylor, and Russell B. Stevenson. 1977. *Environmental Improvement Through Economic Incentives*. Baltimore: John Hopkins University Press.

Anderson, Rune, and Carl-Johan Liden. 1986. "Integration of Environmental Policies with Agricultural Policies: Sweden." Country Information Paper, Organization for Economic Cooperation and Development.

Antle, John M. 1988. "Dynamics, Causality, and Agricultural Productivity." In *Agricultural Productivity Measurement and Explanation*, eds. Susan M. Capalbo and John M. Antle. Washington, DC: Resources for the Future.

Archibald, Sandra O. 1988. "Incorporating Externalities into Agricultural Productivity Analysis." In *Agricultural Productivity Measurement and Explanation*, eds. Susan M. Capalbo and John M. Antle. Washington, DC: Resources for the Future.

Batie, Sandra S. 1983. *Soil Erosion, Crisis in America's Croplands?* Washington, DC: The Conservation Foundation.

Baumol, William J., and Wallace E. Oates. 1975. *The Theory of Environmental Policy*. Englewood Cliffs, NJ: Prentice Hall, Inc.

Fenner-Crisp, Penelope A. 1987. "Pesticide Registration and the Safe Drinking Water Act: A Federal Perspective for Health Standard Setting." *Pesticides and Groundwater: A Health Concern for the Midwest*. Navarre, MN: The Freshwater Foundation.

Great Britain, House of Commons. 1987. "Pollution of Rivers and Estuaries." Report of Environment Committee. London.

Great Britain, Ministry of Agriculture, Fisheries and Food. 1983. "General Information, Farm Waste Management." Booklet 2077.

Institute for Environmental Studies. 1987. *European Environmental Yearbook 1987*. London: DocTer International U.K.

Jensen, Mary. "Pesticide Regulation in San Joaquin County, California." In *Rural Clean Water Program 1988 Workshop Proceedings*. September 12–15, 1988, St. Paul, MN. Raleigh, NC: North Carolina State Univ.

Morandi, Larry. 1988. "Overview of Innovative State Policy Initiatives." *Agricultural Chemicals and Ground Water Protection: Emerging Management and Policy*. Navarre, MN: The Freshwater Foundation.

Nebraska Department of Environmental Control. 1985. "Nebraska Ground Water Quality Protection Strategy." Final Report.

Organization for Economic Cooperation and Development. 1987a. "Integration of Environmental Policies with Agricultural Policies." Report of the Environment Committee, Ad Hoc Group on Agriculture and Environment. Paris, France.

―――. 1987b. "Improved Integration of Water Resources Management With Other Government Policies—Summary and Analysis of Country Overviews." Report of the Environment Committee, Group on Natural Resource Management. Paris, France.

―――. 1988. "Opportunities for the Integration of Environmental and Agricultural Policies." Final Report of the Environment Committee, Committee for Agriculture. Paris, France.

Rainelli, P. 1987. "Intensive Animal Husbandry and the Management of Manure— The French Case Study." Presented at the Organization for Economic Cooperation and Development Workshop, Paris, France.

Rosenthal, Alan. 1988. "Permitting Nonpoint Sources." Report prepared for U.S. Environmental Protection Agency. (Mimeograph)

Segerson, Kathleen. 1988. "Uncertainty and Incentives for Nonpoint Pollution Control." *Journal of Environmental Economics and Management*, 15:87–98.

Tietenberg, Thomas H. 1984. *Environmental and Natural Resource Economics*. Glenview, IL: Scott, Foresman and Company.

U.S. Department of Agriculture. 1988. "A National Program for Soil and Water Conservation: The 1988–97 Update." Review Draft. Washington, DC.

Welling, Roberta. 1988. "Pesticide Regulation & Groundwater Protection in Europe." Report submitted to the German Marshall Fund of the United States.

Young, Michael D. 1988. "Some Steps in Other Countries." *EPA Journal*, Vol. 14, No. 3 (April 1988) 24–25.

Table 3.1A Pesticide Regulations: Registration and Sale

| Country / State | Registration Period[a] | Evaluation Criteria | Classification | Producer / Dealer Requirements |
|---|---|---|---|---|
| Netherlands | Mandatory expiration after a maximum of 10 years; most only allowed 2–3 years | Behavior in soil and water; toxicity; worker safety | Classified into 1 of 2 groups based on leachability | |
| Sweden | 5 years; upon expiration, applicant must justify need for continued registration | | | Test for effects at levels of application |
| United Kingdom | 3 types of permits: <br>1. Standard: 10 years (subject to earlier review) <br>2. Provisional: usually valid for 1 year or season <br>3. Experimental | | | Certification for salespeople planned |
| West Germany | 10 years | Soil, water and air behavior; ground-water contamination risk; waste disposal | Classified into 1 of 3 groups based on leachability | Environmental fate studies Report annual amounts sold Training for salespeople |
| United States (federal) | Permanent with review every 5 years | Toxicity; environmental impacts; expected benefits | | |
| California | | | | Document effects on ground water Dealers must be licensed and record sales to farms |

[a]Registration periods for countries with limited information: 3 years, Japan; 5 years, Canada, Finland, Norway, Spain; 10 years, Austria (in process), Belgium, Portugal.

Table 3.1B Pesticide Regulations: Use Restrictions

| Country / State | Program | Level of Implementation | Basis of Zone Differentiation | Basis of Pesticide Restrictions |
|---|---|---|---|---|
| West Germany | Well protection zones | State | Distance and groundwater travel time | Leachability and persistence |
| Netherlands | Well protection zones; Soil and ground water protection areas | National Provincial | Groundwater travel time | Leachability; Substances must not harm organisms or contaminate soil or water |
| Sweden | Agricultural land management | National | | Bans use on nonarable land |
| Florida: St. Johns Water Management District | Surface water permitting system | District | | Risk of surface water contamination; ground water standards being introduced |

| Country / State | Applicator Requirements | Use Restrictions | Equipment Requirements |
|---|---|---|---|
| Greece | | Aerial spraying restricted | |
| Netherlands | | Restricted use within water protection zones | |
| Sweden | Training for purchasers | Aerial spraying prohibited | Regular and compulsory testing to be introduced for all farm machinery |
| United Kingdom | Certification planned | Aerial spraying restrictions planned | |
| West Germany | | Restricted use within water protection zones | Approval required for new sprayers |
| United States (federal) | Use of restricted pesticides requires certification, but certification requirements vary by state | | |
| California | Certification required for all commercial applicators and advisors | Use of restricted pesticides requires prior approval by county agent | |
| Nebraska | | | Valves required for chemigation wells |

Table 3.2 Sedimentation Regulations

| Country / State | Location Restrictions | Cover Crop | Management Plans |
|---|---|---|---|
| Australia | Restricts planting crops next to water courses | | |
| Denmark | | Green cover crop or pasture is required each fall over a fixed proportion of acreage | |
| United States (federal) | | | Required for cultivating highly erodible soils in order to qualify for federal farm program benefits |
| Pennsylvania | | | Required for farm operations larger than 25 acres |
| Florida | | | Best management practices included in permits |

Table 3.3 Nutrient Regulations

| Country / State | Manufacturer Restrictions | Livestock Restrictions | Application Restrictions | Storage / Disposal Regulations |
|---|---|---|---|---|
| Austria | | | Spreading of fertilizers in some water catchment areas restricted/prohibited Some länder have restrictions similar to Denmark's | |
| Denmark | Cadmium lmit | 2 livestock units/ha | Liquid manure must be incorporated into soil within 24 hours unless applied to crop or pasture; other manure must be incorporated within 12 hours Maximum nitrogen application equivalent to 2.3 livestock units (dairy farms) or 1.7 units (pig farms) Limit of 200 g of cadmium/ha | Farms with more than 30 livestock units need 9-month storage capacity |
| Finland | | | Prohibits spreading of sludge and manure within 50 meters of the edge of a watercourse | |
| Netherlands | 30 ppm cadmium content in mineral fertilizers | Yes | Records to be kept on phosphate content of manure grassland | Plans to introduce regulations |
| Norway | | Yes | | |

| Country / State | Manufacturer Restrictions | Application Restrictions | Storage / Disposal Regulations |
| --- | --- | --- | --- |
| Sweden | Cadmium limit | Application prohibited on previously unfertilized meadows | Storage capacity for 6–10 months required; Special requirements for operations with more than 100 animal units |
| Switzerland | | | Storage capacity sufficient for number of livestock including winter storage |
| United Kingdom | | Application prohibited on previously unfertilized meadows in some protected areas | |
| West Germany | | Volume and timing of manure spreading; Restricted within wellhead protection zones and some water catchment areas; Some länder have restrictions similar to Denmark's | |
| United States | | License required for large animal handling facility to dispose of waste in a watercourse | |
| Nebraska | | Seasonal restrictions based on soil type and nitrate concentrations in ground water | |

# PART TWO

# Policy Applications

# FOUR

# Incentive Policies in Sweden to Reduce Agricultural Water Pollution

KARL-IVAR KUMM

The aim of this chapter is to describe and analyze incentive policies that have been, or might be, used to reduce water pollution from Swedish agriculture. Both measures covering the entire country and measures concentrated on a particular pollution-sensitive area are considered. As a background, a short survey of structural changes in Swedish agriculture during the recent decades is given. These changes have affected water quality and must be considered when discussing remedial policy measures.

## STRUCTURAL CHANGES IN SWEDISH AGRICULTURE[1]

Beginning in the 1920s, the amount of Swedish land under agriculture rapidly decreased. Initially the reduction mainly concerned meadow and natural pastures, but during the 1950s and 1960s, there was also a rapid decrease in arable land. The reversal ended around 1970, and agricultural acreage in Sweden has held nearly steady since that time. The reasons for this stabilization are higher domestic foodstuff consumption, resulting from food subsidies during the 1970s, and a national policy to protect arable land. Today, most of the subsidies have been removed and the arable land protection policy is under reconsideration.

In the postwar era, Swedish farmers greatly intensified their cropping, applying more fertilizers and pesticides, with higher yields per hectare as a result. A smaller number of hectares is thus required to meet domestic demands for foodstuffs. Agricultural production for export has not been profitable. Greater intensification together with the stable use of arable land since 1970 has caused surplus agricultural production in Sweden. The surplus must be subsidized to compete on the world market.

To solve the surplus problem, the cultivated area of agricultural land could decline again, the use of fertilizers and pesticides could be reduced, or both. In fact, policies encouraging both trends have been employed in recent years. During 1988, 15 percent of Sweden's grain area was put into a "soil bank." Several years ago, charges and taxes were introduced on fertilizers and pesticides in an effort to reduce their use. The chemical fees are also motivated by concerns over the environmental consequences of fertilizers and pesticides.

Another environmentally important structural change has been a shift from grassland for hay or grazing to cereals production. This shift relates to a change from cattle to pig production. In addition, grain makes up an increasing proportion of cattle rations.

Animal production has also become more concentrated to certain regions and enterprises. This is particularly true for the expanding pig production sector. To a great extent, this concentration has occurred in areas where the soil and precipitation conditions are such that the abundant supply of manure may cause considerable water pollution. Moreover, concentration of animal production has left many farms completely without animals. These farms are fully dependent on fertilizers for their supply of plant nutrients.

## Consequences of Structural Changes on Water Pollution

The structural changes in agriculture during recent decades have influenced the losses of plant nutrients (mainly nitrogen) to lakes, the sea, and the ground water in the following directions:

1. Abandonment of arable land has *decreased* losses of plant nutrients. A large proportion of the abandoned arable land has been planted with trees and the losses of plant nutrients from forest are lower than from cultivated arable land.

2. The shift in plant husbandry from grassland for hay or grazing to cereals has *increased* the leaching of plant nutrients.

3. The concentration of livestock to fewer but larger herds has also *increased* nutrient leaching. The reason is that many of the animal farms have insufficient land area for spreading the huge amounts of manure. Very excessive fertilizing generally occurs only in connection with manure spreading.

4. The increased use of fertilizers has *increased* nutrient leaching.

During the 1970s, most urban areas in Sweden built advanced sewage works, and today it is common that most of the phosphorus and nitrogen found in lakes and rivers originates from agriculture. Phosphorus is the element that governs eutrophication in most Swedish lakes. In the sea, on the other hand, it is frequently nitrogen that is the governing element. The importance of agricultural nutrients is evident, for example, in the Laholm Bay on the west coast of Sweden, which suffers from severe eutrophication. Sixty percent of the nitrogen entering the bay originates from farms. Excessive nitrogen in ground water is thought to pose health hazards. High nitrate concentrations have been measured in Swedish ground water, particularly in areas with sandy soils and intensive agriculture, such as the Laholm Bay region.

## INCENTIVE POLICIES TO REDUCE
## WATER POLLUTION FROM AGRICULTURE

In Sweden, incentive policies are used to reduce water pollution from agriculture and surplus cereal production. Examples of these policies are:

- Charges and taxes on fertilizers
- Extension service assistance to improve the handling of manure and to reduce the use of fertilizers
- Subsidies for afforestation of arable land

Charges and taxes on fertilizers have been used in Sweden since 1982. The original goal was to finance the costs of surplus cereal production. Today it also has the environmental goal of reducing fertilizer use.

Better manure handling has been the main focus of water protection policies affecting Swedish agriculture. Regulatory policies and extension services are the means used to achieve this goal. Regulatory policies include prescriptions for storage capacity for manure (eight months for cattle and ten months for pigs) and certain periods when manure must not be spread.

Subsidies for afforestation of arable land have had very limited use during the period of "arable land protection" during the 1970s. But in 1988, subsidies for afforestation were reintroduced. The primary aim was to reduce surplus production of cereals. Measures whereby the afforestation is directed to areas where it would also lead to important decreases in water pollution have not yet been used. One of the main goals of this chapter is to compare "directed afforestation" with other water-improving measures in a cost-effectiveness perspective.

### Charges and Taxes on Fertilizers

In order to reduce surplus production in agriculture and to finance the costs of exporting that surplus, a charge on fertilizers was introduced in 1982. It has gradually increased and is now about 20 percent of the price of fertilizers. In 1984, an environmental tax on fertilizers was also introduced. It is now 10 percent of the price of nitrogen and phosphorus fertilizers. Revenues from that tax are used, among other things, for research and extension services on environmental measures in agriculture. Table 4.1 illustrates how charges and taxes on fertilizers have developed over the years.

Figure 4.1 shows that phosphorus (P) and potassium (K) fertilization has

Table 4.1  Charges and Taxes on Fertilizers in Sweden

| Period | Charge (SEK/kg)[a] | | | Tax (SEK/kg) | | | Charge + Tax as a Percent of Fertilizer Cost[b] | | |
|---|---|---|---|---|---|---|---|---|---|
| | N | P | K | N | P | K | N | P | K |
| 1982/83 | 0.30 | 0.58 | 0.18 | — | — | — | 7 | 7 | 7 |
| 1983/84 | 0.60 | 1.16 | 0.36 | — | — | — | 12 | 12 | 12 |
| 1984 (second 6 months) | 0.65 | 1.25 | 0.39 | 0.30 | 0.60 | — | 17 | 17 | 12 |
| 1985 (first 6 months) | 0.72 | 1.38 | 0.43 | 0.30 | 0.60 | — | 17 | 17 | 12 |
| 1985/86 | 0.93 | 1.79 | 0.56 | 0.30 | 0.60 | — | 20 | 20 | 15 |
| 1986/87 | 1.12 | 2.43 | 0.76 | 0.30 | 0.60 | — | 25 | 25 | 20 |
| 1987/88 | 1.12 | 2.43 | 0.76 | 0.30 | 0.60 | — | 25 | 25 | 20 |
| 1988 (first 6 months) | 1.12 | 2.43 | 0.76 | 0.60 | 1.20 | — | 30 | 30 | 20 |

*Source*: National Agricultural Market Board, Jönkoping, Sweden.
[a]1 SEK = $US0.16; N = nitrogen; P = phosphorus; K = potassium
[b]Fertilizer cost excludes charge and tax.

Figure 4.1  Sales of Fertilizers in Sweden, 1961–1986

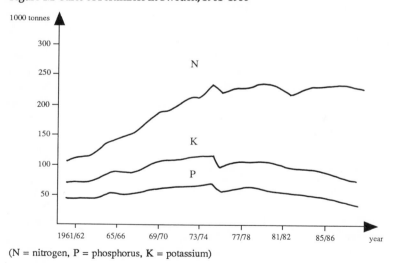

(N = nitrogen, P = phosphorus, K = potassium)

decreased considerably since the charges were introduced. But the reduction of P and K probably largely took place for reasons other than the charges. Studies made in the early 1980s showed, for example, that earlier extension service recommendations regarding P and K fertilization were too high even at the price level that prevailed before the charges (Dock Gustavsson and Sundell, 1983). Therefore, much of the reduction has been a response to better information.

Although phosphorus is of major importance for eutrophication, synthetic fertilizers are not the major contributors, at least not in the short run. The crop rotations and the manure handling are more important. The analysis below is restricted to the environmentally important use of nitrogen fertilizers.

It is difficult to evaluate the effects of the charge and tax on the use of nitrogen fertilizer. At the same time they were introduced and have increased, the relative prices of fertilizers (excluding taxes) and agricultural product prices have changed. In addition, protein bonus payments on grain have increased. The latter changes have increased nitrogen use. At the same time, environmental awareness has led many farmers to reduce their overall use of fertilizers from the excessive levels of the 1970s.

Figure 4.1 shows that sales of nitrogen fertilizer have been roughly constant since the charge and tax were introduced. The upward trend of the 1960s and 1970s was actually broken prior to the tax and charge. The slightly lower sales in 1987 and 1988 can be explained by the fact that a set-aside program was introduced during these years. This program decreased the cultivated area by 9 percent in 1988.

The most profitable level of fertilization for the farmer depends on the ratio between the fertilizer price and the product price. Table 4.2 illustrates how this ratio develops for nitrogen and barley. The price trend for barley is similar to other cereals. The ratio between the prices of nitrogen and barley increased after the introduction of the charge and tax in the early 1980s, but this increase is only partly explained by the charge and tax. The other explanation is that the nitrogen prices, excluding the charge and tax, increased faster than the product prices. The drastic increase in the ratio (from about 4 in 1981 to about 6 in 1985) did not reduce the sales of fertilizer-N, according to Figure 4.1. On the other hand, without these increases, the sales might have increased.

Calculations using linear programming at the farm level show, for example, that a 30 percent increase in the nitrogen price should reduce nitrogen fertilization by 10–15 percent (Mattsson, 1986). This suggests that the charge and tax on nitrogen, together amounting to 30 percent, should have had a considerable effect on nitrogen use. Mattsson's calculations suggest that a twofold increase in the price of nitrogen would reduce the use of nitrogen by 30–40 percent.

The effects of higher nitrogen prices on the amounts of nitrogen purchased have been counteracted by increased protein payments for grain. During the 1980s the protein payments have increased for wheat. This has increased the optimal nitrogen application rate to wheat by slightly less than 10 percent. Protein payments have also been introduced for feed grain. This has probably

Table 4.2 Development of Barley and Fertilizer-N Prices, Including and Excluding the Charge and Tax[a]

| Year | Fertilizer-N (SEK/kg N)[b] | | Barley (SEK/kg) | Ratio of SEK/kg to SEK/kg Barley | |
| | including charge + tax | excluding charge + tax | | including charge + tax | excluding charge + tax |
| --- | --- | --- | --- | --- | --- |
| 1971 | 1.50 | 1.50 | 0.45 | 3.3 | 3.3 |
| 1974 | 2.10 | 2.10 | 0.54 | 3.9 | 3.9 |
| 1981 | 3.90 | 3.90 | 0.96 | 4.1 | 4.1 |
| 1982 | 4.60 | 4.30 | 1.09 | 4.2 | 3.9 |
| 1983 | 5.40 | 4.80 | 1.17 | 4.6 | 3.9 |
| 1984 | 6.50 | 5.55 | 1.22 | 5.3 | 4.5 |
| 1985 | 7.50 | 6.50 | 1.25 | 6.0 | 5.2 |
| 1986 | 7.40 | 6.20 | 1.23 | 6.0 | 5.0 |
| 1987 | 7.10 | 5.70 | 1.16 | 6.1 | 4.9 |
| 1988 | 7.70 | 6.30 | 1.30 | 5.9 | 4.8 |

*Sources*: Agricultural Statistics (1986) and Swedish University of Agricultural Sciences (1988).
[a]1 SEK = US$0.16
[b]Calcium nitrate

increased the economically optimal rate of nitrogen application by approximately 10 percent on farms that produce feed grain for the market (Mattsson, 1986).

To summarize, the charge and tax may have decreased the use of nitrogen fertilizers by 10–15 percent ceteris paribus. The effects of the charge and tax have been offset to some extent by protein premiums for cereals and feed grains. Results from field trials presented by Joelsson et al. (1986) indicate that a decrease in the range of 15 percent or less reduces nitrogen leaching only marginally.

## Extension Service

Some studies have shown that it is possible on many Swedish farms to combine reduced application of fertilizers and better manure handling with better profitability for the farmers. This possibility is found mainly on farms with large numbers of animals and too much manure in relation to the area of arable land. In such cases, the extension service can stimulate the marketing of surplus manure to neighboring farms and reduce purchases of complementary fertilizers. This reduces water pollution from agriculture. The conditions for extension service help are illustrated by a study conducted in the Laholm Bay region in southern Sweden (Joelsson and Kumm, 1984).

The Laholm Bay region and parts of its catchment area have been declared a particularly pollution-sensitive area by the government. The area comprises about 60,000 hectares of arable land divided among 2,500 farms. Livestock keeping is intensive. A large proportion of the livestock consists of pigs, and the area of grassland is thus relatively small. In combination with permeable sandy soils and high precipitation, the presence of vast amounts of manure implies a major risk of nitrogen leaching.

During recent years, serious changes in the ecological balance in Laholm Bay have been observed. These changes have been linked to the large quantities of nitrogen entering the bay. Nitrogen stimulates algal growth, and large quantities of organic matter are formed. Degradation of the organic matter utilizes oxygen, and oxygen deficiency may stress fish and bottom animals. It has been calculated that 60 percent of the nitrogen in rivers emptying into the bay comes from agricultural land (Joelsson et al., 1986).

*Reduced Use of Fertilizers.*  The study by Joelsson and Kumm (1984) was conducted among 36 representative farms in the Laholm Bay area. It showed that the actual nutrient application on many farms was considerably above the economically most profitable level. Very few farms had a suboptimal application rate. By adapting nutrient application to the economically optimal level, it was estimated that the profitability could be improved by an average of 100–150 SEK (US$16–24) per hectare per year on the farms studied. The largest improvement in profitability was estimated to come from reducing purchases of phosphorus fertilizers. However, reduced use of nitrogen fertilizers also contributed to improved profitability.

If over-optimal nitrogen application rates were reduced, the leaching could be reduced considerably. The extension inputs on the 36 farms were made in 1982–1983. Measurements and evaluation of the extension results were made in 1984. It was found that a number of management changes had been made in order to adapt the supply of nutrients to the requirements of the plants. Nitrogen use had been reduced by 14 percent and phosphorus use by 38 percent in comparison with the situation in 1981. In the province as a whole, however, nitrogen use increased slightly from 1981 to 1984. Phosphorus use decreased slightly in the province as a whole, but not as much as on farms that had received special extension advice. Consequently, the evaluations suggest that specific extension inputs can improve the utilization of plant nutrients and reduce the load of nutrients emanating from agriculture. The use of extension was available before the taxes and charges were placed on fertilizer, but these charges have improved the possibility for extension to be effective by reenforcing the incentives to reduce nutrient use.

*Better Manure Handling.*  Some of the farms investigated have so many animals that the manure alone contains more nutrients than their own crops require. In order to utilize this surplus, the manure must be sold to neighboring farms that have no manure of their own. Such trading occurs already but could be increased. Within a certain radius of an animal farm, a suitable manure price will allow both the seller and purchaser to make a profit, even allowing for transport costs. The purchaser can replace some of the fertilizer requirements by cheaper manure. The seller will receive income from surplus manure, which has little productive value on his own farm.

Increased manure trade is associated with organizational difficulties. Farms with compatible supply and demand requirements and reasonable proximity must find each other. A comprehensive extension and information activity is required to make the market work.

The fertilizing effect of manure can be improved by spreading more during the spring and late winter and less during the autumn. In this way, more fertilizer can be saved. Later application also reduces the risk of pollution. On the other hand, increased spreading in the spring frequently requires investments in larger storage space. In addition, there is a risk of soil compaction and delayed seeding when manure is spread in the spring. On none of the 36 farms investigated in the Laholm study was it profitable to increase the storage capacity in order to increase the amount applied in the spring. The calculated deficits were so large that increased storage capacity is simply not profitable even with the prevailing taxes and charges on fertilizer. In this respect, extension advice and current fees are not sufficient to cause increases in manure storage capacity. At present, regulations are being used to force the farmers in the area to increase their storage capacity and spread manure only in some periods of the year.

## Subsidies to Afforestation of Arable Land

Swedish agricultural policy calls for reducing the surplus production of grain, and national environmental policy seeks to reduce the leaching of nitrogen. Both policies can be fulfilled by planting forests on arable land.

A government commission of inquiry (Ministry of Agriculture, 1986) estimated the socioeconomic effects of future surplus production of grain both in the short term (at least for the rest of the 1980s) and for the long term. In the short-term scenario, the costs for machinery, buildings, and land improvement, and so forth will be fixed, whereas in the long term they will be fluid. For southern Götaland, the most productive farming area in Sweden (also the location of Laholm Bay), the calculated socioeconomic deficit of export production is almost 2,000 SEK (US$320) per hectare per year in the short term and about 3,000 SEK (US$480) per hectare per year in the long term. For the individual farmer, however, production is profitable at least in the short term because the producer price is about 200 percent higher than the export price, which is probably closest to the socioeconomic value of Swedish crops.

During 1987 and 1988, farmers were paid to reduce their area of grain cultivation. In 1988, these payments amounted to 700–2,900 SEK (US$112–

464) per hectare depending on the yield level of the area in question. For woodland planting, a one-time subsidy of 2,100–8,700 SEK (US$336–1,392) per hectare was paid. In 1988, the area of grain grown decreased by 260,000 hectares as a result of the set-aside compensation. However, most of this area was fallowed or used for grassland production. Only 5,000 hectares were planted with woodland.

The commission of inquiry found that energy forestry and conventional forestry (spruce and birch, for example) offered the best prospects for profitable conversion from grain producing. However, lower energy prices in the 1980s have reduced interest in energy forestry. Consequently, conventional forest species are probably the major alternative to growing grain. This was also the case during the 1950s and 1960s. Today, however, the general public and politicians largely oppose the planting of woodland. To some extent this may be explained by the movement in the 1970s to preserve agricultural land. Among farmers, the most important reason for resistance is probably the domestic system of price supports for agricultural products. This makes continued agricultural production more profitable than planting woodland, at least in the short term.

In the Laholm district the economic ground rent for the farmer is about 3,000 SEK (US$480) per hectare per year in the short term with continued grain production (income including price support minus total costs except for the cost of land improvement, rent, and appreciation of machinery). In the long term, when land improvement and machinery are also variable costs, the ground rent is about 500 SEK (US$80) per hectare per year. The anticipated long-term ground rent for planting woodland is 500–1,000 SEK (US$80–160) per hectare per year. In the short term, however, planting woodland only leads to costs.

For grain production, the leakage of nitrogen is about 40 kilograms per hectare per year in the Laholm district, with its leaching-sensitive soils. If the land were planted with woodland, then the leakage would probably decrease to 10 kg per hectare or less (Joelsson et al., 1986; National Environmental Protection Board and Central Office of National Antiquities, 1988). The principal measures now being used to reduce nitrogen leaching are improved manure storage capacity, in order to reduce fall and winter spreading, together with increased treatment of municipal wastewater. The cost of reducing nitrogen leaching by means of these measures is about 50 SEK per kilogram (US$3.60 per pound) (National Environmental Protection Board, 1987). Alternatively, nitrogen leaching could be reduced by changing land use from grain production to woodland. In the Laholm district, about 30,000 hectares are used to produce grain. As shown in Table 4.3, if 10,000 hectares were transferred from grain production to woodland, nitrogen leaching would decrease by 10,000 times the leaching reduction of 30 kilograms per hectare, for a total of 300,000 kilograms per year. In this way, it would be possible to save 300,000

Table 4.3 Socioeconomic Comparison Between Planting Woodland on Land Presently Used for Grain Production and Larger Storage Space for Manure with the Aim of Increasing the Spreading in the Spring

| Alternative Measures | Socioeconomic Gain (+) or Cost (−) (million SEK/year)[a] | Reduced Load (tonnes N/year) |
|---|---|---|
| Transfer of 10,000 hectares of grain to forest | | 300 |
| Avoided loss for export production of grain | 18–36 (+) | |
| Ground rent in planting woodland | 5–10 (+) | |
| Larger storage space for manure | 15 (−) | 300 |
| Gain obtained by planting woodland instead of enlarging the manure-storage capacity | 38–61 | 0 |

[a]1 SEK = US$0.16

x 50 = 15,000,000 SEK (US$2,400,000) per year in other water management inputs and achieve the same environmental improvement. If this environmental effect is considered together with the socioeconomic cost of grain production for export, then large sums can be saved if the planting of woodland is chosen instead of deciding to increase the storage space for manure.

The Laholm area and most other areas with large nitrogen leakage from agriculture are generally homogeneous "grain deserts" where some degree of planting woodland would lead to a more diversified countryside. In these areas, more woodland would be a positive feature not only from the leaching viewpoint but also with regard to recreation, flora, and fauna.

Socioeconomically justified planting of woodland may be made economically interesting for the farmers through incentive policies. These may consist of reduced price support given to agricultural products and/or subsidies given to the planting of woodland. With incentive measures to foster the planting of woodland in pollution-sensitive areas and extension inputs designed to unite a better environment with better profitability, the need for costly regulatory measures can be reduced.

## SUMMARY

- Structural changes in Swedish agriculture in recent decades have influenced water pollution. The pollution has been increased by the shift from grassland production to grain production, the concentration of livestock production on certain farms, and the increase of fertilizer use. On the other hand, pollution has been reduced by planting woodland on earlier agricultural land.

- Sweden employs incentives to reduce agricultural surplus production and pollution through subsidies for the planting of woodland, extension inputs for improved manure handling and reduced use of fertilizer, as well as the introduction of fees on fertilizers.
- In Sweden, taxes and charges amount to about 30 percent of fertilizer costs. These fees have had only marginal importance in reducing water pollution, but they are important in financing the costs of exporting surplus grain and paying for research and extension inputs in the environmental sector.
- An extension experiment in a particularly pollution-sensitive area with intensive livestock production has shown that it is frequently possible to find changes that both improve profitability and reduce water pollution. These changes comprise, for example, adapting fertilizer use to the availability of manure.
- If nutrient leaching from agriculture is to be drastically reduced (e.g., by half), it will be essential to decrease grain production and increase the areas of forests and grassland. Reduced use of fertilizers and better handling of manure will not be sufficient.
- If the planting of woodland is to become economically profitable for the farmers on better quality agricultural land, it will be necessary to reduce price supports on agricultural products and/or increase subsidies for planting woodland.

## NOTE

1. Information in this section is based on Andersson (1986), Joelsson et al. (1986), and the National Environmental Protection Board (1986).

## REFERENCES

Agricultural Statistics. 1986. *Official Statistics of Sweden*. Stockholm: Statistics Sweden.

Andersson, R. 1986. "Losses of Nitrogen and Phosphorus from Arable Land in Sweden. Magnitude, Regulating Factors and Measures Proposed." Swedish University of Agricultural Sciences, Uppsala. (In Swedish with English summary.)

Dock Gustavsson, A.-M., and B. Sundell. 1983. "Plant Nutrients in Agriculture." Report 213, Department of Economics and Statistics, Swedish University of Agricultural Sciences, Uppsala. (In Swedish with English summary.)

Joelsson, A., and K.-I. Kumm. 1984. "Advisory Work Concerning the Application of Crop Fertilizers," SNV pm 1852. Solna, Sweden: National Environmental Protection Board. (In Swedish with English summary.)

Joelsson, A., H. Berggren, K.-G. Gustafsson, K. Persson, and R. Skogsberg. 1986. "Measures to Reduce Nitrogen and Phosphorus Leaching into Laholm Bay." County Administration, Halmstad, Sweden. (In Swedish.)

Mattsson, C. 1986. "An Economic Analysis of the Application of Nitrogen Fertilizer and Manure Handling." Report 265, Department of Economics and Statistics, Swedish University of Agricultural Sciences, Uppsala. (In Swedish with English summary.)

Ministry of Agriculture. 1986. "Measures to Reduce the Grain Surplus." Report by Commission of Inquiry, 1986:6, Stockholm, Sweden. (In Swedish.)

National Environmental Protection Board. 1986. *Agriculture and the Environment: A Programme of Action*. Solna, Sweden. (In Swedish.)

———. 1987. *Plan of Action for Control of Marine Pollution*. Solna, Sweden. (In Swedish with English summary.)

National Environmental Protection Board and Central Office of National Antiquities. 1988. "Planting Woodland on Arable Land." Solna, Sweden. (In Swedish.)

Swedish University of Agricultural Sciences. 1988. "Area Calculations—Agriculture." Report 143, Research and Information Centre, Uppsala. (In Swedish.)

# FIVE

# Programs to Abate Nitrate and Pesticide Pollution in Danish Agriculture

ALEX DUBGAARD

Two-thirds of the Danish land area is being used for agriculture, and more than 90 percent of the agricultural area is under arable cultivation. Accordingly, agricultural practices play an important role for the whole ecosystem and the landscape.

Like most other industrialized countries, Denmark has experienced a dramatic increase in the intensity of agricultural production, particularly with respect to chemical inputs like nitrogenous fertilizer and pesticides. In recent years this has created growing public and political disquiet over the environmental effects of agricultural practices.

Since the mid-1980s a number of political initiatives have been taken to remedy environmental problems created by agriculture. The most important are the so-called Aquatic Environment Action Programme, instituted in January 1987, (Ministry of the Environment, 1987) and the Action Plan to Reduce Pesticide Application, instituted in December 1986 (Ministry of the Environment, 1986).

Other important environmental legislation comprises: (a) regulations that restrict drainage of wetland, (b) prohibition of straw-burning from 1990, (c) public support for conversion of conventional agriculture to organic farming, and (d) an extensification program.

The scale and complexity of environmental regulations in regard to agriculture are so great that not all measures against damaging activities can be examined in this chapter. Only the most topical issues will be dealt with—the Aquatic Environment Action Programme and the Action Plan to Reduce Pesticide Application.

This chapter considers both regulations and incentives as policy instruments in this context.

## AQUATIC ENVIRONMENT ACTION PROGRAMME

During the last decade increasing attention has been focused on the rising content of nutrients in ground and surface waters. Excessive amounts of nitrogen in combination with phosphorus has resulted in widespread

117

eutrophication of water bodies—lacustrine as well as marine—with detrimental effects on aquatic life. Nutrient pollution of the aquatic environment has been subject to intensive public and political debate, especially in connection with the so-called NPO Report about nitrogen phosphorus and organic pollution of the aquatic environment (National Agency of Environmental Protection, 1984). In this report agriculture was made "responsible" for most of the nitrate pollution, and phosphorus pollution was attributed mainly to wastewater from urban areas.

The focus on agriculture as the primary source of nitrate pollution must be seen in relation to major changes in agricultural practices over the past two to three decades. In Danish agriculture the use of nitrogen in commercial fertilizers has increased by no less than 450 percent since the mid-1950s. Furthermore, the search for economies of scale through specialization has led to a considerable concentration of livestock production. This implies that some holdings produce excessive amounts of manure in relation to available land, leading to increased leaching of nutrients. It should be emphasized, though, that in spite of the coinciding trends between growing nitrogen intensity in agriculture and increasing nitrogen content in ground and surface waters, agriculture's contribution to nitrate pollution is not yet well defined.

## Regulations to Reduce Nitrate Pollution

In 1985, after a period of intensive political debate and departmental investigations, the NPO Action Plan was presented by the Minister of the Environment. In April 1987 the NPO Plan was replaced by the more comprehensive Aquatic Environment Action Programme (Ministry of the Environment, 1987).

For agriculture the overall objectives of the Aquatic Environment Action Programme are to eliminate pollution from storage of animal manure and silage, and to reduce nitrogen leaching by 50 percent. The most important initiatives in this context are listed below:

1. A stop to run-off and leaching from storage of liquid and solid manure and silage
2. Regulations requiring adequate storage capacity for animal manure— by far the most expensive part of the programme
3. Extended environmental approval of large-scale livestock production units
4. A stop to spreading of liquid manure on unvegetated soil in the period from autumn harvest until November 1
5. Restrictions on the maximum amount of nitrogen in animal manure that may be applied per hectare
6. Compulsory preparation of fertilizer management plans

7.  A maximum limit of 12 hours for working in manure after spreading
8.  Land use regulations that require the planting of autumn catch crops
9.  Programs to support the retirement of environmentally sensitive land

The most important of these regulations are addressed in more detail below.

*Stop to Run-Off From Storage.* These efforts seem to have been quite successful; less than 10 percent of the livestock farms had still not complied with standards in 1987 (Agricultural Organizations, 1989).

*Adequate Manure Storage Capacity.* Originally regulations demanded a nine-month storage capacity for all livestock farms with more than 31 livestock units (a livestock unit is the equivalent of one dairy cow or three sows with respect to manure production). However, political disputes and agricultural lobbying led to a compromise in 1988 modifying the requirements for storage capacity. This has resulted in a highly complicated legislation creating in fact a possibility for individual assessment of the need for storage capacity at each of Denmark's 30,000 or so livestock farms with more than 31 livestock units. It soon became clear that there was no political willingness to furnish environmental control agencies with the resources needed to enforce this legislation. Recognizing the lack of enforcement capacity, the government decided to transfer the responsibility for implementing storage capacity standards to the agricultural advisory service being run by the agricultural organizations.

*Application of Animal Manure.* Present regulation sets a limit for the application of animal manure equivalent to the manure output from 2.3 livestock units per hectare per year on dairy farms and 1.7 livestock units on pig farms. Farms with a livestock density exceeding the limits above may prove compliance with standards by presenting a written agreement with neighboring farms to receive excess manure. Actual compliance with such regulations, when manure is being spread, is virtually impossible to control.

*Fertilizer Management Plans.* Investigations indicate that farmers as a group are applying 5–10 percent more nitrogen than economically advantageous. Improved fertilizer management may therefore have some impact by convincing farmers to voluntarily reduce the amount of nitrogen applied.

*Autumn Catch Crops.* The purpose of the regulation requiring planting of autumn catch crops is to reduce nitrate leaching from bare fallow land. In 1990 land under catch crops must make up 65 percent of the cultivated area of each farm unless the land is already covered by winter crops, grass, sugar beet, or other vegetation. No monitoring or controls system has been implemented in relation to catch crops, leaving it in reality to farmers to decide to what extent they are willing to comply with the standards for autumn crop cover. Nevertheless, economic considerations have led to a considerable conversion of land from spring sown crops to winter cereals—also counting as catch crops according to legislation. This may bring actual practice up to official standards, even if for other reasons than legislative requirements. In 1988, the change in cropping pattern seems to have brought the percentage of land covered by crops in the autumn up to the requirements for 1990 for the country as a whole.

## Actual and Targeted Nitrogen Use

The government foresaw that implementation of the Aquatic Environment Action Programme would lead to a reduction in the use of nitrogen (in inorganic fertilizers) by about one-third between 1987 and 1990.

Figure 5.1 shows the development in the application of nitrogen in

**Figure 5.1   Actual and Targeted Nitrogen Use in Danish Agriculture (kilograms of pure nitrogen in commercial fertilizer per hectare)**

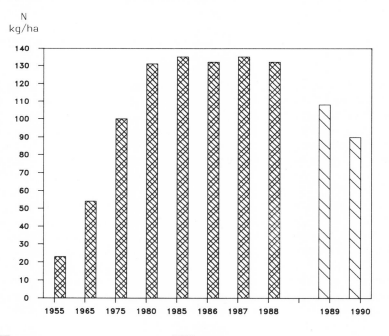

commercial fertilizers up to 1988 and the targeted reduction in nitrogen use according to the Aquatic Environment Action Programme. As seen from this figure, nitrogen consumption has been practically unaffected so far by the implementation of measures to improve nitrogen utilization, and there is little chance of realizing the targeted reduction of nitrogen use by 1990.

To bind the government to decisive action, a majority in Parliament had a resolution passed in 1987 demanding that a tax on nitrogen should be imposed in case agriculture failed to meet the required reduction in nitrogen use. More specifically, the resolution requests that the government impose a levy of 3 DKr (US$0.40) per kilogram pure nitrogen in commercial fertilizers in 1990 if nitrogen consumption had not fallen by 20 percent in 1989, and 6 DK (US$0.80) per kilogram of nitrogen in 1991 if consumption had not fallen by one-third in 1990.[1] The taxation rates suggested would increase the price of nitrogen by about 75 and 150 percent, respectively, in 1989 and 1990. According to the resolution, the tax proceeds should be returned to agriculture.

To provide background information for decisionmakers, the Institute of Agricultural Economics has investigated the economic effects of selected nitrogen control policies such as a tax on nitrogen in commercial fertilizers and a nitrogen quota (see Dubgaard, 1987a; Rude, 1987).

## Taxation as a Means of Controlling Nitrogen Use

By levying taxes on polluting activities, society can introduce a set of prices for the private use of social resources such as the use of air and water for the discharge of wastes. Thereby, the social costs of pollution can be internalized to polluters and cost-minimizing firms will cut back on emissions until the marginal cost of a further reduction equals the tax.

Nonpoint-source pollution, like nitrate leaching, cannot be monitored on a widespread basis at realistic costs. This makes the application of an emission-based tax infeasible. Instead, the polluting input, i.e., nitrogenous fertilizer, can be taxed.

Economic measures of controlling the use of nitrogenous fertilizers in Danish agriculture have been studied using nitrogen response functions[2] (Rude et al., 1986). In the optimizing procedure the costs of potassium, phosphorus, harvesting, and drying were specified as linear functions of yield. Pesticide application, on the other hand, was represented by a fixed spray program.

The findings indicate that the total use of nitrogen in commercial fertilizers would be reduced by about 25 percent if the average price of nitrogen was increased by about 150 percent (Rude, 1987; Dubgaard, 1987a). This is close to the policy target mentioned above.

A 150-percent nitrogen tax would reduce land rent by about 25 percent on good soil and considerably more on poorer soils. A tax reimbursement scheme would therefore have to be implemented, if significant producer (landowner) losses are to be avoided. An administratively fairly simple scheme would be to refund a flat rate per hectare.

The resulting tax burden would vary considerably between crops. A cropping pattern of cereals and peas would suffer the smallest penalty in absolute as well as in relative terms. Consequently, the present cropping pattern would probably change from oilseed rape toward grain legumes as a break crop.

## Quota Regulation of Nitrogen Application

Alternatively, the use of nitrogen could be controlled by imposing a quota on nitrogen in commercial fertilizers. If a market is established for the rights to purchase nitrogen in commercial fertilizers, an optimal distribution of available nitrogen may be found by the market. This approach is similar to issuing (transferable) discharge permits in the case of point sources of pollution where cost-effective monitoring of emissions of pollutants is possible.

Quota regulation has certain advantages compared to input taxation. It is often emphasized that input quotas would have less effect on farm income than an input tax, provided that they are allocated to farmers free of charge. However, if tax proceeds are reimbursed by a lump sum per hectare, the distributional effects would tend to be the same in both alternatives. It may be a psychological advantage, though, that money does not have to circulate through a distribution system in the quota alternative.

However, the predictability of the quantitative outcome of input quota regulation is no doubt a more important advantage. Using input quotas, regulatory authorities do not have to make estimates of the likely response by farmers to changes in price relations. The total amount of inorganic nitrogen purchased would be given in advance, whereas the distribution of available nitrogen between crops and regions and the price of quotas would be determined by the market.

Furthermore, quota regulation is also insensitive to price fluctuations. Input taxes, on the other hand, will have to be adjusted in case of (major) shifts in price relations if a constant effect on input levels is to be maintained.

However, the fixity of inputs in the quota regulation alternative may also be a disadvantage if the private optimum application level for a restricted input exhibits great fluctuations from year to year due to climatic or economic conditions. In that case, it will probably not be efficient to control the level of application by a fixed annual input quota.

This problem will be addressed later in relation to control on pesticide application. For nitrogenous fertilizer, on the other hand, the optimum level of application would usually not fluctuate to such an extent that quota regulation could be considered inefficient.

## The Effects of a Nitrogen Tax or
## Nitrogen Quota on Animal Manure Management

A cost-minimizing behavior by farmers will often lead to an application of animal manure with the primary purpose of disposing of it rather than utilizing its nutrients. In the western parts of Denmark, especially, intensive livestock production and excessive amounts of manure represent a greater nitrate pollution problem than application of commercial fertilizers. As mentioned previously, new regulations prescribe maximum application rates for animal manure. However, in practice it is virtually impossible to monitor compliance with this scheme. Economic measures may therefore be necessary in order to achieve the intended improvement in animal manure management.

A tax or a quota on nitrogen in commercial fertilizer could contribute to the improvement of animal manure management because the shadow price of nitrogen in manure would increase as a result of the higher price of the synthetic substitute. This would give farmers an incentive to improve the technology used for handling manure. However, further research is needed to assess how much this is likely to improve the utilization of nitrogen in animal manure.

## ACTION PLAN TO REDUCE PESTICIDE APPLICATION

The application of pesticides is the other major area of concern in relation to the environmental effects of chemicals used in agriculture. In Denmark the issues considered most important are the side effects of pesticides on flora and fauna and the danger of pollution of ground water.

### Targeted Reduction in the Use of Pesticides

In response to public and political pressure, in December 1986 the Danish government presented an Action Plan to Reduce Pesticide Application, which addresses the use of pesticides comprising all agrochemicals—herbicides, fungicides, insecticides, and growth regulation products (Ministry of the Environment, 1986). The action plan calls for a 25 percent reduction in total pesticide application by 1990. By 1997, the goal is to reduce pesticide use by 50 percent compared to average pesticide use in the period 1981–1985.

The decision to reduce pesticide application is interpreted as an equivalent percentage reduction in the amount of active ingredients used as well as the number of treatments. (The number of treatments is the number of times the whole agricultural area can be treated with the purchased amount of pesticides, assuming that a standard dosage is applied.)

A 50 percent reduction in the number of treatments is a stronger demand than a similar percentage reduction in the quantity of active ingredients. This is due to the fact that a considerable reduction in the quantity of active ingredients used will come about by itself through the introduction of new, much more biologically active substances with a considerably reduced dosage per treatment.

The use of the number of treatments as a measure of application intensity is based on the assumption that the frequency of spraying is an important indicator of the side effects on flora and fauna from pesticide application (or the level of kill of target species as well as other species). The quantity of active ingredients used is seen more as an indicator of the risks concerning the prevalence of pesticide residues in crops and the risk of ground water pollution by pesticides (Kjølholt, 1989).

The development of pesticide application and the differences between present application and the politically specified targets are seen in Figure 5.2. In 1988 the use of pesticides, measured by the quantity of active ingredients, was in line with the 1990 target. The calculated number of pesticide treatments has also decreased considerably since the record level of 1984. However, the reduction can be attributed mainly to a decrease in the application of fungicides due partly to relatively weak fungus attacks in 1988 and temporary changes in cropping patterns. Thus, the decline in the number of treatments may level off before the 1990 target has been reached.

The action plan prescribes only prevention activities such as improved advisory services and research as a means of achieving the specified targets. It is doubtful, though, that further education and research will lead to the targeted 50 percent reduction in pesticide application by 1997[3]—a doubt that is also expressed in the action plan itself.

## Taxation as a Means of Controlling Pesticide Use

On request of the National Agency of Environmental Protection, the Institute of Agricultural Economics has conducted a study to provide policymakers with information about the effects of using economic measures to control pesticide application (Dubgaard, 1987b).

Pesticides are not a homogeneous group of products. There are great variations in the amount of active ingredient used per treatment for different types of pesticides, and likewise considerable variation in prices per unit of active ingredient. The heterogeneity of pesticides makes it difficult to design a taxation scheme that would not overpenalize certain pesticides and underpenalize others. For example, a flat rate per kilogram of active ingredient would rest on the implicit assumption that adverse environmental effects of pesticides vary in proportion with the amount of active ingredient used. This is probably not so. Suggesting an ad valorem tax, on the other hand, one would assume that the more expensive pesticides would be the most damaging, which also seems unrealistic.

Figure 5.2   Actual and Targeted Pesticide Use in Danish Agriculture

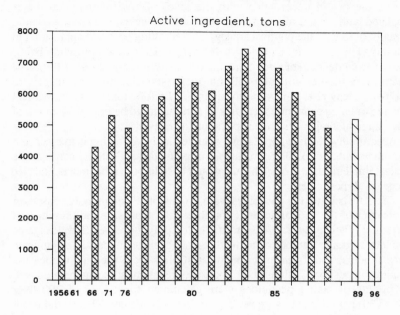

Active ingredient, tons

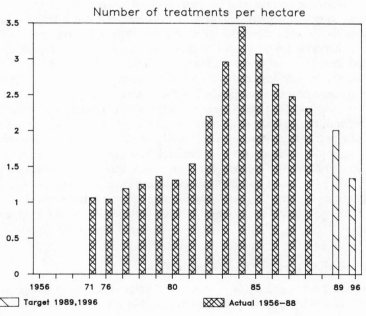

Number of treatments per hectare

Target 1989,1996            Actual 1956–88

Toxicity and/or decay rate might be used as more specific criteria for varying the tax in accordance with the level of environmental damage associated with the use of a particular pesticide. However, such criteria would not really fit in with the political strategy of controlling pesticide application in Denmark. The really toxic or slowly decaying pesticides are presently being removed from the market through regulatory measures (Sørensen, 1989). The remaining pesticides will probably not differ significantly with respect to toxicity or decay rate. It must be considered, therefore, that the main political objective of using economic measures of control would be the achievement of an overall reduction in pesticide application intensity.

Accordingly, the taxation scheme assumed in the following is in essence a tax on the number of pesticide treatments or pesticide application intensity. The practical implementation of such a tax would be to impose a flat rate per labeled dosage on all pesticides.

The effects of taxing pesticides were investigated using models based on the concept of the economic or action threshold, that is, the minimum pest population level for which it is profitable to apply a prespecified dosage of pesticide. To transform the economic threshold decision models into aggregate policy models, data from experimental test plots were used as proxies for variations in pest populations and response to treatment at the aggregate level. The effects of taxing pesticides were calculated for a levy of 200 DKr (US$26.30) per labeled dosage per hectare for all pesticides. This would result in an increase in the average pesticide price of about 120 percent.

Based on entomologists' judgment, it was assumed that a levy of this magnitude would induce technological improvements resulting in a 15–20 percent reduction in pesticide application compared to the present level. The estimated total effect of levying a tax of 200 DKr per labeled dosage is a reduction of pesticide application by 40–45 percent, which would be quite close to the targeted reduction specified by the government.

A levy of 200 DKr per labeled dosage would reduce land rent in crop production by about 15 percent on good soil. The income transfer effects of a pesticide tax can be neutralized by reimbursing the tax proceeds by, for example, a lump sum per hectare. However, due to an uneven distribution of the tax burden between crops this would result in a redistribution of income from farmers specializing in crops like winter cereals and sugar beets to farmers specializing in roughage and dairy production. A mixed farm would just about be in balance with respect to tax paid and reimbursed.

## Quota Regulation of Pesticide Application

Because of the heterogeneity of pesticides and great variations in dosage, the administration of a pesticide quota system would be much more complicated and costly than in the case of nitrogen quotas. However, administration and transaction costs might not be the most important objections to quota regulation of pesticide use. Large variations in pest population levels from year to year would probably be a much more serious obstacle to an efficient quantitative regulation of pesticide application.

For example, field trials show that the private optimum treatment level for insecticides in spring barley was fluctuating between 10 and 60 percent of the area under this crop in the period 1983–1987 (Hansen, 1989). The need for fungus control also displayed considerable variations. From 1981–1987 optimum fungicide application fluctuated from about 30 percent above to about 40 percent below the average treatment level (Jørgensen, 1989).

With such large annual variations in the benefits of pest control, the socially optimal application level would also fluctuate considerably, and it would be extremely difficult for a control agency to specify appropriate use levels for individual years. In practice, it is most likely that a fixed annual quota would have to be imposed, implying that actual application levels might deviate considerably from social optimum levels.

In practice, it is probably also impossible to determine an optimum tax on pesticides. Nevertheless, a taxation solution would be a much more flexible control measure, allowing pesticide application to vary from year to year in response to changes in pest population levels, climatic conditions, cropping patterns, and other variables. It seems reasonable to assume, therefore, that a taxation approach to pesticide control would be socially less costly than a quota approach.

## CONCLUSIONS

At present, Danish environmental policy in relation to agriculture is characterized by the existence of rather ambitious programs and legislation aiming at considerably reducing the intensity of agricultural production and promoting environmentally favorable practices. However, the attempts so far to enact the intentions of these programs clearly demonstrate the problems associated with regulatory approaches to controlling agricultural pollution.

Even for point sources of pollution, controls are difficult to enforce due to the diversified structure of agriculture with a large number of relatively small production units. To ensure compliance with standards, a considerable enforcement capacity is called for—a need that often will not be met by sufficient allocations of resources to the regulatory authorities concerned. For this and for other reasons, economic measures will often dominate regulatory approaches.

## NOTES

The author is grateful to John B. Braden for helpful suggestions on the content of an earlier draft of this manuscript.

1. This does not necessarily imply that the specified nitrogen taxes will in fact be implemented in case agriculture fails to realize the targets of the Aquatic Environment Action Programme. The resolution may be repealed by a Parliament majority, which at present seems the most likely outcome.

2. As an example, the nitrogen response function estimated for spring barley (on heavy soil) is

$$Y = 31.4 + 0.2239N - 0.00076N^2$$

where Y = yield in kilograms per hectare (kg/ha) and N = nitrogen use in kg/ha. At 1988 price relations the optimum nitrogen rate is 121 kg/ha. Expected average yield is 4.73 tonnes/ha at this nitrogen level.

3. The general opinion within the agricultural advisory service (run by the agricultural organizations) is that the targeted reduction in the number of treatments will not be achieved (Elbek-Pedersen, 1989).

## REFERENCES

Agricultural Organizations. 1989. *Survey of the Environmental Achievements by Agriculture*. Copenhagen, Denmark: The Agricultural Unions and the Smallholders Unions. (In Danish.)

Dubgaard, Alex. 1987a. "Reconciliation of Agricultural Policy and Environmental Interests in Denmark: Regarding Controls on Nitrogen Fertilizer." *Multipurpose Agriculture and Forestry: Proceedings of the 11th Seminar of the European Association of Agricultural Economists*, eds. M. Merlo et al. Kiel, Federal Republic of Germany.

————. 1987b. *Taxation as a Means to Control Pesticide Use*, Report No. 35. Copenhagen, Denmark: Institute of Agricultural Economics. (In Danish with English summary.)

Elbek-Pedersen, H. 1989. "The Advisory Services' View of the Action Plan to Reduce Pesticide Application." In *Miljø Danmark*, No. 1–2. Copenhagen, Denmark: National Agency of Environmental Protection. (In Danish.)

Hansen, L. Monrad. 1989. *Registration of Pest Populations in Spring Barley, 1988*. Lyngby, Denmark: Plant Protection Centre. (In Danish.)

Jørgensen, Lise Nistrup. 1989. "Regulation of Fungicide Application by Means of Economic Damage Thresholds." In *Economic Aspects of Environmental Regulations in Agriculture: Proceedings of the 18th Symposium of the European Association of Agricultural Economists*, eds. A. Dubgaard and A. Hjortshøj Nielsen. Kiel, Federal Republic of Germany: Wissenschaftsverlag VAUK.

Kjølholt, Jesper. 1989. "Declining Use of Pesticides." In *Miljø Danmark*, No. 1–2. Copenhagen, Denmark: National Agency of Environmental Protection. (In Danish.)

Ministry of the Environment. 1986. "Action Plan to Reduce Pesticide Application." Copenhagen, Denmark. (In Danish.)

——. 1987. "Aquatic Environment Action Programme." Copenhagen, Denmark. (In Danish.)

National Agency of Environmental Protection. 1984. "Survey of Water Pollution by Nitrogen, Phosphorus, and Organic Materials." Copenhagen, Denmark. (In Danish.)

Rude, S. 1987. *The Impact upon Agriculture of the Aquatic Environment Action Programme*, Report No. 34. Copenhagen, Denmark: Institute of Agricultural Economics. (In Danish with English summary.)

Rude, S., A. Dubgaard, and B. Laursen. 1986. "Economic Investigations of Nitrogen Fertilizer Controls." Unpublished report, Institute of Agricultural Economics, Copenhagen, Denmark. (In Danish.)

Sørensen, Niels-Erik. 1989. "Old Pesticides Risk Prohibition." In *Miljø Danmark*, No. 1–2. Copenhagen, Denmark: National Agency of Environmental Protection. (In Danish.)

# SIX

# National Agroenvironmental Incentives Programs: The U.S. Experience

KATHERINE H. REICHELDERFER

Modern American Agriculture is built on a system of positive incentives provided by the government—incentives to develop land (Homestead Act) and water (Reclamation Act) for agricultural production; incentives to remain in farming (parity pricing), to capital-intensify farming (farm credit), to produce particular commodities (target pricing), to reduce production of certain commodities (acreage reduction), to market for export (Export Enhancement Program), and, of course, to conserve soil and employ environmentally benign production practices. Free choice by farmers to voluntarily participate in supportive programs, or to vote for program choices by referendum, has long been the predominant federal approach to achieving change in the agricultural sector. Historically, direct and indirect positive incentives have been the most popular instruments for agricultural policy implementation.

Agricultural legislators, administrators, and interest groups have consistently and fairly effectively fought against any regulatory action perceived to have onerous consequences for the agricultural sector or for large groups of farmers (Batie, 1987; Bosso, 1987). Until very recently, even the employment of negative incentives to achieve agricultural policy objectives was rare. Voluntary behavior in response to positive incentives appears to remain the mechanism of choice for achieving current national agricultural policy objectives.

The favored status of incentives as a policy instrument has important implications for the evolution and performance of agroenvironmental policies and programs. As agricultural policy increasingly addresses environmental quality and resource conservation objectives, the lessons gained from past experience with agriculturally related conservation and environmental incentives programs should provide some clues about what can and cannot be expected to work well in the future.

This chapter briefly reviews the major U.S. agroenvironmental incentives programs of the last 50 years and identifies factors affecting the successes and failures of those programs. Federal pesticide regulation and regulations dictating environmental impact assessments for agricultural projects are excluded from consideration, even though they pose negative incentives, because they represent a regulatory vis-à-vis a strict incentives approach. The overview is restricted to those programs offering farmers and/or resource owners nonregulatory incentives. These include (1) a direct payment to modify behavior in a specified way that leads to improved environmental quality; (2) a monetary disincentive to behave in a specified fashion that degrades environmental quality; or (3) free technical assistance in modifying behavior. The majority of U.S. agroenvironmental incentives programs falling into these classifications have focused on soil conservation as the sole or a primary objective.

## NATIONAL RESOURCE CONSERVATION INCENTIVE PROGRAMS, 1935–1985

A variety of incentives have been applied to encourage improved management of soil and water resources. Major policy instruments include technical assistance as an indirect subsidy, direct subsidies, incentives for long-term land retirement, and cross-compliance disincentives. Neither taxes nor fees have been employed at the federal level as negative incentives for agroenvironmental improvement. The provisions of major national incentive programs of each type of policy instrument listed above are briefly reviewed next.

### Technical Assistance Programs

One approach employed extensively by the federal government is the provision of technical assistance, an incentive in that it subsidizes the development of human capital and improves the flow of information to farmers.

In the area of resource conservation, the primary technical assistance program has been the Conservation Technical Assistance (CTA) program, authorized by the 1935 Soil Conservation Act and administered by the Soil Conservation Service (SCS). The CTA, operated in cooperation with the nation's nearly 3,000 local soil conservation districts, provides technical support to farmers who voluntarily seek assistance in preparing and implementing soil conservation plans. The CTA accounts for the majority of federally provided technical assistance, although the Cooperative Extension Service and Forest Service also provide information and assistance in resource conservation. CTA expenditures grew from $286 million in 1986 to $366 million in 1988, and currently represent close to 90 percent of total, on-farm technical assistance and extension regarding conservation (U.S. Department of Agriculture, 1988). The program has been criticized periodically for its failure to target assistance to areas with the greatest erosion problems.

The CTA program, while encouraging soil conservation, may have discouraged conservation of wetlands. Prior to 1977, the program covered technical assistance for drainage and leveling of wetlands for conversion to cropland. After nearly 57 million acres of cropland had been drained under the program, technical assistance was suspended for most wetlands unless the assistance would improve wildlife habitat.

## Conservation Subsidies

Direct subsidies for the adoption of soil conservation technologies also have a long history. The Agricultural Conservation Program (ACP), administered by the Agricultural Stabilization and Conservation Service (ASCS), was authorized by a 1936 amendment to the Soil Conservation and Domestic Allotment Act of 1935. The ACP provides cost-sharing assistance to farmers for implementation of approved conservation practices such as contour farming, terrace construction, sod-waterway installation, and irrigation improvements. Cost-share payments to a single farmer may not exceed $3,500 per year. About $177 million was distributed through ACP cost-sharing in 1988 (U.S. Department of Agriculture, 1988). Similar, though smaller scale programs for on-farm conservation cost-sharing are the ASCS Water Bank Program ($8.4 million in 1988) and SCS's Great Plains Conservation Program ($20.5 million in 1988).

Soil Conservation Service programs providing federal financial assistance to local organizations include the Small Watershed Program, initiated in 1954 and directed in part to the reduction of soil erosion, sedimentation and runoff; and the Resource Conservation and Development Program.

In addition, ASCS administers the Forestry Incentives Program (FIP), under which cost-sharing is provided for establishment of tree plantings for conservation purposes. At its zenith, between 1978 and 1982, 1.1 million acres of cropland were converted to forestland under FIP (U.S. Department of Agriculture, 1983).

A number of critical evaluations of conservation cost-share programs have been conducted over the years. A 1977 report by the General Accounting Office (GAO) concluded that many of the practices cost-shared by USDA were misdirected toward production rather than conservation. A 1983 follow-up study argued that ACP funds should, in addition, be directed toward reduction of erosion damages rather than reductions in the physical quantity of erosion (U.S. General Accounting Office, 1983). As a result of such criticism, there have been several redirections of the ACP program since the late 1970s. A portion of ACP funds now is earmarked annually for direction toward critical resource problem areas, and cost-share rates may now be tailored to reflect the value of soil erosion reduction expected.

## Land Rental for Cropland Conversion and Retirement

One sure way to prevent the on- and off-farm costs associated with soil erosion from cultivated land is to take the eroding land out of crop production. Thus, two major programs have been implemented to encourage widespread conversion of cropland to grassland or forests. The earliest of these, the Soil Bank program, was initiated in 1956.

The Soil Bank program authorized voluntary participation in long-term (3-

to 15-year) contracts under which farmers were paid annual land rents in return for diverting crop acreage into conserving uses. Any land used for field crop production was eligible for the program. A total of 28 million acres was enrolled in the Soil Bank. All contracts expired by 1972.

The Conservation Reserve Program (CRP), authorized by the 1985 Food Security Act, is similar to the Soil Bank program in that it offers annual land rental payments and cover establishment cost-sharing in return for the conversion of cropland to grassland or forests under a 10-year maintenance contract, which prohibits any commercial use of the land. However, the CRP differs from the Soil Bank in several important ways: (1) CRP eligibility is restricted to land that meets specific definitions of "highly erodible" or poses specified environmental hazard; (2) real rental rates for the CRP are higher than for the Soil Bank, and are solicited through a quasi-bid system, and (3) the CRP is explicitly a multiple objective program, designed to meet agricultural supply control, water quality, wildlife habitat, and farm income as well as soil erosion reduction goals. Also unlike the Soil Bank, limits are placed on the proportion of cropland from any one county (25 percent) that may be enrolled in the CRP without special authorization.

The CRP was initiated in 1986 and has undergone several modifications over subsequent years. The first sign-up for the program was held in March 1986 under an initial implementation scheme that identified 69 million highly erodible acres eligible for enrollment, and under which rental rate bids from potential participants were successful only if they were less than or equal to an unannounced maximum acceptable rental rate. In subsequent sign-ups, eligibility criteria were expanded to include more acreage eligible under different definitions of "highly erodible," and maximum acceptable rental rates were preannounced. A one-time bonus payment for corn acreage was offered in 1987 to encourage greater CRP enrollment in the corn belt. In 1988, ASCS made several additional changes. To encourage tree planting on CRP land, erodibility requirements were relaxed for enrollees who plant trees. To achieve greater water quality benefits, land to be used as filter strip areas between cropland and bodies of water was made eligible for the CRP, regardless of the erodibility of such land. Following the drought of 1988, harvest of hay and forage was permitted on CRP lands in drought-stricken areas. These and other periodic changes represent increasing flexibility as the program matures toward its 1990 finale. Additional changes are likely.

As of spring 1989, about 30 million of the mandated 40–45 million acres of cropland have been enrolled in the CRP. A total of $1.6 billion was budgeted for the CRP in 1989. But serious questions are arising about whether it is possible to meet the full enrollment goal by 1990 within that budget constraint (Hertz, 1989).

## Cross-Compliance Incentive Programs

The 1985 Food Security Act also authorized three new cross-compliance programs for conservation purposes: sodbuster, swampbuster, and conservation compliance. The sodbuster provisions require that farmers who convert highly erodible native range or woodland to crop production must do so under an approved conservation plan to maintain soil erosion at or below the soil loss tolerance level, or forfeit eligibility for any USDA program payment. In similar fashion, swampbuster provisions require that farmers who convert wetlands to crop production lose eligibility for USDA program benefits unless USDA determines that conversion would have only a minimal effect on wetland hydrology and biology.

Conservation compliance requires that farmers cultivating highly erodible land begin to implement approved conservation plans on such lands by January 1, 1990, and complete implementation by 1995 or lose eligibility for USDA program benefits, Strict adherence to the soil loss tolerance rate will not be a criterion for plan approval. It will be left to SCS field offices to judge whether plans are economically as well as technically feasible alternatives for meeting the compliance requirement.

## EVALUATING THE EFFECTS OF INCENTIVES PROGRAMS

In 1988 a total of $2 billion in federal funds was spent on voluntary conservation incentives programs. These funds were supplemented by an estimated $1.8 billion in private, local, and state funds (U.S. Department of Agriculture, 1988). Total annual expenditures, most of which address soil conservation goals, represent around one-half to two-thirds of the $5.8 billion per year value of on- and off-farm losses associated with soil erosion from cropland (U.S. Department of Agriculture, 1988). Does past experience with the performance of conservation incentive programs suggest that we can expect significant returns to program expenditures of this magnitude?

There is no question that conservation investment has accelerated over the last 50 years, with consequent reduction in total soil erosion and its associated social costs. But several questions remain with respect to the relative contribution and cost-effectiveness of incentive programs in achieving conservation progress: What portion of observed, private conservation investment activity would have occurred in the absence of incentives? Have the returns that are independently attributable to incentives programs been maximized? To what extent is potential response to conservation incentives offset by concurrent provision of counteracting commodity program incentives? Research addressing these questions is summarized as follows.

## Macroeconomic Influence on the Impact of Incentives

Farmers will be induced to invest in conservation structures, apply new conservation practices, or enter into long-term agreements for land retirement only if they can expect the present value of private benefits to exceed private costs. Conservation technical assistance, cost-sharing, and land rental payments all reduce the private costs of conservation, thus increasing the probability that, other things being equal, private benefits will exceed costs. However, the present value of expected benefits is not a constant. In point of fact it is highly variable, moving over time as a function, in part, of interest and exchange rates.

Nielsen et al. (1989) in analyzing actual farm-level conservation and land improvement investments in 1980–1986 find that farmers' decisions to invest appear to be more strongly influenced by real interest rates and farmland values than by the availability of ACP cost-share supplements. Although they do find that ACP subsidies have a positive effect on conservation investment, their analysis suggests that the subsidy incentive can be overwhelmed by the influence of macroeconomic factors. In other words, even though there is always some margin for investment, macroeconomic forces shift that margin. A given level of incentives may be ineffective in inducing desired levels of conservation investment during periods, such as the early 1980s, when real interest rates are high, land values are low, and the present value of expected conservation benefits is low. On the other hand, the exact same level of incentives may be unnecessary to induce widespread conservation investment during periods when land values and farmer's expectations are high, and real interest rates are low. There is a distinct range of macroeconomic conditions over which each level of incentives will induce conservation investment above and beyond that which would otherwise occur. Because U.S. conservation programs have not utilized a system of variable incentive levels, the values of which could be adjusted as macroeconomic conditions change, we might conclude that the incentives offered through those programs have had a significant impact only when macroeconomic conditions coincidentally fall into the range under which the fixed incentive level is effective.

Nielsen et al. (1989) specifically tested the responsiveness of investment to ACP subsidies, but their findings are relevant to performance of the CRP as well. CRP enrollment was initiated during the peak of the farm crisis, when farmland values reached their lowest values in many years, and farmers' expectations were likely just as low. Although maximum acceptable rental rates for CRP bids have increased since 1986, their rate of increase has not been as great as the rise in expected net returns to land in crop production, especially following the drought of 1988. As farmers' expectations shift toward increasing future commodity prices, the CRP may seem, even at modestly increased rental rates, an unattractive alternative to crop production.

The implications of these relationships for the CRP are the opposite of those for investment incentives, namely: (1) conservation and environmental incentives for land retirement are most costly or least effective (at fixed rates) during precisely those periods of time when public concern for the social costs of agricultural production is greatest—periods of high commodity market prices and sectoral expansion; and (2) incentives for land retirement may be unnecessary during sectoral or general economic downswings, although their availability eases consequent exit from the sector, and their ties to environmentally sensitive lands shift the distribution of acreage remaining in production toward land with lower associated social costs.

## Cost-Effectiveness of Conservation Incentive Programs

The conservation technical assistance and cost-share programs that evolved under the New Deal era of the 1930s were originally designed with particular care to distribute transferred capital equally throughout the agricultural sector. As a consequence, they later came under attack for having failed to target subsidies appropriately to those regions and production operations on which soil conservation would yield the greatest social benefits. An evaluation of all national conservation technical assistance and cost-share programs estimated that the benefit-cost ratio for erosion measures generated by those programs in 1983 ranged from 0.3 to 0.9 in aggregate, and exceeded 1.0 only for the subset of measures implemented on cropland with erosion rates exceeding 15 tons per acre per year (Strohbehn, 1986). The fact that more than 80 percent of the land treated under these programs was eroding at rates under 15 tons per acre per year, and 40 percent was eroding at rates less than 5 tons per acre per year, suggests that significant gains in returns to federal conservation expenditures could be accomplished through program targeting (Strohbehn, 1986). The notion of targeting efforts to lands from which erosion rates and fate incur the highest social cost is straightforward and logical. Its actual implementation is less so, as it implies a regional redistribution of federal funds, with possible political ramifications.

Conservation Research Program implementation, too, has been found lacking in its potential to generate maximum returns to expenditure. Taff and Runge (1988) suggested that the CRP is "so encumbered with secondary objectives that it costs more and accomplishes less than it should" (p. 16). Surely, evaluation of the CRP is complicated by a lack of information on priortization of the program's multiple objectives. Still, a multiple-objective analysis finds that the "net government cost [of the 1986–1987 CRP] could have been reduced while simultaneously increasing the extent to which [both] erosion and supply control objectives were met" (Reichelderfer and Boggess, 1988, p. 9). The revealed preference of CRP administrators appears to be maximization of the number of acres enrolled rather than the benefits achieved through acreage enrollment.

Because there are no criteria that identify the degree of offsite and on-farm damages associated with parcels of land eligible for the CRP or subject to conservation compliance, there is no mechanism for assuring that net social benefits are optimized, and no guarantee that they even exceed the program's unit transaction costs. Proposed solutions to this problem include the use of a true bidding process, which matches bid values to the value of land's CRP enrollment (Phipps, 1987); and the differentiation of conservation and supply control objectives into separate programs, each targeting land with characteristics that make it most appropriate for its independent objective (Taff and Runge, 1988). Such suggestions for improved efficiency presume (1) there is a practical mechanism for characterizing each unit of land's erosion potential productivity on continuous scales; and (2) associated market and nonmarket benefits of lands' retirement can easily be measured. Unfortunately, the data required to do this are not readily available. Data collection would add considerably to the cost of program implementation, and it is unclear whether increased efficiency gains would be sufficient to offset added administrative costs of the program (Harte, 1988).

## COINCENTIVES AND COUNTERINCENTIVES

An incentive is "something that incites to action," according to Webster's dictionary. Applied to a system in which there is no other interference, an incentive will induce a given, often preestimable change in behavior. However, when applied to a system already rife with incentives, a new incentive will likely not act independently. It can become, in effect, a counterincentive or a coincentive. Counterincentives, in acting against existing incentives for opposite or inconsistent targeted behavior, will have less effect on behavior than they otherwise would if acting independently. Coincentives, by supplementing existing incentives for similar behavior, may bring about synergistic reactions, the combined behavioral effect of coincentives being greater than the sum of the incentives acting independently.

### Commodity and Conservation Program Interactions

The concepts of counter- and coincentives are relevant to the evaluation of conservation incentive programs because these programs are overlaid upon agricultural markets that are distorted by commodity and related farm programs. To some extent, the interactions between commodity program and conservation program incentives will determine how effective each will be. For example, although the CRP was originally envisioned as a substitute for a portion of acreage that would otherwise be retired through annual acreage reduction programs, these programs have instead become strong competitors for CRP enrollment. At current CRP rental rates and current deficiency payment rates, it pays many farmers more to continue short-term acreage retirement through commodity program participation than to enroll land in the CRP. Either CRP rental rates (and the associated public cost of the CRP) must go up, or deficiency payment rates must go down to make the CRP an attractive enough option to bring much more land into the reserve.

While the CRP offers counterincentives to commodity program participation, it may create a coincentive that reinforces the long-term trend in development and use of land-saving agricultural inputs. The extent to which increased environmental hazard resulting from continued intensification on land remaining in production would offset some of the environmental gains from large-scale acreage retirement is an open question. The trade-offs between land intensive and extensive production may require more study before we tie up too much more land in long-term retirement programs.

Cross-compliance disincentives perform exceptionally well in assuring that commodity program participants adhere to minimum standards for protection of society's interests in soil conservation. Whether they can lead to successful enhancement of either environmental or agricultural policy goals is an entirely different question. The consistency aspect of compliance schemes may also prove to be their downfall. For example, sodbuster, swampbuster, and conservation compliance were not just made consistent with other farm programs, they were inextricably linked with them by virtue of the fact that the enormity of the penalty for noncompliance is a function of the attractiveness of the other programs' benefits. This relationship works fine, as a coincentive, when there are conditions of surplus and low commodity prices, such as there were when the legislation was formulated. But, as stocks deplete, commodity prices rise, and prospects improve for high, market-determined farm income, the tight linkage between programs will make the cross-compliance provisions ineffective. By tying these programs' incentives to the existence of other farm programs, their success in protecting the environment becomes a direct function of unrelated programs' benefits. Furthermore, disregarding the contribution of program nonparticipants to environmental problems leads to slippage in the achievement of conservation goals even when cross-compliance is an effective disincentive for program participants.

## State-Federal Policy Interactions

State-level agroenvironmental policies can also provide either coincentives or counterincentives to federal programs. Over the last five years, in particular, state governments have been active in proposing, passing, and implementing legislation concerning soil conservation, surface- and ground-water protection, and agricultural pesticide use. The policy instruments employed by states to implement this legislation run the gamut from programs that provide incentives for adoption of beneficial management systems to laws that limit land use or regulate production practices.[1] The states are more prone than is the federal government to use taxes, fees, fines, regulations, and liability rules, either exclusively or in combination with positive incentives, to affect farm practices.

Intervention by state or local governments rather than the federal government is particularly well justified where the site specificity of an agricultural externality and/or political-economic situation limits the need for resolution of market failure to small geographic areas (Chapter 1, this volume). Federal intervention presumably addresses problems that cross geographic boundaries or are recognized as national priorities despite site-specific aspects of their manifestation. In recent years, the distinction between the state and federal approaches to agroenvironmental problems has blurred under federal legislation that directs state action. For example, the Clean Water Act (P.L. 92–500), as amended in 1987, requires states to manage nonpoint sources of water pollution and includes a 50-percent grant program to carry out state ground-water protection activities. The states have discretion in determining the policy approach and instruments they will employ to meet the federal mandate. This institutional arrangement is meant to establish state programs that act as coincentives to federal water quality priorities. But, in reality, the nature of federal-state policy interaction is heavily dependent upon the degree to which programs are coordinated within the state and with other federal programs. Interagency coordination has been identified as an important issue by states developing ground-water protection strategies (Batie and Diebel, 1989).

State programs are most likely to provide effective coincentives when they are designed to increase, directly or indirectly, the private benefits of participation in federal agroenvironmental incentives programs. An example of direct enhancement of private benefits is provided by Minnesota's Reinvest in Minnesota (RIM) program, under which the state has augmented federal CRP rental payments. By increasing CRP bid-to-land rent ratios in designated areas, the RIM program payments have significantly increased CRP participation rates in Minnesota relative to other lake states (Dicks, 1987). The State gains from its ability to target CRP acres to areas of particular state concern. Ogg (1986) called this a "two-layered system of targeting," which creates state coincentives for federal programs as well as a federal coincentive for state priorities.

In a less direct fashion, state-imposed regulations or negative incentives also can act as coincentives for generally positive federal agroenvironmental incentives programs. Placing taxes on agricultural chemicals, as has been done by Iowa, for example, may raise the cost of production by a sufficient amount to induce voluntary adoption of state or federally sponsored best management practices or to make participation in the CRP a viable option. State regulations that prohibit particular production practices will similarly induce a change in behavior that may, or may not, complement federal priorities. Even the threat of state regulatory action is viewed as an inducement for farmer participation in federal programs offering positive incentives for voluntary change in management practices. The point often being made to farmers is that if they don't avail themselves of the opportunities provided through the paternalistic federal programs, the state has no option but to impose restrictive regulation of farm practices.

Potential federal-state program conflicts may arise under a range of circumstances. For example, as federal programs evolve toward a focus on agricultural contamination of ground water, they may provide counter-incentives against programs of states primarily concerned with surface-water quality problems. Or, federal programs that attempt to limit entry into the agricultural sector as a way to deal jointly with excess output and externalities may be counteracted by State incentive programs that encourage new entry.

In any case, market conditions also play a critical role in determining the extent to which state and federal programs complement or conflict with one another. If a fixed, federal incentive payment level is insufficient under specific macroeconomic and market conditions to induce a desired change in behavior on its own, the addition of state coincentives can push the total incentive value into the effective margin defined by general economic conditions. On the other hand, if federal incentives alone fall within the margin that effectively induces change under existing macroeconomic conditions, the addition of state coincentives may act to encourage sectoral expansion and create slippage in the achievement of federal program objectives.


SUMMARY AND CONCLUSIONS

National conservation incentive programs have been successful in garnering social benefits, but they have not always worked as well as they could have. There are three primary reasons they have failed to meet their potential: (1) macroeconomic conditions are not always conducive complements to fixed incentive levels, (2) program implementation schemes have not capitalized on the potential to maximize returns through targeting, and (3) conservation incentives can be counteracted by commodity program incentives. It is easy to criticize incentive programs for their lack of targeting (a point that is getting hammered to death). It is much more difficult, but perhaps more important, to judge the extent to which the availability of incentives, regardless of their distribution, has affected conservation behavior independent of the influence of macroeconomic and market forces, and in relation to other counterincentives and coincentives. Because the current set of incentives programs is providing models for proposed, future agroenvironmental programs, it may be useful to draw some conclusions from past experience.

Two general lessons emerge. First, it is patently clear that the absolute cost and cost-effectiveness of new agroenvironmental incentives programs will be determined more by the manner in which the incentive instrument is implemented than by the nature of the incentive itself. With broad administrative discretion and multiple, unweighted program objectives, a given legislated incentive instrument can be used in a myriad of ways, each implementation method having distinct, associated costs and benefits. Second, the apparent influences of macroeconomics and market forces, commodity program provisions and state-level programs suggest that new incentive policies and programs need to be designed in anticipation of shifting social, economic, and political conditions—not tied to the short-term conditions existing at the time of policy formulation.

For example, the success of any future incentives offered through technical assistance or cost-sharing for adoption of low-input, sustainable agricultural systems will depend as significantly upon whether macroeconomic and agricultural market conditions provide coincentives for adoption, upon the strength of counterincentives posed by commodity program base acreage and deficiency payment provisions, and upon the degree of state support via coincentives, as they will upon the mere availability and level of new federal incentives. Likewise, the expected success of proposals to expand the CRP to meet additional environmental quality objectives is limited by the increasing value of land remaining in production and affected by the extent to which other federal and state programs limit or encourage acreage expansion.

Past experience indicates that the most effective national agroenvironmental incentives programs will (1) take into account the variation in site-specific environmental benefits of program implementation; (2) provide long-term incentives for shifts in agricultural research and production technology; (3) account for agricultural and environmental and state-federal policy interactions; and (4) provide flexibility to vary incentive levels as agricultural and general market conditions change.

Using macroeconomic indicators to either vary the rate of incentives or trigger an "on-off switch" for incentive programs is a conceptually appealing approach to enhancement of incentive program benefits. If the relationships among interest and exchange rates, farm net returns, and agroenvironmental incentives in affecting farmer behavior were known, incentive payment levels could be geared directly to farm economic and macroeconomic indicators so that their values would rise or fall in predetermined increments as the margin of effectiveness shifts in response to changing economic conditions. For instance, the research reported by Nielsen et al. (1989) suggests that as interest rates rise, the level of conservation investment incentive offered farmers should also rise in order to obtain a constant rate of desired, private conservation investment. Alternatively, economic indicators could be employed to switch from one agroenvironmental policy approach to another, if

Figure 6.1 Hypothetical Conditions for Shifts in Incentive Programs and Incentive Levels

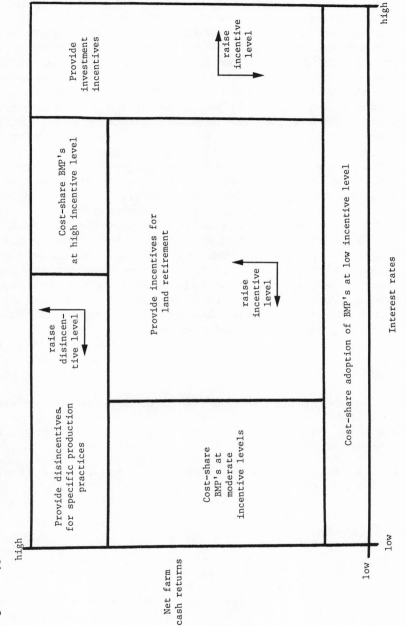

different policy instruments are found to vary in their response to macroeconomic and market conditions. For example, because monetary incentives may be unnecessary to induce land retirement during agricultural recession, and are ineffective, within a reasonable range of levels, during periods of high demand and low interest rates, entry to CRP-type programs could be discontinued as economic conditions change. As such programs are "switched off," incentive programs that are more appropriate to existing economic conditions could be "switched on." That is, as interest rates rise above certain levels, incentive programs supplementing long-run private investment in environmentally beneficial equipment or structures could replace land retirement incentives; as agricultural demand rises and/or interest rates fall below given levels, programs to cost-share adoption of best management practices could replace land retirement incentives. The system depicted in Figure 6.1 is a purely hypothetical illustration of how economic indicators might be used to trigger change and lend flexibility to agroenvironmental incentive programs in order to increase overall program cost-effectiveness.

There is currently an inadequate empirical basis for coordinating incentive programs to capitalize on macroeconomic and market conditions and related coincentives. But one thing is clear—simultaneous consideration of these interacting factors precludes partial ex ante assessment of agroenvironmental program options. Further research on the price elasticity of response to incentives under uncertain market conditions should prove particularly fruitful in designing more effective incentive programs.

## NOTES

The author gratefully acknowledges the contributions by Randall Kramer, whose compilation of information on historical conservation programs contributed extensively to this chapter. The author also appreciates review comments and suggestions by John Braden and David Trechter on an earlier draft.

1. See Batie and Diebel (1989) for a comprehensive review of the wide variety of state strategies for ground-water protection from agricultural contamination existing as of 1988.

## REFERENCES

Batie, Sandra S. 1987. "Institutions and Ground Water Quality," in *Agricultural Chemicals and Ground Water Pollution Control*, ed. L. Canter, pp. 22–40. Norman: University of Oklahoma.

Batie, Sandra S., and Penelope L. Diebel. 1989. *Managing Agricultural Contamination of Ground Water: State Strategies*. Blacksburg: Virginia Polytechnic and State University.

Bosso, Christopher J. 1987. *Pesticides and Politics.* Pittsburgh: University of Pittsburgh Press.

Dicks, Michael. 1987. "CRP Halfway to Goal," *Agricultural Outlook,* November: 19–21.

Harte, Paul R. 1988. Letter to the editor of *Choices* 3: 41–42.

Hertz, Milton. 1989. "The Conservation Reserve Program: Progress and Prospects," In *Outlook 89: Proceedings of the 65th Agricultural Outlook Conference,* pp. 466–471. Washington, DC: U.S. Department of Agriculture.

Nielsen, Elizabeth G., John A. Miranowski, and Mitchell J. Morehart. 1989. *Investments in Soil Conservation and Land Improvements: Factors Explaining Farmers' Decisions,* AER-601, Jan. Washington, DC: U.S. Department of Agriculture, Economic Research Service.

Ogg, Clayton W. 1986. "Erodible Land and State Water Quality Programs: A Linkage," *Journal of Soil and Water Conservation* 41(6): 371–373.

Phipps, Tim. 1987. "The Conservation Reserve: A First Year Report," *Resources* 86: 14–16.

Reichelderfer, Katherine, and William C. Boggess. 1988. "Government Decision Making and Program Performance: The Case of the Conservation Reserve Program," *American Journal of Agricultural Economics* 70(1): 1–11.

Strohbehn, R., ed. 1986. *An Economic Analysis of USDA Erosion Control Programs: A New Perspective,* AER-560, Aug. Washington, DC: U.S. Department of Agriculture, Economic Research Service.

Taff, Steven J., and C. Ford Runge. 1988. "Wanted: A Leaner and Meaner CRP," *Choices* 3(1): 16–18.

U.S. Department of Agriculture. 1983. *Conversion of Southern Cropland to Southern Pine Plantings: Conversion for Conservation Feasibility Study,* Washington, DC: Office of Budget and Program Analysis.

————. 1988. *Cropland, Water and Conservation Situation and Outlook Report,* AR-12, Sept. Washington, DC: Economic Research Service.

U.S. General Accounting Office. 1983. *Agricultural's Soil Conservation Programs Miss Full Potential in Fight Against Erosion,* GAO/RLED 84–48. Nov. Washington, DC.

# SEVEN

# California's Proposition 65: A New Regulatory Trend?

GLORIA E. HELFAND
SANDRA O. ARCHIBALD

Traditionally, regulatory action in the United States has taken the form of endowing a governmental agency with the power to regulate in the public interest. For example, the federal Clean Air Act (42 U.S.C. 7409 et seq.) requires the Environmental Protection Agency to develop national ambient air quality standards and to supervise the state implementation of those standards; the Food, Drug, and Cosmetic Act (21 U.S.C. 300(f) et seq.) authorizes the Food and Drug Administration to control the use of additives in food as well as the safety of drugs and cosmetics. It is probably safe to say that virtually all federal and state regulatory legislation takes that same general form.[1]

California's Proposition 65 (California Health and Safety Code Section 25249.5 et seq.), however, breaks from that trend, perhaps in response to a distinct disappointment with governmental regulators, or perhaps in recognition of the limits of the traditional command-and-control approach. Rather than relying on state agencies to protect the public from toxic substances in food, drinking water, and the workplace, Proposition 65 instead seeks to control human exposure to toxic substances with fundamental changes in the regulatory approach. Through its warning requirements, it assumes that consumers with greater information are better judges of when risks are "acceptable" than is a governmental agency; and through its prohibition on discharges of toxic materials, it endows consumers with the right to uncontaminated drinking water, giving manufacturers the burden of proving that they are not infringing on that right. Both these changes are intended to provide strong incentives to firms to reduce their use of hazardous substances. Although the success of Proposition 65 in achieving these goals cannot yet be determined definitively, the regulatory mechanisms it has set out represent a significant change in the regulation of hazardous substances.

## THE MAJOR PROVISIONS OF PROPOSITION 65

Proposition 65, the Safe Drinking Water and Toxic Enforcement Act of 1986, was written in large part by several private environmental organizations and became law through the initiative process.[2] It was strongly opposed by businesses, trade associations, and agricultural interests. The voters of California enacted it in November 1986 by nearly a two-to-one margin. This overwhelming margin has been attributed to voters' beliefs that state and federal agencies were not protecting them adequately from toxic substances, and that a new approach, less reliant on bureaucracies, would help solve the inadequacy (Business Education Partnership, Inc., 1988).

The heart of the act lies in two provisions: Section 25249.5, which prohibits contamination of drinking water with carcinogenic or reproductively toxic substances; and Section 25249.6, which prohibits a business from exposing any individual to a carcinogen or a reproductive toxicant without first providing a "clear and reasonable warning." The two parts, known respectively as the discharge prohibition and the warning requirements, have in common a list of chemicals "known to the state to cause cancer or reproductive toxicity" (Section 25249.8(b)). The governor was required to publish such a list within four months of its passage, and to revise the list at least once per year thereafter. Governor George Deukmejian delegated the task of identifying which chemicals to list to a Scientific Advisory Panel of 12 scientists. Currently, 296 chemicals (261 carcinogens and 35 reproductive toxicants) are on the list (State of California, 1989a).

Although these two parts of the act have in common the list of carcinogenic and reproductively toxic chemicals, they differ substantially in their approaches and their intents. For most goods subject to the warning requirement, consumers have a choice whether to expose themselves to the hazard or not. For instance, people have the option of not drinking alcoholic beverages, or of finding a job in a workplace without toxic substances, if the risks to them are greater than the benefits. However, people have much less choice over their source of drinking water—unless they use only relatively expensive bottled water, many can get drinking water only from the local utility, and they have little control over the quality of that water. Perhaps this "public good" aspect of how water is provided explains the differences between the treatment of hazardous substances under the proposition.

## Discharge Prohibition

Under Section 25249.5, businesses are prohibited from knowingly discharging any carcinogen or reproductive toxicant into any drinking water source after the chemical has been listed for 20 months, unless no "significant amount" of the chemical will enter a drinking water source, and unless the discharge conforms with all other existing laws and regulations. "Significant amount" is defined as any detectable amount, except an amount for which lifetime exposure poses "no significant risk" for carcinogenic substances, or for which there is "no observable effect," assuming exposure at 1,000 times the level in question for reproductive toxicants. "No significant risk" is not defined in the law.

This provision represents a major shift from the "innocent until proven guilty" approach underlying the U.S. legal system. Under many other pollution laws, a polluter is assumed to have caused no damage unless the harm is proven in court. Food safety laws, on the other hand, ex ante prohibit use of potentially harmful chemicals through licensing and registration of chemicals. Proposition 65 combines some aspects of both these forms. If the polluter emits any measurable level of any listed chemical into a water body that could potentially be used for drinking water, the polluter must be able to show that this discharge will cause no significant risk. This provision thus leads to a major shift in designated rights: whereas previously the discharger could pollute unless it was proven that he violated a statute or otherwise caused harm, now the burden of proof rests on the discharger to show that his actions impose no danger.

## Warning Requirements

Section 25249.6 prohibits a business from "knowingly and intentionally" exposing anyone to a carcinogen or reproductive toxicant "without first giving clear and reasonable warning" after the chemical has been listed for 12 months. Exceptions to this requirement are federal preemption of state authority, lifetime exposure posing "no significant risk" for a carcinogen, or a reproductive toxicant with "no observable effect" at 1,000 times the level in question.

This provision does not prohibit any use of chemicals, even if they are carcinogenic or cause reproductive problems; instead, as long as a business notifies the affected party, exposing someone to the chemical at harmful levels is legal (assuming no conflicts with other laws or regulations, of course). It assumes that consumers, once informed of the risks they face by purchasing or working with a product, will make wise decisions about the relative risks and benefits. Unlike most regulatory actions, which assume that the government should and will protect the public interest through controls on business behavior, this section prefers to leave the risk-balancing decision to the affected public. In a sense, it forces consumers to "internalize" the adverse effects of substances, by forcing them to be aware of the risks.

Proposition 65, then, approaches the control of toxic substances in a new regulatory framework. Instead of setting up an agency to determine acceptable business behavior for controlling toxic substances, it shifts much of the burden directly onto individuals and firms. The following section will highlight some of the important innovations accompanying this way of thinking.

## THE INNOVATIONS OF PROPOSITION 65

Most pollution control laws designate an agency to determine appropriate methods for polluters to comply with the requirements of the law. For example, an agency may be asked to determine ambient air and water quality standards, or to specify legal limits for pesticide residues in food. Agencies may even designate appropriate cleanup technologies. Under Proposition 65, though, neither the discharge provision nor the warning section requires any agency to determine standards of any sort. Once a chemical is classified by a recognized scientific body as a carcinogenic or reproductively toxic substance, the act specifies exactly what is to happen: discharges of the chemical into sources of drinking water must cease unless they pose no significant risk, and businesses must inform customers and workers if the firms expose them in any way to a listed chemical at levels determined to be harmful.

This formulation of the law shows a major change from the traditional approach to regulating toxic substances. The following discussion highlights some of those innovations.

### Faith in Markets Versus Faith in Government

As noted, most food safety and pollution control laws rely on a governmental agency to protect the public interest. Such laws reflect an assumption that the governmental agency is indeed acting in the broad interests of the public. However, in recent years people seem to believe that this model of public behavior does not completely explain how government works.

One alternative theory has suggested that politicians and regulators may act not only for the public good; rather, they may have their own goals and objectives, which may differ from those of the public. This theory of the "captive regulator" asserts that reliance on government to solve the ills of society may not always work: if regulators and those they regulate are concerned with helping each other ("I'll scratch your back if you'll scratch mine"), they may not serve the public (see, e.g., Stigler, 1971; Peltzman, 1976). Proposition 65 can be seen as a response to the view that many federal and state agencies are captured, or at least too heavily influenced, by those they are supposed to regulate. Instead of giving government further authority over polluters, it sets up an almost government-free way of controlling toxic substances, in some sense privatizing regulation.

A related theory suggests that, regardless of reason, government agencies just have not been able to solve today's problems with hazardous substances. Perhaps because they have been saddled by laws with clumsy command-and-control regulatory mechanisms, or because of bureaucratic inertia, or for any number of reasons, regulators are perceived as not having protected the public adequately. Proposition 65 may have arisen just to find a way around this apparent failure of the existing agencies.

This phenomenon is perhaps best exemplified by the warning requirement. As noted, the warning section does not prohibit use of any carcinogenic or reproductively toxic substance. Rather, if a business might expose someone to such a chemical at harmful levels, the business must inform the person of the risk. The affected person himself must then decide on the most appropriate response: to accept the risk or to seek alternatives. No agency of any sort must intervene in the consumer's decision. Instead, the consumer is given increased information with which to make a sound decision on exposure to a chemical, and the firm that is exposing people to the chemical has a strong incentive (removal of the warning) to eliminate or reduce use of the toxic substance. As David Roe, one of the authors of the proposition, noted, "If one company's product sits on the shelf with a cancer warning and a competitor's doesn't, it's not hard to foresee which one a consumer will choose" (Roe, 1988). The proposition has thus set market incentives to reduce the use of toxic substances as a way of bypassing government.

Not only does the proposition set up nongovernmental ways for people to avoid toxic substances; it also sets up an enforcement mechanism that does not depend on the actions of an agency. Under the so-called "bounty hunter" provision of the act (Section 25249.7(d)), anybody can bring legal action against violators of the act, as long as the person bringing action gives sixty days' notice to the state attorney general and the local district attorney, and the latter are not "diligent" in prosecuting the case themselves. If a citizen suit is successful, the plaintiffs earn 25 percent of the penalties, which can be as high as $2,500 per day of violation. Government officials are given the first chance to bring action, but private citizens can bring enforcement if public officials, for whatever motivation, do not choose to act. Again, this provision manifests the distrust of the law's authors toward government's ability to regulate in a timely and effective manner.

According to the Coase theorem, any definitive allocation of property rights can lead to an efficient market solution, no matter whether the polluter is unequivocally permitted to pollute, or the victim of pollution clearly has the right to an unpolluted environment (Coase, 1960). In either case, efficiency can result if the two parties can bargain—as long as the marginal benefits of an additional unit of pollution outweigh the marginal costs imposed by that unit of pollution, there are gains from exchange. The discharge provision can be viewed as a partial market mechanism that changes the allocation of property rights. Instead of an agency setting a standard for a chemical, citizens are entitled to uncontaminated drinking water; if a discharger wants to emit chemicals into a source of drinking water, the discharger must prove that its emissions will not cause any significant harm. Proposition 65 makes a definitive reallocation of property rights, with those who demand safe drinking water having the clear right; however, current implementation of the act leaves no room for the Coasian negotiation over what a reasonable level of pollution might be. As a result, the efficiency gains from trade are lost.

This shift in rights has also created strong incentives for industries to act on their own to discover the risks of toxic substances and to control their use, privatizing risk assessment. The burden of proof is now clearly on businesses to determine their actual exposure levels and to demonstrate that their actions will not expose people to toxic chemicals (or, if exposure is unavoidable, to warn people of a significant risk). Therefore, the best way for firms to protect themselves is to avoid the use of those chemicals, to substitute away from those chemicals to less dangerous ones, or to adopt alternative technologies that do not use harmful substances in toxic amounts. Indeed, it is probably even in their interests to conduct accurate toxicity tests of listed chemicals whose significant risk levels have not yet been estimated, in order to avoid future lawsuits. Under most pollution control laws, in which an agency has the responsibility to determine whether exposure is safe and at what levels, firms may have incentives to delay testing as long as no regulation takes effect until the chemical is shown to be unsafe. Proposition 65, though, by assuming a chemical is unsafe (once listed) until shown not to be harmful, makes it more likely that risk assessments will be done in a timely, cost-efficient manner. David Roe notes that no significant risk levels have been set for chemicals in the two years since the proposition passed (Totten, 1989). If this goal is met, and firms do change their incentives toward working with toxic substances, the act will probably be considered a success by its proponents.

In spite of the claims for increased emphasis on markets and less emphasis on government regulation, Proposition 65 limits, but in fact does not remove, government's role in controlling hazardous chemicals as much as it shifts the branch of government. Although executive-branch regulatory agencies are clearly bypassed as much as possible, this law leaves much interpretation and much enforcement to the judicial branch. If interested parties cannot agree on interpretations of actions or law, courts may very well have to decide such issues as whether warnings used by firms are adequate, whether "bounty hunters" have brought justified action, or whether a discharger has complied with the no significant risk standard. To some extent, then, the success of Proposition 65 will depend on the role of government as much as traditional laws do, but with an important difference: whereas regulatory agencies (after taking input from affected parties) can enact their own compromises into regulations, any party to a Proposition 65 dispute can walk away from a compromise and seek judicial interpretation. Proposition 65 thus requires compromises to be Pareto improving, because a loser can use litigation to break any coalition for that compromise.

## Attitudes Toward Risk,
## Risk Assessment, and Risk Management

When economists approach questions of regulating in the face of risk and uncertainty, they focus on the trade-offs among increased safety, increased information, and increased costs. Even if zero risk were attainable (a highly dubious proposition), economists often argue that the costs of zero risk are far higher than the benefits; society could be better off by taking some resources away from risk avoidance and spending it on increasing society's well-being in other ways. Economists would not advocate regulating chemicals until the risk of getting cancer from one was no greater than the risk of getting cancer from any other. Instead, the most efficient way to prevent deaths would be to allocate money to controlling exposure to the chemicals where the most lives could be saved per dollar spent, or, put another way, economists would advocate controlling exposure where the costs per life saved were minimized. With this criterion, instead of the risk factors for different chemicals being equalized, the risk per dollar of avoidance is equalized.

Proposition 65 has, from an economist's perspective, a schizophrenic attitude toward controlling toxic substances. On the positive side, it recognizes that there may be acceptable levels of exposure above zero, and it emphasizes human exposure to chemicals rather than ambient concentrations of them. On the negative side, once a chemical is identified as being carcinogenic or reproductively toxic, there is no flexibility at all in current implementation of the law as to whether or how it is regulated—the provisions of the proposition relate equally to substances that are easily avoided and to substances that cannot be replaced and serve valuable purposes for society.

All of Proposition 65 is phrased in terms of human exposure to toxic substances: discharges to drinking water are prohibited unless they cause no significant risk, and consumers must be warned about exposure to the chemicals under the same standard. If the goal of the proposition is, as stated, to protect the people of California from toxic substances in drinking water and to inform them about exposure to chemicals in other contexts, then measuring effects in terms of human exposure makes far more sense than setting standards for water bodies.

As noted, the law specifically accepts that people may be exposed to toxic chemicals when they pose no significant risk. This statement recognizes that zero risk may not be attainable, but "no significant risk" is more realistic, especially when costs are considered. Because the ability of scientists to detect trace amounts of chemicals in drinking water has increased dramatically in recent years, setting a standard of zero exposure (and therefore zero risk) would require increasingly stringent and increasingly expensive regulation of firms. By setting a limit on exposure to "no significant risk," the law shows an acceptance of some realities about the dangers of toxic substances and the costs of abating to zero exposure. Indeed, the law's exclusion of any local, state, or federal agency, including public water systems, from its purview can be viewed either as a weakness or as an implicit assumption that the benefits of their activities exceed the risks.

Nevertheless, once a chemical is placed on the list of known carcinogens and reproductive toxicants, current implementation of the law allows no flexibility in its regulation. Instead, as described by Catherine St. Hilaire (1989), Proposition 65 combines risk assessment and risk management. Risk assessment, the determination that a chemical poses a risk (and what its level of risk is at different concentrations), is the realm of toxicologists and other related scientists; risk management, the determination of how (and how much) to control human exposure to a chemical, is the realm of policymakers. Proposition 65 does not separate these two activities, though, showing a trade-off between abandoning zero risk and a requirement for exclusion of benefits consideration. As soon as risk assessment has shown that a substance is carcinogenic or reproductively toxic, it is subject to the discharge prohibition and warning requirements to the same degree as all other listed chemicals. Indeed, the no significant risk level has been interpreted by the Health and Welfare Agency as requiring uniform levels of risk among chemicals to meet this standard. The discharge prohibition does not distinguish between chemicals that are easily avoided (and should perhaps be controlled even more stringently) and chemicals that have no good substitutes and serve important social functions (and perhaps should be permitted more flexibility). The warning requirement can better handle these distinctions, if warnings describe the role of the chemical and its risk factor; how the warning requirement is to be met is still open to debate.

In most federal pollution control laws, federal agencies are given a fair degree of discretion in deciding how much to regulate chemicals. Most standards are set in terms of emissions or ambient pollution levels, rather than in terms of risk to the affected population; and, either implicitly or explicitly, there is often a desire for all the pollution to go away.[3] In these regards, Proposition 65 again deviates from the norm for pollution control, resembling more closely the patterns for food safety laws.[4] Here, human exposure—at what is unlikely to be a level of zero—is the target for regulation, and agencies are given limited discretion in determining what safe levels of the chemicals are. The lack of discretion in regulating the chemicals is perhaps the most debatable of these changes. On the one hand, the law seems clearly intended to circumvent regulatory bottlenecks. On the other hand, agencies can serve the valuable function of balancing the gains from reduced human exposure against the losses from reduced ability to use a chemical. By removing agencies' abilities to make those trade-offs, Proposition 65 gains in clarity of intent but loses in flexibility.

Proposition 65 thus exhibits some major changes from existing environmental and food safety laws. It shows a distinct distrust of government agencies, some (as yet limited) movement toward market mechanisms, a focus on human exposure, and an acknowledgment that zero risk may be either unattainable or undesirable. In some of its provisions, it reflects economic principles such as consumer sovereignty, a recognition that we each must "internalize" the side effects of new technologies (reflected in the warning requirement), and the importance of designating property rights (in the discharge requirement). In other provisions, it rejects those principles, such as by not allowing any flexibility in regulating chemicals of different importance in their uses, and not allowing any negotiation of pollution rights between consumers of drinking water and dischargers. Whether these innovations will better achieve their goals than existing legislation is still debatable, as the proposition is still being implemented and is not yet in its final form. Some of the issues that have already arisen in its implementation are the subject of the following section.

## IMPLEMENTATION OF PROPOSITION 65: IS IT MEETING ITS GOALS?

As discussed, Proposition 65 could lead to significant changes in how toxic substances are controlled. However, the effects of the act are still largely uncertain. Proposition 65 has alternatively been labeled "extreme and unnecessary" by industry and "revolutionary" by environmentalists. Three years after its enactment, it has been characterized by "quiet compliance and responsible enforcement" (Kizer et al., 1989). The basic provisions of the law are now in force, although many critical policy parameters and issues remain to be resolved.

Two key principles have guided the implementation. First, science is to be given a preeminent role in developing new regulations; second, the regulated should clearly know the rules for compliance. These principles are considered essential to avoid any unintended negative economic consequences from what could be an expensive set of regulations.

### Organizing for Implementation

Implementation has proceeded quite rapidly, as much of the timetable is specified in the law. In the same month (November 1986) that Proposition 65 became law, a working group was convened by the governor to assess the issues related to its implementation. Just two months later, the governor designated the state Health and Welfare Agency the lead agency, with the undersecretary carrying primary responsibility for implementation. A cabinet-level working group of related departments was designated to assist the lead agency in implementation (State of California, 1989a).[5]

Proposition 65 is administered by relatively few state employees (fewer than 100 are involved). This lean structure assures that the law takes advantage of existing regulations and laws already in place, just as the working group promotes coordination among agencies with implementation responsibility.

## Incorporating Science: The Scientific Advisory Panel

Within three months of the enactment of Proposition 65 (by February 1987), the governor had appointed twelve eminent scientists from the fields of epidemiology, oncology, pathology, reproductive toxicology, teratology, and toxicology to advise him on which chemicals were to be regulated under Proposition 65. Scientists from the California Department of Health Services and other related departments provide staff support. It was by this means that the administration assured a solid scientific grounding for deciding which chemicals are subject to the law and at what levels they are dangerous.

## Identifying Carcinogens and Reproductive Toxicants

Simultaneous with the appointment of the Scientific Advisory Panel (SAP) was the announcement of the initial list of 26 carcinogenic and 3 reproductively toxic chemicals. An additional 200 chemicals were named for further study. The 26 carcinogens were those with clear evidence of human carcinogenicity identified by the International Agency for Research on Cancer of the World Health Organization and the National Toxicology Program of the U.S. Public Health Service. Those identified as being reproductively toxic were so classified by the U.S. Occupational Safety and Health Administration. The remainder had sufficient evidence of carcinogenicity in animal tests, but the addition of these chemicals to the list as potentially harmful to humans was to be determined by the Scientific Advisory Panel within one year. As of July 1989, the list included 261 carcinogens and 35 reproductive toxicants, well beyond the initial candidate list (State of California, 1989a). More chemicals probably will be added. Additional candidate chemicals are coming from the SAP, Department of Health Services, Department of Food and Agriculture, and the state Water Resources Control Board. The list includes alcoholic beverages (in abusive amounts), tobacco, and a range of chemicals including well-known human carcinogens such as benzene, arsenic, lead, asbestos, vinyl chloride, chromium, and ethylene oxide. Urethane, found in red wine, and a nitroso compound found in bacon and cured meats are also on the list. Naturally occurring toxins, such as aflatoxin, are listed as well.

The SAP's procedures involve a review of the available scientific evidence for each candidate chemical. Because this approach is rather slow, many would like to see the SAP accept the judgments of other authoritative bodies as to the classification of specific chemicals. In the spring of 1989, a superior court judge ordered the SAP to determine whether the federal Environmental Protection Agency is an authoritative body and to consider whether other organizations meet this designation. Although the panel recognized the EPA as an authoritative body, it has decided that it would recognize the EPA's classification of chemicals as carcinogens or reproductive toxicants only if the decision had been reviewed by the EPA's own science advisory board and published in the Federal Register (13CRR 10, 47). This issue, still being debated, can significantly affect the speed of listing and the number of chemicals listed under Proposition 65.

## Assessing Risk

The issue of assessing risk has not been well resolved, as a result of the vagueness of the original language of the law and of the limited scientific data available upon which to make determinations of risk. Vagueness in language encompasses such fundamental areas as what is meant by "no significant risk" or "known to cause" cancer or reproductive toxic effects. Even such terms as "exposure," "sources of drinking water," "discharges," and "clear and reasonable warnings" were either left undefined or were so imprecisely specified as to preclude immediate implementation.

The lack of specificity may have contributed to the proposition's broad voter appeal, but it has since been the source of continued debate. For example, Proposition 65 defines "significant amount" as a detectable amount *unless* the level constitutes "no significant risk," which itself was not defined in the act. Because industry groups have so clearly had the liability placed with them, they have demanded clear and precise resolution of these issues. Informal advisory groups with representatives from environmental and consumer organizations, industry and agriculture, lawyers and scientists have worked with the state Health and Welfare Agency to develop both definitions and implementing approaches that have become regulations.[6]

Regulations have been developed for operation of the Scientific Advisory Panel, definitions of critical terms, and the establishment of no significant risk levels for common chemicals. Also addressed are aspects of the discharge provision including the application to waste facilities and pesticides. The interim regulations for foods, cosmetics, drugs, and medical devices follow those contained in other state and federal regulations, on the assumption that until new risk assessments are completed under Proposition 65, no significant risk will result from appropriate use under those regulations. As levels that constitute no significant risk or no observable effect are promulgated, the interim regulations will be deleted (State of California, 1989a).

The determination of whether the use of a listed chemical presents a significant risk to those exposed to it requires knowledge of the potential for the chemical at a given dose to result in harmful effects (e.g, tumors or reproductive problems). A major problem that all regulation relying on risk assessments has faced to date is the lack of complete and scientifically sound information on this dose-response curve (Archibald et al., 1988). Currently, for example, of the 53 pesticides classified by the EPA as potentially oncogenic, potency factors (the slope of the dose-response curve) for only 28 have been developed. This lack of data equally plagues the implementation of the act as it does other regulations dependent upon such risk assessments.

A definition of no significant risk was essential; without it, given the language of the proposition, the allowable levels of exposure would be driven to the level of detection. "No significant risk" has been defined in the regulations as the risk of one excess case of cancer per 100,000 people exposed for a lifetime. Clearly a compromise, industry believes this to be quite conservative whereas many environmental groups believe a more stringent standard is called for.

Although the definition for no significant risk was lacking in the proposition, providing at least some flexibility in establishing standards for carcinogens, the opposite is true for reproductive toxicants. The law specifies a safety factor set so that allowable exposure is 1,000 times lower than the no observable effect level; this level is 10 to 100 times higher than traditional safety factors for reproductive toxicants. A legislative effort to modify this provision failed, but it is likely to be raised again.

What constitutes an exposure to a listed chemical? State regulators have now made several key decisions. First, levels of many naturally occurring chemicals that are ubiquitous in the environment are generally considered beyond the control of industry and thus not the intended focus of the act. As a result, the presence of these chemicals in food or food products is not classified as an exposure under the law. Second, in certain cases where water contains background levels of listed chemicals, only additions to these levels are considered in determining allowable discharge levels.

The Health and Welfare Agency defines the likely exposure level for foods as the amount that results from "reasonably anticipated use at the average rate of consumption by the typical consumer."[7] These average dietary intakes are available for determining exposure, and in some cases differences for age and sex are considered. Where available, they are included in the current regulations.

The state continues to conduct risk assessments and determine acceptable exposure levels; as more risk assessments are completed they will be incorporated into regulations. Historically, this process has been a slow one. It appears, from casual observation, that demand for risk assessment by those now liable for exposing consumers or workers to listed chemicals could increase.

As of mid-1989, no significant risk levels have been established for about 40 chemicals (Totten, 1989). The first regulations (February 1988) included risk levels for 31 chemicals and safe harbor, or legally acceptable, language for conveying warnings to workers, consumers, and the public.

## Establishing "Clear and Reasonable Warnings"

The most visible warnings focused on lifestyle exposures, specifically requiring strong warnings on alcohol and non-cigarette tobacco products. Regulations regarding warnings on food and consumer products were required in order to meet the legal timetable. On the recommendation of the Scientific Advisory Panel, the state allowed FDA standards to apply to food, drugs, cosmetics, and medical devices on an interim basis for carcinogens. It is expected that as chemicals are assessed for risk under the proposition, FDA standards will be replaced by state standards, if they are stricter (Russell, 1989).

Environmental groups and the food industry have challenged this exemption in court, but for different reasons. Environmental groups opposed the interim regulations for food. Food industry representatives claimed that FDA regulation of products pre-empted Proposition 65. A federal interagency working group assigned to study the issue concluded in late 1988 that "there was no evidence of major interstate economic burden from Proposition 65 and thus no grounds for federal intervention" (Russell, 1989). Given current trends of returning jurisdiction to states, many believe it unlikely that preemption will occur.

Debate over the form of warnings continues without consensus among affected parties (Pam Jones, personal communication, July 1989). The proposition provides industry with flexibility in meeting the warning requirements, with the result that a myriad of different types of warnings have emerged. To avoid citizen suits about failure to warn, companies and groups of companies have placed advertisements in newspapers to warn that chemicals "known to the state of California to cause cancer, birth defects or other reproductive harm are contained in the following facilities," which are then listed. Other firms post such warnings in the workplace where appropriate. Product labels would satisfy the warning requirement, but other means are also appropriate.

The strategy to deal with consumer product warnings is not yet well developed. Retail stores do not want responsibility for posting warnings on grocery and other shelves; producers do not want them on the product label. Two groups of product manufacturers (food/consumer products and oil/gas products) voluntarily set up toll-free telephone lines to provide information on their products and announced the numbers in many stores and newspaper ads. Challenging the appropriateness of such a warning mechanism for tobacco products, environmental and consumer groups initiated legal action under the bounty hunter provision. In less than a month, the state attorney general sued eight tobacco companies for failure to comply with the warning provision (*People* v. *Safeway Stores Inc.*, Calif SuperCt, San Francisco County, No. 897576, Sept. 30, 1988: 12 Crr 1016). The immediate response from a large retail chain was to threaten to remove the products from the shelves if the tobacco companies themselves failed to provide the necessary product warnings. The defendants agreed to settle out of court by providing in-store labels or warning language on individual products.

The Ingredient Communication Council's effort to seek a judgment that the toll-free telephone warning system is adequate (*ICC* v. *Van de Kamp*, Calif SuperCt, Sacramento County, Docket No. 504601, filed Sept. 27, 1988; 12 CRR 1515) is not yet resolved. Currently, about 45 companies rely on the 800 number for warnings involving nearly 10,000 products (Roberts, 1989).

## Clarifying the Discharge Provision

The first drinking water restriction became effective October 27, 1988 (Section 25249.9). The discharge provision has raised concern over the potential for agricultural runoff water containing pesticides and fertilizers to reach drinking water sources. Field tests by major manufacturing companies indicate that no detectable amounts of listed chemicals would reach water sources, assuming good management practices were followed. Companies who may face liability under Proposition 65 for such discharges have not ruled out the possibility of removing products in the future. This has already led to new research into substitute chemicals (Totten, 1989).

## Enforcing Compliance

Under the 'so-called bounty hunter provision to Proposition 65, 60 days following notification of public authorities, an individual may bring suit to a business or enterprise for violations of the warning or discharge requirements of the law. To date, only seven citizen suits to enforce the law have appeared. In all the cases in which enforcement action has proceeded, state or local government has elected to bring suit, leaving the private enforcement provision as yet untested (Roberts, 1989). Some of the legal challenges to the act itself are discussed below.

The question of whether federal laws preempt Proposition 65 is the subject of several suits in both state and federal courts and remains unsettled. Industry has challenged the constitutionality of Proposition 65 on the grounds that it is preempted by the federal food and drug laws (*Committee for Uniform Regulation and Labeling (CURL)* v. *Allenby*, DC N Calif, No. C88-070 EFL, filed Feb. 26, 1988; 12Crr 300) and the federal Occupational Health and Safety Act (*Chemical Manufacturers Association* v. *California Health & Welfare Agency*, DC E Calif, No. Civ-S-88-1615-Lkk JFM, filed Dec. 16,

1988;12 Crr 1543). On the other side, environmental and labor groups have challenged the interim regulations exempting from Proposition 65 many substances subject to federal standards (*AFL-CIO et al.*, v. *Deukmejian*, Calif SuperCt, Sacramento County, No. 88C11393, filed May 31, 1988).

To date, then, Proposition 65 is being interpreted and put into force, but many of its issues are yet to be settled. On the positive side, interested parties are participating in the development of regulations, and many compromises have been worked out; on the negative side, not all the issues have been settled in this fashion, and many are being left to the courts. Indeed, as noted earlier, any party can destroy a consensual compromise by seeking to litigate the issue rather than settle it by negotiation. What compromises are developed, then, must be better to all affected parties than what they expect they could get out of the legal process.


## IMPLICATIONS FOR AGRICULTURE

Agriculture is one of the largest industries in the state of California, and it is not intended to be exempt from the requirements of Proposition 65. Nevertheless, most of the implications for agriculture depend to a large extent upon the outcome of a number of currently unresolved issues. This section will review a few questions that have arisen about the effects of the act on agriculture.

Of critical importance is how consumers will respond to clear and reasonable warnings added to food products. Will people use them as useful sources of information and make their own comparisons of different goods, as the authors of the act clearly intended? Or will the warnings confuse, aggravate, or be ignored by the public? Some experts believe that generic warnings may dilute the effect of more significant risk warnings, such as those for cigarettes. One study of saccharin labels found that people did reduce their consumption of saccharin in response to the warning label, but the authors expressed concern that too many labels would be viewed as "crying wolf" too often, and that labels would become less effective over time and in quantity (Schucker et al., 1983). Another study of labeling "good products" (that is, shelf labels in grocery stores identifying products with low or reduced fat, sodium, cholesterol, or calories) again found that they did induce changed consumption habits, although this study found that consumers did not respond instantly; the authors here felt that permanent labeling helped their success (Levy et al., 1985). What is most clearly known about warning, then, is that little is known about its effects. Whether consumers will substitute away from foods or jobs with warnings on them, if the costs of the food are lower or the pay from the jobs is higher, is yet to be answered.

When product warnings are required in California but not in other states, a number of unresolved issues arise. The costs of labeling and separating products destined for California markets alone could be high, and industry claims that these costs may be passed on to consumers all over the country. If 90,000 products must have warning labels, the costs could be as high as a 2 percent tax on the food dollar of every person in the United States. This itself establishes grounds for federal preemption, because it poses a burden on interstate commerce. State experts disagree that the problem will be of this magnitude; at a risk level of 1 in 100,000, they claim, only a few products will need warnings, and it is unlikely that food products will be affected (Roberts, 1989).

Special regulations for "economic poisons" (pesticides) have been adopted as emergency rules by the Health and Welfare Agency. Briefly, it is presumed that, as long as those applying pesticides in the course of doing business follow existing policies and state and federal regulations designed to avoid drinking water contamination, they are unlikely to discharge listed chemicals at levels banned under the law. This presumption does not apply if it can be shown that the person responsible for the application had actual knowledge that similar applications under similar circumstances had resulted in a significant amount of a listed chemical passing into a source of drinking water[8] (State of California, 1989b, Notice of Emergency Rule Making Section 12405). If these regulations stay in force, agriculture will not have to worry about its use of pesticides, and their concerns over the act will be greatly reduced; whether these regulations will withstand a court challenge has not been tested. Without these regulations, the chemical industry and agricultural organizations argued, a defendant would have to independently prove what experts have already proven. In addition, it was argued that failure to adopt this regulation would place businesses that use economic poisons in the position of liability with risk of penalties when they were not economically or scientifically able to monitor whether their chemicals affected drinking water sources. Secondary effects on crop quality and production costs were also cited.

At a minimum, companies must review their products and perform risk assessments. Chevron undertook risk assessments for its entire product line. For the 50 Ortho home-use products, none required warnings, providing evidence for many that current regulations may be assuring similar environmental and health protection.

The final resolution of the 1,000-fold safety factor for reproductive toxicants has potential implications for agriculture. It has already been demonstrated that this level would encompass such everyday items as bread, vanilla, and orange juice on the basis of their alcohol content; of more serious concern is the potential for application to synthetic fertilizers (Elin Miller, personal communication, July 1989). If this level is not changed, a multitude of warnings will be necessary, both diluting the effectiveness of warnings for more serious risks and imposing a large cost on industry and the consumer. Additionally, some substances necessary for human health in small doses, such as vitamin A, are toxic at higher doses. Under the 1,000-fold safety factor, substances that contain necessary amounts of such substances might be required to carry warnings, if the levels at which they are necessary are within that factor. The Health and Welfare Agency has avoided this problem by listing the chemical only at megadose quantities; at lower levels, the list of reproductive toxicants specifically states that vitamin A is necessary for normal reproduction.

Other issues of concern to agriculture include: (a) chemicals that are listed but are not covered under the current exemptions; (b) the fate of the temporary exemption from food and drugs; and (c) the standards for what constitutes a drinking water source. These standards are not yet resolved, leaving unclear when runoff from a farm is a discharge subject to the proposition. Given the nature of the implementation to date, experts believe that surprises are unlikely (Roberts, 1989), but so many issues are left unsettled that agriculture in California still has reason to be concerned over the implementation of the law.

Where consensus on these parameters has not been achieved, the courts must decide. The impacts and costs of this law for agriculture depend critically on the outcome of these debates. The advantage of this law over environmental and health and safety regulations is that it has not rigidly incorporated into the law specific risk standards for carcinogens, such as the zero-risk standard of Delaney, thus allowing these critical parameters to change over time as we learn more about long-term health effects. The rigidity of the 1,000-fold safety factor with respect to reproductive toxicants, however, presents a real constraint. In the most extreme case, each unique chemical in each unique use must have its safety factor individually determined, resulting in an incredibly expensive regulatory system where no benefits can be specified and no costs can be considered.

## CONCLUSIONS

At least in intent, Proposition 65 reflects a substantial change in attitudes from previous pollution and food safety legislation. It shifts the burden of proof for discharges into drinking water: dischargers must now be able to show that they are not causing harm, rather than consumers having to show that they are harmed by the dischargers' actions. For other exposures to dangerous substances, businesses are required only to warn consumers of the risk—consumers themselves must then choose whether they want to live with the exposure.

Some of the changes initiated by Proposition 65 are clearly positive. For instance, Proposition 65 leaves the risk-benefit trade-off to individuals, with the exception of drinking water (which one could argue deserves the prohibition requirement, given its status as a public good). In the long run, education of consumers and workers about the true nature of these risks as well as the range of benefits derived from modern technology is critical if the goals of the act are to be fully realized (Kizer et al., 1988). At a minimum, it is likely to force industry to become more aggressive in acquiring data regarding health risks. It may force industry to assume this educational role and to be more open with its own information, a necessary condition for improving the quality of health and environmental risk assessments. This may be the most important impact of all.

One important goal was to force a scientific basis into policy decisions. As such, Proposition 65 is an experiment in how well science is brought to bear in the decisionmaking process. The law affects every area of risk assessment and management as well as its communication to the public (Russell, 1989).

It is claimed that more exposure limits have been set in California in two years than the federal government has set in twelve years (Totten, 1989). Under the 1976 Toxic Substances Control Act, the EPA has set regulatory limits for just 15 chemicals (Roberts, 1989). In one year, Proposition 65 set safe harbor levels on over 40 chemicals. It has succeeded in requiring warnings on alcohol and noncigarette tobacco products where federal warnings were then lacking, and it is developing standards for known human carcinogens, including benzene, vinyl chloride, chromium, and arsenic, for which the FDA has no standards.

Perhaps for the first time, industries that use hazardous substances have been given strong incentives to rethink their use of the chemicals. Because of both the discharge restrictions and the required warnings, firms are likely to seek alternative chemicals or technologies that allow them to avoid or reduce use of listed chemicals. Just as consumers will be made more aware of the trade-offs involved in the use of hazardous substances by the warning requirements, firms will also have to consider how necessary their use of toxic chemicals is and whether they can do without them.

Many of these advantages of Proposition 65 are still somewhat speculative, as the implementation of the act is still in process. In fact, perhaps one of the major problems with the act has been that so many of its provisions are unclear that many of its key issues are not resolved. Although the manner of implementation by the state, using careful, coordinated management and broadly based consultation with affected parties, has to date mitigated many concerns about the act's adverse effects, concerns still exist over its effects. A spokesman for the Environmental Working Group, a coalition of trade associations and individual companies, gives full recognition to the Health and Welfare Agency for making the law workable, but believes at the same time that the full impacts of the law are yet to be felt. Specifically, the law's limits on discharges of listed chemicals into drinking water sources have just begun.

Under them, industry will be forced to very low discharge levels, particularly given the 1,000-fold safety factor governing reproductively harmful chemicals (Totten, 1989).

The costs of this law have not yet been assessed. Compliance costs have been declared large by industry representatives (Totten, 1989). In addition to the short-run compliance costs, in the long run it is likely that capital investments may be required if cost-effective substitutes are not available.

With this risk-only regulatory framework, the benefits of regulation are assumed and the costs are ignored, restricting any ability to determine trade-offs or to know whether improved health does result from the rules. In many cases it is likely that reduction in use of listed chemicals will provide net societal benefits; in other cases, though, it is possible that society will gain more from the use of a chemical than from its dangers. Proposition 65, by using a framework that does not consider the economic benefits of the listed chemicals, shows no recognition of the possibility that these chemicals may provide irreplaceable social benefits.

Because of its innovative approach, politicians and interest groups within and outside California are monitoring the progress of Proposition 65 very closely. If it succeeds in improving public health without severe costs, it may be duplicated in many other places; if its apparent costs exceed its benefits, its future is unclear. Based on the number of people who supported it, many Californians do not feel adequately protected from toxic substances in their food, water, and workplaces under current laws. How realistic those fears are may be revealed as the act is implemented; as the public is made more aware of the benefits and costs of different chemicals, perhaps even wiser forms of regulation can result.

## NOTES

1. Section 409 of the Food, Drug, and Cosmetic Act, the Delaney Amendment, proves an exception to this in its specification of a zero-risk standard for potentially carcinogenic chemicals in processed foods.

2. The initiative process allows private citizens or organizations, by gathering signatures on petitions, to put legislation on a statewide ballot; if a majority of the voters in the state vote for the initiative, it becomes law without having to go through the legislature or the governor's office.

3. Perhaps the best example is the 1972 Federal Water Pollution Control Act Amendments (Public Law 92-500, 33 U.S.C. 1251 et seq.), which had as a stated goal zero discharge by the year 1985.

4. The Food, Drug, and Cosmetic Act (21 U.S.C. Section 300(f) et seq.) prohibits sale of products until safety has been demonstrated. With the exception of the Delaney Clause (Section 409), however, the *de minimis* safety level is recognized as one in one million.

5. These include the Department of Health Services; the Department of Food and Agriculture; the Department of Industrial Relations; the Environmental Affairs Agency; the Resources Agency; and the Business, Transportation, and Housing Agency.

6. These regulations are published in Division 2 of Title 22 of the California Cope of Regulations, following the list of chemicals, which is contained in Section 12000.

7. In determining the levels at which the chemical is actually present, the implementing regulations allow the use of methods recommended by federal and state agencies or learned scientific bodies with regard to methods and levels of detection. Reasonably, if a chemical is not detected, no exposure can occur.

8. Similar conditions are defined to cover such factors as soil conditions, crop type, weather conditions, and location of and proximity to a source of drinking water (State of California, 1989b).

## REFERENCES

Archibald, S. O., C. Bruhn, N. Dowling, A. Fan, T. W. Hazlett, B. K. Hurd, S. Lane, R. Marsh, and L. T. Wallace. 1988. *Regulating Chemicals: A Public Policy Quandary.* Davis: University of California Agricultural Issues Center.

Business Education Partnership, Inc. 1988. "Facts About Controlling Toxic Substances." *California's Proposition 65: A Practical Guide for Compliance.* Sacramento: California Chamber of Commerce.

Coase, R. H. 1960. "The Problem of Social Cost." *Journal of Law and Economics* 3:1–44.

Kizer, K. W., T. E. Warriner, and S. A. Book. 1988. "Sound Science in the Implementation of Public Policy". *Journal of the American Medical Association* 260:951–955.

———. 1989. "A Case Report on California's Proposition 65: In Reply." *Journal of the American Medical Association* 261:2501.

Levy, Alan S., Odonna Mathews, Marilyn Stephenson, Janet E. Tenney, and Raymond E. Schucker. 1985. "The Impact of a Nutrition Information Program on Food Purchases." *Journal of Public Policy and Marketing* 4:1–13.

Peltzman, Sam. 1976. "Toward a More General Theory of Regulation." *Journal of Law and Economics* 19:211–240.

Roberts, Leslie. 1989. "A Corrosive Fight Over California's Toxics Law. *Science* 243:306–309.

Roe, David. 1988, "California Law Has a Built-In Toxin Alarm." *Wall Street Journal*, April 22.

Russell, Cristine. 1989. "Proposition 65: California's Controversial Gift. *APF Reporter* 12:951–956.

St. Hilaire, Catherine. 1989. "Sound Science and the Interpretation of Risk," Presented before the Western Food Industry Conference, University of California at Davis.

Schucker, Raymond E., Raymond Stokes, Michael Stewart, and Douglas Henderson.

1983. "The Impact of the Saccharin Warning Label on Sales of Diet Soft Drinks in Supermarkets." *Journal of Public Policy and Marketing* 2:46–56.

State of California. 1989a. "The Implementation of Proposition 65: A Progress Report." Sacramento: Health and Welfare Agency.

————. 1989b. "Notice of Emergency Rule Making: Safe Drinking and Toxic Enforcement Act of 1986," Title 22. Sacramento: Health and Welfare Agency.

Stigler, George J. 1971. "The Theory of Economic Regulation." *Bell Journal of Economics and Management Science* 2:3–21.

Totten, Glenn. 1989. "Controversial Proposition 65 Provokes Industry Outrage, 'Quiet Compliance' as It Marks Second Anniversary as Law." *Chemical Regulation Reporter*, May 5, pp. 169–174.

# EIGHT

# Water Quality and Agriculture: The Case of the Murray-Darling Basin in Australia

WARREN F. MUSGRAVE

The Murray-Darling river system, which drains a large part of southeastern Australia, is hydrologically and politically complex. Its hydrological complexity springs from the size and considerable geological age of the area it drains. Its political complexity springs from the fact that the system contains within its boundaries parts of four states of a federation, although only three states border the River Murray, which is the focus of this chapter. The constitution of the federation confers responsibility for land and water on the states, apart from situations where matters relating to defense, overseas trade, and foreign affairs (including, for example, world heritage listings) are raised. These latter concerns are the responsibility of the commonwealth (federal) government. This political complexity, which is typical of a federation, is complicated by the dominant role of the commonwealth in public finance and the provision in the constitution that trade between the states shall be free, a provision that the High Court has tended to interpret very literally.

The landscape through which the streams of the basin flow is naturally saline. Consequently, the waters of these streams are also saline. The incidence of salinity is much more pronounced to the west and south of the system. The introduction of European settlement has increased the rate of mobilization of salt, but the inertial forces of the political system have made amelioratory action difficult. This is particularly true of policies such as subsidizing the price of water, which provide incentives for users to use irrigation water relatively liberally, thereby exacerbating the incidence of salinization of the surface waters and soils of the basin. Recent action has led to organizational and institutional developments that show promise of changing this situation. The purpose of this chapter is to describe the river system and to outline the recent initiatives. The latter, in particular, should be of interest to policymakers and advisors concerned with analogous resource management problems.

## SOME DETAILS OF THE SYSTEM[1]

The Murray-Darling Basin (Figure 8.1) covers one million square kilometers, about one-seventh of the land area of Australia. It covers 75 percent of New

South Wales (N.S.W.), 56 percent of Victoria (VIC.), 15 percent of Queensland (QLD), 8 percent of South Australia (S.A.), and all of the Australian Capital Territory. About 2 million people live in the basin or depend on it for their water supply. The greatest part of the inflow into the rivers of the basin comes from mountains on its eastern and southern borders. Most of the basin is undulating or flat, and the system acts largely as a drain, which receives little inflow and experiences substantial losses from seepage and evaporation. Of the inflow that occurs, some is saltier than the sea.

Although the Murray-Darling system is the fourth longest river system in the world, its yield is low; the volume of water coming from the total catchment represents only 5 percent of Australia's total runoff. Despite this, about three-quarters of all the domestic, industrial, and agricultural water used in Australia is used in the basin. It is the source of water to 16 large urban centers within its boundaries as well as to some outside them. Forty percent of the water supply of the state of South Australia comes from the River Murray. Clearly the basin is of major importance to the Australian economy.

Irrigation was introduced into the Murray Valley in the 1880s. Early failure of a number of pioneering private ventures was due, at least in part, to the construction of water storages that were too small to cope with the highly variable rainfall and the high rates of summer evaporation. In fact, the size of storage necessary to ensure the viability of an irrigation venture deterred continued private investment of any magnitude. This dearth of private investment implied that such development was uneconomic, but this did not deter the government from filling the breach, albeit on occasions in partnership with private parties. This persistence with irrigation possibly reflected optimistic technological expectations of the times, reinforced by strong public sentiment in favor of development, irrigation, and settlement of the "inland."

The ensuing program of irrigation development was influenced greatly by the earlier experience of British colonial authorities in India and Egypt. Large storages were built in the eastern and southern mountain ranges bordering the valley, and a number of irrigation settlements were established, usually on resumed (condemned) land, some considerable distance from the storages. As indicated, government involvement in these irrigation settlements was considerable and continues to be so. The responsible state agencies are substantially engaged in land and water management. In the past, they have discharged their responsibilities very benignly; so much so that the hypothesis that they had been "captured" by the irrigation communities could have been reasonably entertained. The upshot has been a system of water allocation that operates at high reliability and within which prices have been charged that have often been below the short-run variable costs of supply and invariably below the total of all long-run costs. This neglect of market considerations in the development and operation of irrigation in the Murray-Darling system has resulted in the development of an area greatly in excess of that which could

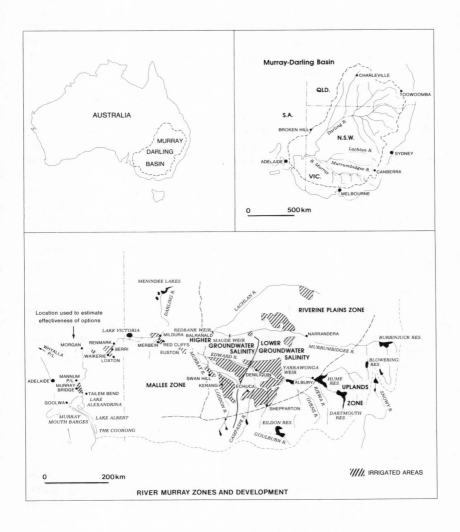

RIVER MURRAY ZONES AND DEVELOPMENT

have been justified on economic grounds alone, and the adoption of irrigation practices that have prompted relatively high levels of water use.

Today almost the entire flow of the river is regulated. There are more than 400 reservoirs in the catchment; those designed primarily for flow regulation have a total capacity of 30 million megaliters (ML) or 1.4 times the estimated mean annual flow of the system. The total amount of water currently reaching the lower Murray, because of diversions upstream, is of the order of only about 5 million ML annually. With total annual usage of about 10 million ML, the water resources of the system are heavily committed.

The river system becomes increasingly turbid and saline as it flows westward. Even though much of the salinity comes from natural sources, irrigation activity raises water tables, which has accelerated the mobilization of salt, thereby causing serious local problems. Further, through a combination of drainage of surplus irrigation water into the rivers and a reduction in their flow, irrigation has contributed to a rise in salt levels in the waters of the rivers above those that would occur naturally. Thus there is a pattern of localized externality problems associated with the rising water tables and of more widespread effects associated with drainage and the flow of the rivers. These problems would, almost certainly, have been less severe had public policy encouraged more parsimonious water use. Dryland salinity caused by rising water tables following extensive clearing of upland country has contributed to the situation.

Most of the economic costs of salinity are concentrated in South Australia. The average annual cost of rising water tables and of land salinization in the Riverine Plains Zone is estimated to be A$65 million, and the average annual cost of in-river salinity is estimated to be A$50 million (Murray-Darling Basin Ministerial Council, 1988). Most of these costs would be third-party or external effects.

## INTERGOVERNMENT COOPERATION

Recent years have seen significant policy responses to the problems of the system. A number of these responses have been market oriented, some have been regulatory, and others have been organizational. The circumstances that prompted these reforms were various and included an increasing concern over land degradation in the lower basin and salinity in the River Murray itself; stronger political pressure from South Australia over the quality of water obtained from the Murray for urban and irrigation purposes; and increased financial pressure on the relevant state agencies, leading to an appreciation that continued reliance on expensive engineering stratagems alone to combat problems was not possible. The most striking development has been an apparent willingness on the part of the lower basin states to increase their collaboration in the management of the most degraded parts of the system.

The River Murray has been the subject of concern since before the creation of the Australian Federation in 1901. A prolonged period of debate within a context of changing economic, political, and technical circumstances eventually saw the emergence of a situation where the scope for disagreement had been so narrowed and the benefits of cooperation perceived to be so great relative to the costs of continued interstate competition that, in 1915, a system of integrated management was introduced (Paterson, forthcoming). A new body, the River Murray Commission, was established that had responsibility for the main stem of the Murray, its headwaters, and for the lower Darling River. This responsibility essentially took the form of the management of the regulation and allocation of the water under a prearranged formula. The commission consisted of representatives of each state and the commonwealth. Over the ensuing period the commission acquired new powers relating to its original objectives concerned with regulation and allocation.

In 1983, the powers of the commission were further extended to include responsibility for monitoring water quality and formulating water quality objectives. This was a response to increasing concern over the quality of the waters of the River Murray. As this concern increased, dissatisfaction with the River Murray Commission appeared. This dissatisfaction sprang from the facts that the powers of the commission were limited to one particular part of the system, albeit the part where the problems were most severe; that its control extended to the waters of the river only, rather than to its tributaries and the land of the basin; that the range of its responsibilities was limited; and that its modus operandi was highly regulatory within a fairly rigid formula. In discussing the history of the commission up to this time, Paterson (forthcoming) pointed to the previous success of the organization in that, by and large, its functions and the way it performed them received little criticism and that it successfully survived the few crises that it experienced. Paterson argued that this history should not be discounted, and that the commission was an appropriate body at the time of its establishment and for almost 70 years after. He argued that the history of the commission, its structure, and its method of operation provide some important lessons for those who would pursue interstate compacts over water resources.

According to Paterson "it could be said that by the late seventies the political mandate of 1914 was exhausted; system attributes had reached the limits of the circumstances envisaged in the 1914 Agreement and directly new phenomena required accommodation" (forthcoming, ms. p. 15). Chief among those new phenomena was the quality of the water of the whole Murray-Darling system. As the condition of the Murray, in particular, deteriorated, the inadequacies of the existing commission arrangements became increasingly apparent and the subject of debate, but several years were to pass before the inertia of the past, both political and bureaucratic, subsided and the political conditions for change came into being.

If the weight of political opinion was shifting to favor change it would have been consistent with broad shifts in legal opinion. The history of cooperative agreements between sovereign states in relation to the management of jointly owned natural resources is marked by an unwillingness to trade sovereignty for mutual economic benefit, and by the rigidity of the procedures agreed to even when such a sacrifice of sovereignty is made. Although water flowing from a state still tends to be regarded in law as being legitimately under the control of that state up to the point where it reaches the border with another state (Caponera, 1985), increasing awareness of the hydrology of river basins, particularly with regard to ground water and the environment, and of the capacity of upstream states to affect the well-being of downstream states, has resulted in a greater acceptance of limitations being placed on state sovereignty in order to protect the rights of interested parties. This attitude is coming to be accepted in law (Caponera, 1985; Goldie, 1985).

In 1985, a group of state and commonwealth ministers met and agreed to replace the commission with a new Murray-Darling Basin Commission. This new organization differed from the old commission in terms of the greater spread of its responsibilities, both functionally and geographically, and in terms of its freedom of action.

Perhaps of more significance than the reform of the commission was the establishment of a ministerial council to which the new commission was made responsible. The council, which is made up of the ministers holding responsibility for the water, land, and environmental portfolios in each of the four governments represented on the commission, oversees the management of the basin. The state of Queensland, which contains a major part of the upper basin, has observer status on the council, although there is provision for that state to join at any time should it so wish. Although this means that the whole basin is not within the jurisdiction of the council, the problems of major concern are predominantly contained in the area within the council's jurisdiction.

Under the new agreement, proposals for land, water, and environmental policies and for management within any one state may be brought to the attention of the council, if they have the potential to impinge on the welfare of another state. This is not automatic, and so there is no guarantee that such issues will be considered by the council (Taylor, 1988). The important point, however, is that the possibility is there and this provides scope for initiative and flexibility of action that was not present under the old agreement. A further important development is that the agreement resulted in the establishment, by the council, of a Community Advisory Committee, which is intended to reflect the concerns of the people of the basin, and which provides further scope for bringing issues to the attention of the commission or the council. Finally, the commission may bring any consideration to the attention of the council by majority vote—that is, by the agreement of at least two of the states. Separate opinions may also be presented (Taylor, 1988). In summary, the agreement provides for a diminution of the sovereignty of the states over a wide range of only broadly defined issues.

Too much cannot be made of the facts that this new system of management and policymaking covers much of the basin and provides for the consideration of the full range of environmental, land, and water issues, provided they have a bearing on the waters of the basin (Taylor, 1988). Any consideration of salinity control measures, by either regulation or incentives, would have been of severely restricted value without these sweeping reforms of the organizational and institutional arrangements for the management of the basin. Important in this respect are the creation of the council and of the Community Advisory Committee. Both are potentially forceful sources of political pressure.

On the other hand, the new arrangements represent a significant departure from the circumstances that helped ensure the survival of the old commission, particularly with respect to its "apolitical" nature, and the restrictions on its scope, which left intrastate responsibilities and activities—particularly those of the various state bureaucracies—more or less intact. The active involvement of ministers through the ministerial council and the extension of the commission's responsibilities to include functions with an intrastate dimension meant that this could no longer be the case. The impact on the perceptions of costs and benefits held by those affected by the new arrangements could prove of critical importance. In this respect, Paterson makes the significant observation that "no agreement between sovereign states can long survive if the balance between benefits from the agreement is outweighed by net costs to even one of the parties, even in a transient way" (forthcoming p. 20). Important to the potential for success of the new arrangements is the fact that they have been put into place after the states had made considerable progress in placing their own resource and environmental management under "internal cross-jurisdiction political authority, which allows each State to speak with one voice on the basis of internally rationalized policy" (Paterson, forthcoming, p. 20).

## POLICY ACTION

The new arrangements described in the previous section provide an interstate framework for the management of an asset owned in common, the value of which is to be maximized by the employment of suitable policies. This approach to the problems of the basin is consistent with the analytical approach urged by Quiggin (1988). A further desirable feature of the new arrangements is that they should provide feedback to the owners of the asset (the individual states), which will provide incentives for them to establish cognate policies consistent with the maximization of the value of the commonly owned asset.

In a direct attack on the water quality problem and the associated land degradation, the ministerial council has adopted a salinity and drainage strategy intended to reduce river salinity and to provide an opportunity to ameliorate the waterlogging and salinization of agricultural land. The objective of the strategy is "to maximize net benefits to the Basin subject to the overall objectives of the Council" (Murray-Darling Basin Ministerial Council, 1988).

The specific objectives of the strategy are:

- Improve water quality in the River Murray for all beneficial uses—agricultural, environmental, urban, industrial, and recreational.
- Control existing land degradation, prevent further land degradation, and, where possible, rehabilitate land resources, to ensure the sustainable use of these resources in the Murray and Murrumbidgee valleys.
- Conserve the natural environment of these valleys and preserve sensitive ecosystems with respect to salinity (Murray-Darling Basin Ministerial Council, 1988).

An economist would argue with the parochialism of objectives expressed in terms of the maximization of regional rather than national benefits, but be satisfied with the same objectives expressed in a way that would be compatible with the idea of maximizing the value of an asset held in common. The economist's enthusiasm would be further increased by the knowledge that economic analysis played a significant role in the determination of the components of the strategy.

The strategy provides each state with a clear statement of its obligations and rights under the scheme. The states are free to pursue their own programs within the resulting framework, and there is scope for cooperation (trade) between them. Three "baseline conditions" are part of the strategy:

1. Current river salinity levels are adopted as the *baseline* for evaluating responsibility for all future actions that affect river salinity.
2. Each state will be responsible for its future actions that affect river salinity.
3. No actions will be allowed that increase the overall net cost of river salinity (Murray-Darling Basin Ministerial Council, 1988).

The dilemma of basin management is that amelioration of land degradation is inconsistent with the improvement of water quality. Lowering water tables and reducing land surface salting adds to the salt load entering the rivers. Yet there is strong pressure on the states to do these things in order to preserve the irrigation enterprises of the lower basin and their associated communities. The council's salt strategy tackles this problem head-on by providing for the states to undertake, within agreed limits, land management or other developments within their own boundaries that will increase the salinity load of the River Murray, and for governments (state and commonwealth) jointly to fund cost-effective salt interception schemes, which will reduce salinity to a more than compensating extent. The first of these provisions will enable states to protect and rehabilitate land; the second should enable a net reduction in River Murray salinity, after allowing for the contribution to salinity of natural drainage. The net present value of the strategy, expressed in 1986 prices over a thirty-year project life and calculated on a regional basis, which does not correct for subsidies, is estimated to be A$335.1 million with a present value of total costs of A$335.5 million (Murray-Darling Basin Ministerial Council, 1988). The discount rate used was 5 percent.

Any state is permitted to transfer its contribution to the salt interception works to another state but it must, at the same time, surrender proportionally its right to undertake land reclamation works that increase river salinity. This possibility for trade between the states adds desirable flexibility to the strategy.

Central to the development of the strategy has been the determination of the preferred balance between measures to rehabilitate land—which adds to the amount of salt entering the river—and the construction of works that are calculated to prevent this happening. This determination was aided by a benefit-cost analysis of the options identified by the council's working party. The benefit-cost analysis was supplemented by a "snapshot" determination of the optimal mix of stratagems using a single period mixed-integer linear programming model of the problem (Murray-Darling Basin Ministerial Council, 1987). These analyses are not discussed in this chapter because they are not central to its purpose.


## DISCUSSION

In effect, the ministerial council has adopted a new constitution for the collective that "owns" the lower basin. This collective is made up of the three riparian River Murray states, New South Wales, Victoria, and South Australia, along with the commonwealth. Under the salinity strategy, the rights of the member states have been modified and augmented. A "starting position" is suggested that is defined in terms of the initial river salinity situation. The adoption of the strategy by the council obliges the states to contribute in an agreed-upon way to the construction of interception works that will reduce the salt load of the river. This agreement will entitle them to embark upon approved land management schemes, which will increase the salt load of the river. These schemes will enable rehabilitation and protection of lands that have been degraded, or are under the threat of degradation by rising water tables or salinization. In effect, in contributing to the cost of the salt interception works, a state will be creating a salt credit, which gives it the right to add salt to the river over and above its baseload entitlement. As indicated, there is provision for these credits to be transferred between the states.

The ministerial council's salinity strategy has established important macro-settings for the future management of the basin. By linking the attack on land degradation with in-river salinity control in an explicit but flexible way, the council has established an important link between the management of the commonly owned asset and the internal policies of the participating states. Targets and regulation play an important part in this strategy; the key component, however, is the provision of incentives for the states to conduct their internal affairs in a manner consistent with the objectives of the strategy.

This incentive dimension of the strategy may project its shadow down to the micro level within the states, thereby encouraging individual water users to act in ways consistent with the objectives of the strategy. Although the states have yet to articulate, jointly or singly, explicit policies to promote such behavior at the micro level, a number of important initiatives have been taken that are highly consistent with those objectives. Of particular interest is a consolidated attack on land salinization in Victoria, which is based on a catchment approach and places a heavy reliance on public education. If successful, this program should have a significant impact on the position of Victoria with regard to the River Murray.

Further important initiatives have been taken by all the participating States with regard to water allocation and pricing. It is too early to assess their impact, but these initiatives promise to lower the intensity of water use in irrigation and so lessen the pressure on water tables, reduce the rate of increase in land salinization, and thereby contribute to the attainment of the objectives of the council's salinity strategy. Striking among these innovations have been a number of initiatives in relation to water pricing and marketing.

All Australian states have, until recently, employed essentially the same water doctrine, which is characterized by a high degree of attenuation of user rights. In particular, transferability is restricted by the attachment of water entitlements to land, the life of entitlements tends to be poorly defined, and the reliability of supply is ill-specified and insecure. This attenuation has been attacked by the introduction of the transferability of entitlements, separate from land in all three states, the auctioning of "new" water in some Murray tributaries in Victoria, and the first known use of the new concept of capacity sharing (Dudley and Musgrave, 1988), also in Victoria. All of these innovations are constrained to some extent or other. For example, nonirrigators are not permitted to bid in the Victorian water auctions, water transfers can be made on an annual basis only, and capacity shares are available to bulk suppliers of water only. Although these constraints—along with political concern over the impact of the operation of relatively unfettered water markets on the welfare of irrigators and their communities—may impede further progress toward the development of water markets, what has been done so far should serve to facilitate the attainment of the objectives of the salinity strategy.

## CONCLUSION

The spatially diverse, nonpoint-source and multiparty nature of the pollution problems of the lower Murray-Darling Basin mean that traditional incentive policy of the Coasian or Pigovian type is not likely to be able to contribute very much to their solution. The ministerial council has opted, however, for a strategy that contains the scope for flexibility of action and the retention of options for participants at both the macro- and the microlevels of the planning of water and land use. Such features are traditionally associated with strategies relying on incentive. In particular, at the macrolevel of the states, the agreement redefines property rights in such a way as to have created negotiable instruments defined in terms of the pollutant of concern. Further, the states that are party to the agreement have accepted the obligation to share in the construction of salt interception works in order to undertake land management schemes that are of value to them both politically and economically. Entering into the agreement means that they are prepared to forgo their existing right to undertake such land management schemes unilaterally. Under the agreement, in order to regain this right, the states will agree to contribute to the funding of the salt interception schemes. In other words, the prospect of regaining the right to undertake certain land management works will provide an incentive for them to support the salt intervention effort.

The council has replaced an interstate compact, which had been rendered inadequate by the emergence of a grave pollution problem, with a new and more complex arrangement intended, among other things, to solve that problem. The intention is that the net benefits of the new compact should be such as to make it attractive for participants to support its continued operation, as was the case with its predecessor for about 70 years. Whether this will prove to be the case, only the future will tell.

## NOTES

Without implication, the author would like to acknowledge the helpful comments of Chris Alaouze, John Burton, Geof Kaine-Jones, and John Paterson.
1. This section draws on an unpublished manuscript written by John Burton.

## REFERENCES

Caponera, D. A. 1985. "Patterns of Cooperation in International Water Law: Principles and Institutions." *Natural Resources Journal* 25:563–587.

Dudley, N. J., and W. F. Musgrave. 1988. "Capacity Sharing of Water Reservoirs." *Water Resources Research* 24:649–658.

Goldie, L. F. E. 1985. "Equity and International Management of Transboundary Resources." *Natural Resources Journal* 25:665–699.

Murray-Darling Basin Ministerial Council. 1987. "Salinity and Drainage Strategy Background Paper." Background Paper No. 87/1, Canberra.

———. 1988. "Draft Salinity and Drainage Strategy." Discussion Paper No. 1, Canberra.

Paterson, J. Forthcoming. "The River Murray and Murray Darling Basin Agreements: Political Economic and Technical Foundations." *Water International*.

Quiggin, J. 1988. "Murray River Salinity—An Illustrative Model." *American Journal of Agricultural Economics* 70:635–645.

Taylor, P. V. 1988. "The New Agreement on the Murray-Darling–How Will It Work?" New South Wales Department of Water Resources, Sydney, Australia.

# PART THREE

# Environmental Policies and Agricultural Competitiveness

# NINE

# Environmental Regulation and Agricultural Trade Competitiveness

C. FORD RUNGE

On January 1, 1989, the European Community announced a ban on all beef imports from the United States containing hormones used to help increase cattle growth. Citing health risks, the EC action touched off a cycle of retaliation that has affected the world trading system. This apparently isolated example of health regulations acting as trade barriers is part of an emerging pattern of environmental and health issues with major consequences for the world economy. These consequences are especially important to trade between developed and developing nations. Consider these other developments:

- During 1988, the American Soybean Association conducted a campaign emphasizing the health risks of palm oil, which competes directly with soybean oil in the processed food market. Palm oil is produced almost entirely in developing countries, notably Malaysia and coastal Africa.
- In 1988, a major controversy broke out over Italy's shipment of tons of hazardous wastes to Nigeria. The wastes, expensive and difficult to dispose of in the EC, were shipped for disposal where regulations are considerably less stringent. After the action provoked an international incident, the shipment was returned.
- In 1987, the Sandoz chemical plant in Basel, Switzerland, was the site of an environmental calamity, when tons of fertilizers and chemicals spilled into the Rhine River, killing fish and aquatic life along hundreds of miles. Largely lost amidst the public uproar was the fact that the majority of the toxic products spilled, although manufactured in Switzerland, were destined for markets in developing countries.
- In February, 1989, the Natural Resources Defense Council released a report citing significant health risks from the use of Alar, a growth retardant, on U.S. apples. U.S. regulatory agencies may ultimately ban its use, but no controls are in force over continued applications outside the United States. The Alar episode coincided with a scare over Chilean fruit (a major source of U.S. winter supplies) that resulted in a temporary ban on these fruit imports.

These examples are part of an emerging problem: environmental and health risks are increasingly traded among nations along with goods and services. These risks are the opposite of services—they are environmental and health disservices traded across national borders. These problems arise directly from the transfer of agricultural technology, and will increasingly affect international investment flows, trade and development, and the relative competitiveness of U.S. agriculture.

This pattern of trade arises from three sources. The first is the increasing role of chemicals and fertilizers promoting agricultural productivity. These production inputs have been responsible for dramatic increases in yields, and have made agriculture an important meeting point for environmental, health, and trade issues. Food and human health are intimately connected. Agriculture is increasingly dependent on chemical and fertilizer inputs; it also is a major trade sector in developed and developing countries. This links environmental and health concerns to agricultural trade policy as never before.

The second source of the problem is the emergence of a two-tiered international structure of environmental regulation. Increasingly stringent rules and regulations in developed countries result from a rising concern with environmental quality and human health. In most developing countries, however, food production and agricultural development remain the primary focus of concern. This creates incentives to export restricted agricultural and industrial chemicals—or whole production processes—from north to south.

Third, when products carrying risks are imported into developed country markets, competing producers may demand protection, converting environmental and health concerns into nontariff trade barriers. As international trade increases, the linkages from environmental and health concerns to agriculture take on significance for organizations such as the General Agreement on Tariffs and Trade (GATT), which has made them a focus of the agricultural trade negotiations.

In developed countries, increased costs of production resulting from stricter regulations put producers in a less competitive cost-price squeeze, adding to their incentives to fight imports through environmental or health restrictions. In developing countries, meanwhile, heavy use of pesticides, herbicides and fertilizers marketed without regulation is leading to major health and environmental impacts.

This chapter considers these issues from an economic and political perspective, and concludes with some suggestions for policy reform at both domestic and international levels.

## Growing Chemical and Fertilizer Use

U.S. pesticide, herbicide, and fungicide sales grew at an average of 6 percent per year between 1965 and 1974, fluctuated throughout the 1970s, and fell along with farm financial conditions and acreage cut-backs in the 1980s (Tables 9.1–9.3). Like other inputs to agriculture, the demand for these products is largely derived from the demand for grain and oilseeds, which are heavily export dependent (Runge et al., 1988). Corn, a major U.S. export crop, receives the largest levels of pesticide treatments. Application rates increased from 1.2 pounds per acre in 1966 to 3.1 pounds per acre in 1982. In 1985, atrazine was applied on over 60 percent of surveyed acreage, and alachlor on 40 percent (Swanson and Dahl, 1989, p. 21). Table 9.4 shows herbicide and insecticide use by crop.

Given the derived demand from row crops to input uses, margins in the pesticide business fell during the market declines of the 1980s. From the perspective of the U.S. chemical industry, softening domestic demand for farm inputs stimulated a search for foreign marketing opportunities. By 1986, the U.S. pesticide industry exported 34 percent of its total sales value ($1.4 billion) compared with 26 percent in 1965 (Swanson and Dahl, 1989).

Part of the incentive to increase foreign sales arises from the substantial fixed costs of bringing new products to market in the face of internal research and development expenses and U.S. Environmental Protection Agency registration requirements. Research and development in the industry is a major expenditure due to specialized personnel, manufacturing specifications, and tight government controls. Large quantities of chemicals must now be screened to find those that target specific markets and conform to environmental regulations.

In 1986, according to Swanson and Dahl (1989, p. 43), pesticide researchers screened 13,500 compounds for every one registered by the EPA, compared with 5,500 compounds screened per registration in 1967. The time lag between product discovery and marketing likewise rose from an estimated 5 years in 1967 to 10 years in 1986. These fixed costs create powerful incentives, once a chemical is registered and in use, to build long-term markets. If domestic markets tighten due to market or regulatory factors, foreign markets are all the more crucial in spreading these fixed costs over sufficient sales volume. Finally, this process is likely to make entry into the pesticide industry by smaller firms more difficult, concentrating industry activity in larger firms with international marketing strategies.

Despite current criticism of their use in agriculture, chemicals and fertilizers promoting agricultural productivity have been responsible for much of the global increase in agricultural output, without which billions of people would be both poorer and more hungry than they are today. In the postwar period, agricultural productivity gains throughout the developed and developing world have been powered by significantly increased applications of these inputs.

According to the International Fertilizer Development Center (Baanante, et al., 1989), agricultural production increased from 1961–1963 to 1983–1985 at

Table 9.1 Sales of Pesticides (total)—Synthetic Organics[a]

| Year | U.S. Sales Quantity[b] (million lb) | U.S. Sales Value (million $) | Value ($/lb) | Exports Value (million $) | Exports Quantity[b] (million lb) | Imports[c] Value (million $) | Imports[c] Quantity[b] (million lb) | U.S. Usage[d] Value (million $) |
|---|---|---|---|---|---|---|---|---|
| 1965 | 763 | 497 | 0.65 | 131 | 299 | 9.7 | 5.5 | 376 |
| 1966 | 822 | 584 | 0.71 | 168 | 348 | 14.6 | 9.1 | 431 |
| 1967 | 897 | 787 | 0.88 | 194 | N/A | 16.2 | 15.4 | 609 |
| 1968 | 960 | 849 | 0.88 | 239 | 465 | 19.1 | 16.8 | 629 |
| 1969 | 929 | 851 | 0.92 | 197 | 395 | 15.2 | 10.9 | 669 |
| 1970 | 881 | 870 | 0.99 | 217 | 394 | 17.1 | 17.6 | 670 |
| 1971 | 946 | 979 | 1.03 | 248 | 413 | 26.7 | 23.9 | 758 |
| 1972 | 1,022 | 1,092 | 1.07 | 226 | 381 | 35.1 | 27.2 | 901 |
| 1973 | 1,199 | 1,344 | 1.12 | 362 | 590 | 43.2 | 32.1 | 1,025 |
| 1974 | 1,365 | 1,815 | 1.33 | 563 | 668 | 51.3 | 32.2 | 1,303 |
| 1975 | 1,317 | 2,359 | 1.79 | 664 | 592 | 108 | 55.1 | 1,803 |
| 1976 | 1,193 | 2,410 | 2.02 | 615 | 558 | 134 | 65.7 | 1,929 |
| 1977 | 1,263 | 2,808 | 2.22 | 767 | 595 | 108 | 52.4 | 2,149 |
| 1978 | 1,300 | 3,041 | 2.34 | 935 | 660 | 216 | 114 | 2,322 |
| 1979 | 1,369 | 3,631 | 2.65 | 1,113 | 650 | 236 | 110 | 2,754 |
| 1980 | 1,406 | 4,078 | 2.90 | 1,210 | 650 | 308 | 115 | 3,176 |
| 1981 | 1,291 | 4,652 | 3.60 | 1,204 | 526 | 338 | N/A | 3,786 |
| 1982 | 1,147 | 4,432 | 3.86 | 1,257 | 531 | 320 | 167 | 3,495 |
| 1983 | 1,017 | 4,054 | 3.99 | 1,280 | 496 | 303 | 143 | 3,077 |
| 1984 | 1,108 | 4,730 | 4.27 | 1,497 | 615 | 375 | 197 | 3,608 |
| 1985 | 1,022 | 4,437 | 4.34 | 1,363 | N/A | 449 | N/A | 3,523 |
| 1986 | 940 | 4,234 | 4.50 | 1,424 | N/A | 423 | N/A | 3,233 |

*Source:* Reproduced from Swanson and Dahl (1989) p. 57.
[a]Total sales of synthetic organic pesticides by U.S. manufacturers.
[b]Quantity sales of active ingredients for U.S. sales. Quantity of total ingredients (active plus inert) for exports and imports.
[c]Imports include synthetic organics plus nonorganics.
[d]U.S. sales minus exports plus imports.
N/A = Not Available

Table 9.2 Sales of Herbicides—Synthetic Organics

| Year | U.S. Sales[a] | | | Exports | |
| --- | --- | --- | --- | --- | --- |
| | Quantity[b] (million lb) | Value (million $) | Value ($/lb) | Quantity[b] (million lb) | Value (million $) |
| 1965 | 184 | 211 | 1.15 | 39 | 29 |
| 1966 | 222 | 258 | 1.16 | 44 | 37 |
| 1967 | 288 | 430 | 1.50 | N/A | 45 |
| 1968 | 319 | 483 | 1.52 | 71 | 65 |
| 1969 | 311 | 496 | 1.59 | 67 | 58 |
| 1970 | 308 | 498 | 1.62 | 76 | 62 |
| 1971 | 317 | 563 | 1.78 | 83 | 66 |
| 1972 | 354 | 629 | 1.78 | 88 | 68 |
| 1973 | 447 | 764 | 1.71 | 140 | 104 |
| 1974 | 529 | 1,048 | 1.98 | 190 | 179 |
| 1975 | 645 | 1,452 | 2.25 | 200 | 250 |
| 1976 | 558 | 1,450 | 2.60 | 198 | 245 |
| 1977 | 585 | 1,621 | 2.77 | 210 | 288 |
| 1978 | 640 | 1,783 | 2.78 | 231 | 348 |
| 1979 | 703 | 2,166 | 3.08 | 256 | 430 |
| 1980 | 768 | 2,558 | 3.33 | 256 | 486 |
| 1981 | 724 | 2,909 | 4.02 | 222 | 500 |
| 1982 | 663 | 2,866 | 4.32 | 219 | 509 |
| 1983 | 604 | 2,676 | 4.43 | 221 | 593 |
| 1984 | 684 | 3,131 | 4.58 | 289 | 707 |
| 1985 | 636 | 2,884 | 4.54 | N/A | 622 |
| 1986 | 579 | 2,527 | 4.36 | N/A | 625 |

*Source*: Reproduced from Swanson and Dahl, 1989, p. 58.
[a]Total sales of synthetic organic pesticides by U.S. manufacturers.
[b]Quantity of sales of active ingredients for U.S. sales. Quantity of total ingredients (active plus inert) for exports and imports.
N/A = Not Available

an annual rate of 2 percent in developed countries and 3.2 percent in developing countries. About two-thirds of these increases were due to increases in yields, as distinct from increases in area planted (Baanante et al., 1989, p. 2). Fertilizer use, which increased tenfold in developing countries and doubled in developed market economics from 1961–1963 to 1983–1985, is "possibly the most potent single factor in raising productivity" (Food and Agriculture Organization, 1987a). Table 9.5 shows per hectare fertilizer use in kilograms of nutrient in 1985. Table 9.6 shows the 1985 contribution of fertilizer to agricultural production expressed in cereal equivalents.

In Indonesia, for example, rice production grew at an average rate of 5 percent per year from 1968 to 1984. By 1985 the country was an exporter rather than an importer of rice. Roughly half of this increase is attributed to

Table 9.3 Sales of Insecticides—Synthetic Organics

| | U.S. Sales[a] | | | Exports | |
|---|---|---|---|---|---|
| Year | Quantity[b] (million lb) | Value (million $) | Value ($/lb) | Quantity[b] (million lb) | Value (million $) |
| 1965 | 473 | 237 | 0.50 | 86 | 230 |
| 1966 | 482 | 273 | 0.57 | 108 | 265 |
| 1967 | 489 | 301 | 0.61 | 122 | N/A |
| 1968 | 511 | 304 | 0.59 | 148 | 349 |
| 1969 | 493 | 294 | 0.60 | 118 | 286 |
| 1970 | 444 | 307 | 0.69 | 128 | 272 |
| 1971 | 497 | 343 | 0.69 | 147 | 283 |
| 1972 | 540 | 381 | 0.71 | 127 | 247 |
| 1973 | 605 | 471 | 0.78 | 198 | 384 |
| 1974 | 692 | 645 | 0.93 | 296 | 406 |
| 1975 | 546 | 765 | 1.40 | 323 | 323 |
| 1976 | 502 | 808 | 1.61 | 272 | 287 |
| 1977 | 545 | 1,000 | 1.84 | 355 | 313 |
| 1978 | 509 | 1,038 | 2.04 | 390 | 312 |
| 1979 | 522 | 1,212 | 2.32 | 475 | 299 |
| 1980 | 492 | 1,230 | 2.50 | 485 | 289 |
| 1981 | 423 | 1,380 | 3.27 | 472 | 216 |
| 1982 | 374 | 1,265 | 3.38 | 490 | 214 |
| 1983 | 307 | 1,082 | 3.53 | 475 | 191 |
| 1984 | 312 | 1,308 | 4.19 | 545 | 216 |
| 1985 | 292 | 1,291 | 4.42 | 519 | N/A |
| 1986 | 272 | 1,423 | 5.23 | 534 | N/A |

Source: Reproduced from Swanson and Dahl, 1989, p. 59.
[a]Total sales of synthetic organic pesticides by U.S. manufacturers.
[b]Quantity of sales of active ingredients for U.S. sales. Quantity of total ingredients (active plus inert) for exports and imports.
N/A = Not Available

massive subsidies for fertilizers and chemicals. The trade-off is that these benefits were not without external costs. Robert Repetto, of the World Resources Institute, documents the substantial ecological damages of such policies, including water pollution, destruction of breeding habitat for coastal fish populations, and the elimination of natural predators. This has led in turn to insect infestations and subsequent overapplications of pesticides, at levels that actually have harmed crop harvests (Repetto, 1985).

In summary, increasing production and consumption of chemicals and fertilizers over the last 40 years has created a major and beneficial flow of trade. But this trend has been accompanied by significant disservices. The point is not to end the use of these chemicals, but to use them responsibly and knowledgeably. Modern chemical inputs require substantially more

Table 9.4 Farm Herbicide and Insecticide Use by Crop (in million pounds active ingredient)

| Crop | Herbicide Quantity | | | | | Insecticide Quantity | | | | |
|---|---|---|---|---|---|---|---|---|---|---|
| | 1966 | 1971 | 1976 | 1982 | 1987[d] | 1966 | 1971 | 1976 | 1982 | 1987[d] |
| Row crops | | | | | | | | | | |
| Corn | 46.0 | 101.1 | 207.1 | 243.4 | 196 | 23.6 | 25.5 | 32.0 | 30.1 | 24.3 |
| Soybeans | 10.4 | 36.5 | 81.1 | 125.2 | 104 | 3.2 | 5.6 | 7.9 | 10.9 | 9.1 |
| Cotton | 6.5 | 19.6 | 18.3 | 17.3 | 16 | 64.9 | 73.4 | 64.1 | 16.9 | 15.5 |
| Grain sorghum | 4.0 | 11.5 | 15.7 | 15.3 | 11 | 0.8 | 5.7 | 4.6 | 2.5 | 1.8 |
| Peanuts | 2.9 | 4.4 | 3.4 | 4.9 | 6 | 5.5 | 6.0 | 2.4 | 1.0 | 1.2 |
| Tobacco | N/A | 0.2 | 1.2 | 1.5 | 1 | 3.8 | 4.0 | 3.3 | 3.5 | 2.3 |
| Total | 69.8 | 173.3 | 326.8 | 407.6 | 334 | 101.8 | 120.2 | 114.3 | 64.9 | 64.2 |
| Small grain crops | | | | | | | | | | |
| Rice | 2.8 | 8.0 | 8.5 | 13.9 | 10 | 0.3 | 0.9 | 0.5 | 0.6 | 0.4 |
| Wheat | 8.2 | 11.6 | 21.9 | 18.0 | 14 | 0.9 | 1.7 | 7.2 | 2.4 | 1.8 |
| Other[a] | 4.9 | 5.4 | 5.5 | 5.9 | 7 | 0.3 | 0.8 | 1.8 | 0.2 | 0.2 |
| Total | 15.9 | 24.0 | 35.9 | 37.8 | 31 | 1.5 | 3.4 | 9.5 | 3.2 | 2.4 |
| Forage crops | | | | | N/A | | | | | N/A |
| Alfalfa | 1.3 | 0.6 | 1.6 | 0.3 | | 3.6 | 2.5 | 6.4 | 2.5 | |
| Other hay[b] | | | | 0.7 | | 0.1 | | | 0.1 | |
| Pasture and range[c] | 10.5 | 8.3 | 9.6 | 5.0 | | 0.3 | 0.2 | 0.1 | | |
| Total | 11.8 | 8.9 | 11.2 | 6.0 | | 4.0 | 2.7 | 6.5 | 2.6 | |
| Total | 97.6 | 207.2 | 373.9 | 451.4 | | 107.4 | 126.3 | 130.3 | 70.7 | |

*Source*: Reproduced from Swanson and Dahl, 1989, p. 22.
[a]Includes barley, oats, rye, and other mixed grains in 1966; barley, oats, and rye in 1971 and 1976; and barley and oats in 1982 and 1987.
[b]Blanks indicate that hay is included in the alfalfa figure.
[c]Blanks indicate that the quantity was less than 50,000 pounds active ingredients.
[d]Estimated
N/A = Not Available

information for safe and efficient  use. Among traditional farmers, this knowledge is often lacking. Especially in LDCs, the inputs themselves are aggressively marketed and subsidized, but farm-level education (including basic literacy necessary to read package instructions) is seldom given comparable attention. High levels of human poisoning in LDCs due to overapplication of pesticides are common. For example, per capita pesticide poisonings in the seven countries of Central America are 1,800 times higher than in the United States (Leonard, 1989, p. 4).

Responsible use of powerful chemical agents also requires attention to land-use patterns. On lands where crops are heavily irrigated, surface- and ground-water pollution is likely unless runoff and drainage are carefully controlled. On hilly or deforested lands, where soil fertility is most likely to be low, heavy applications of these chemicals flow rapidly into rivers and streams. Regulating which lands are appropriate for using these chemicals is an important step just now beginning to be done in North America and

**Table 9.5  Per Hectare Fertilizer Use in Kilograms of Nutrient, 1985 (kh/ha)**

| | | | |
|---|---|---|---|
| *By Regions* | | *In selected developing* | |
| World | 87.1 | *market economies* | |
| Developed market economies | 115.5 | *(continued)* | |
| North America | 85.1 | Africa (continued) | |
| Western Europe | 226.1 | Cameroon | 8.1 |
| Oceania | 32.3 | Ethiopia | 4.7 |
| Others | 164.6 | Ghana | 4.4 |
| Developing market economies | 41.6 | Côte d'Ivoire | 11.8 |
| Africa | 11.8 | Kenya | 42.1 |
| Near East | 52.3 | Malawi | 11.4 |
| Far East | 55.8 | Nigeria | 10.8 |
| Latin America | 41.4 | Senegal | 5.5 |
| Centrally planned economies | 138.0 | Sudan | 7.5 |
| Europe | 129.6 | Tanzania | 7.6 |
| Asia | 158.4 | Zambia | 15.5 |
| | | Latin America | |
| *In selected developed* | | Brazil | 42.5 |
| *market economies* | | Mexico | 69.3 |
| North America | | Colombia | 64.3 |
| Canada | 49.8 | Peru | 20.1 |
| United States | 93.7 | Near East | |
| Western Europe | | Turkey | 53.8 |
| Denmark | 241.8 | Iran | 60.9 |
| France | 300.9 | Syria | 40.5 |
| Federal Republic of Germany | 427.3 | Jordan | 36.9 |
| Netherlands | 783.3 | Far East | |
| Switzerland | 436.2 | Pakistan | 73.7 |
| United Kingdom | 355.5 | Bangladesh | 59.2 |
| Oceania | | Indonesia | 94.7 |
| Australia | 23.5 | India | 50.3 |
| New Zealand | 892.2 | Philippines | 35.8 |
| Others | | Malaysia | 116.5 |
| Japan | 430.4 | | |
| Israel | 220.3 | | |
| South Africa | 66.7 | *In selected centrally* | |
| | | *planned countries* | |
| *In selected developing* | | Czechoslovakia | 336.5 |
| *market economies* | | Hungary | 252.7 |
| Africa | | Romania | 146.0 |
| Angola | 5.8 | Soviet Union | 109.3 |
| Burkina Faso | 3.9 | China | 167.3 |

*Sources*: *FAO Fertilizer Yearbook*, 1986, reprinted in Baanante et al., "The Benefits of Fertilizer Use in Developing Countries," International Fertilizer Development Center, Muscle Shoals, Alabama, 1989.

Table 9.6 Contribution of Fertilizer to Agricultural Production in Cereal Production Equivalents, 1985

| | Total Nutrient (N+P$_2$O$_5$+K$_2$O) Consumption, in million mt | Increased Production per Unit of Nutrient, in Cereal Equivalents | Increased Production Due to Fertilizer, in Cereal Equivalents |
|---|---|---|---|
| Africa | 3.44 | 5 | 17.2 |
| Asia | 40.69 | 10 | 406.9 |
| Latin America | 7.38 | 7 | 51.6 |
| Total | 51.51 | | 475.7 |

*Sources*: Derived from data in *FAO Production and Fertilizer Yearbooks*. Printed in Baanante et al., "The Benefits of Fertilizer Use in Developing Countries," International Fertilizer Development Center, Muscle Shoals, Alabama, 1989.

Western Europe. In Minnesota, for example, a land-targeting scheme is part of the Reinvest-in-Minnesota program, which promises to reduce erosion and improve ground-water quality by guiding land use toward high-productivity, low-vulnerability terrain (Larson et al., 1988).

## Structure of Environmental Regulation

Unfortunately, land-use restrictions of this kind, rare in the United States, are essentially nonexistent in developing countries. Patterns of land use in LDCs give greatest priority to shorter term food production goals at the expense of environmental quality considerations.

These differences in priorities require some analysis because they are not without cause. In the developed countries of North America and Western Europe, the "food problem" is solved. The farm problem arises not from too little food and land in production, but generally too much. As predicted by Engels' law, the incomes of developed countries have increased, and the share of this income spent on food has fallen in proportion to other goods and services. In contrast, environmental quality and health concerns have grown in importance with increasing income levels. They are superior goods in the sense that they play a larger role in the national budget as national incomes increase (Runge, 1987).

In low-income developing countries, the share of national resources devoted to food and agriculture remains large, creating substantial markets for yield-increasing chemicals and fertilizers. Environmental quality and occupational health risks are widely perceived as less pressing concerns than economic development. Even if environmental and health risks are acknowledged, the income levels of most developing countries do not permit a structure of environmental regulation comparable to that in the north.

This difference in priorities creates a two-tiered structure of international environmental regulation. Stricter regulatory regimes in developed countries, when paired with lax or nonexistent regulations in developing countries, increase the north-south flow of environmental risks. A kind of "environmental arbitrage" results, in which profits are gained by exploiting the differential in regulations (Nolan and Runge, 1989, p. 6). In the United States, for example, the Federal Insecticide, Fungicide and Rodenticide Act (FIFRA), the Safe Drinking Water Act (SDWA) and the 1990 Farm Bill are all likely to be amended in ways that effectively constrain land use choices (Batie, 1988; Benbrook, 1988). These are but several examples of restrictions that may lead firms to expand in foreign markets where regulatory oversight is less constraining.

This environmental arbitrage results from conscious policy choices that reveal differences in the value attached to environmental quality by rich and poor countries. As these paths of institutional innovation increasingly diverge, so will the differential impact of environmental constraints on producers in North America and, say, Argentina and Brazil. The competition implications of these trends are not lost on U.S. producers. They and others in developed countries have been quick to see the trade relevance of environmental and health standards. Growing consumer concerns with the health and environmental impacts of agriculture create a natural (and much larger) constituency for nontariff barriers to trade, justified in the name of health and safety. It is doubtful, for example, that beef-offal merchants in the European Community could have blocked competitive U.S. imports solely in the name of superior French or German beef kidneys. But the hormones question created a large, vocal, and committed constituency for denying the United States access to this market.

## Regulation as Protectionism

U.S. consumers are made increasingly aware of environmental and health risks posed by imported agricultural products produced with chemicals that are restricted in domestic markets. In the Caribbean Basin, an important example is fruit and vegetable production. Although Caribbean farmers are encouraged to use pesticides, herbicides, and fertilizers, regulations against some of these products in North America are rapidly becoming barriers to market access. The beef hormone dispute between the United States and European Community is another example showing the difficulty of separating regulatory from trade issues in an open world economy.

Unfortunately, despite recent attempts to deal with these issues in forums such as the General Agreement on Tariffs and Trade (GATT), international responses have been inadequate, in part because the problem itself has not been clearly recognized. The Food and Agriculture Organization (FAO) of the United Nations has worked to develop comprehensive rules affecting food and agricultural health and safety (Food and Agriculture

Organization, 1987b). These rules are called the "Codex Alimentarius." Unfortunately, there are no agreed-upon standards for health and sanitary regulations except for a few items, and none are regarded as binding in law. This work has not been given the force and backing of international institutions. The World Bank/International Monetary Fund (IMF) system, recently acknowledged the importance and severity of ecological factors in project development and planning, but it has not confronted the broader trade and development implications of environmental and health issues.

A continuum of reactions to this issue exists. It stretches from those who insist that U.S. environmental and health standards ought to be those of the world (presumably including Western Europe, where there are no doubt those who feel similarly self-righteous) to those who contend that each country (and perhaps state) should be sovereign to interpret health and environmental standards as it sees fit.

In view of differences in levels of economic development and national priorities, however, it is clear that neither extreme can prevail. Jeffrey James (1982) suggested that despite valid arguments for improved health and environmental regulations in LDCs, "it does not follow from this that countries of the Third World should adopt either the same *number* or the same *level* of standards as developed countries" (p. 260). James suggests what may be called *intermediate* standards, "in the same sense and for the same basic reason as that which underlies the widespread advocacy of intermediate technology in the Third World." This does not necessarily imply only a downgrading of U.S. regulations, but also implies an upgrading of LDC norms.

If GATT remains an important forum for discussion of these issues, these distinctions may prove useful in developing a basis for "special and differential treatment" of LDCs under GATT law. While this treatment often creates serious long-run distortions, the terms under which it is granted, as James (1982) emphasizes, may actually reduce current regulatory differentials by raising LDC norms.

## Research and Policy Needs

The global consequences of failure to confront these problems are increasingly clear, in both environmental and trade terms. The Brundtland Commission Report (World Commission on Environment and Development, 1987), undertaken by the United Nations and the World Commission on Environment and Development, has underscored the need for international action on a wide range of environmental issues. Despite such calls to action, little has yet been done to move effectively to reduce environmental and health hazards at the international level.

Beyond ecological considerations are shorter-term problems of trade distortion and market access. These distortions threaten more liberal international trade in ways that are damaging to both developed and developing country interests. U.S. and European farmers are placed at competitive disadvantages by the two-tiered structure of regulation. LDC farmers, meanwhile, are not only likely to be denied access to developed country markets, but technological choices in the south may become biased, making farmers more dependent on purchased chemical inputs at the same time that markets for their products are foreclosed. In periods when rapid growth in trade is one of the only avenues out of debt and deficits, these distortions cannot be dismissed as unimportant.

How can the complex relationship between national environmental and trade policies be addressed? One response, sometimes heard in the United States, is to loosen the environmental regulatory constraints affecting U.S. producers. This is bad policy, because it is inconsistent with the importance attached to the environment and health both at home and abroad. However, it is important to recognize that tight regulatory constraints *do* have cost and competitiveness implications, and that the perception that foreign competition does not face similar constraints breeds animosity and protectionism. If U.S. agricultural interests do not help to define the environmental constraints of the 1990s in ways that are least likely to harm global competitiveness, these constraints may very well reduce our comparative advantage as low-cost producers of many agricultural products. Yet the agricultural establishment faces a credibility gap with many environmental groups. It is vital that the agricultural community grasp the economic and political point that it is soil, water, and the general quality of the environment on which continued competitiveness ultimately depends.

Second, because of the many national interests involved, the trade side of these problems requires strengthened multilateral institutions, which rationalize domestic regulations in the interest of environmental quality and health and safety. The key is to recognize the inherently international character of environmental quality and health—issues that are similar in nature to human rights. Only the force of international standards defining the duties of nations, corporations, and individuals, can hope to resolve these difficult issues. This does not, as I have emphasized, suggest that these standards cannot be different, depending on national levels of development and microlevel differences such as land-use patterns. Attention should also be given to the important role of subnational governmental jurisdictions, such as states and regions.

To begin this process, the United States must take the lead in urging existing multilateral institutions to coordinate their efforts. These include the agencies of the United Nations (notably the United Nations Environment Program, the World Health Organization, and the Food and Agriculture Organization), GATT, and the World Bank/IMF consortium. A broad-based effort from these groups, which already have considerable expertise and experience, is a first condition for success. Some of this coordination is under way. GATT, IMF and the World Bank, for example, have agreed to work more closely on issues of trade, aid, and development. The use of environmental and health regulations as trade barriers would provide an especially appropriate focal point for these efforts.

In addition, an international accord on environmental and health regulations would be appropriate, similar in nature to the 1988 Montreal Protocol agreed to by 40 nations to reduce emissions shown to be harmful to the ozone layer. Its purpose would be primarily invocational—to call for the rights, duties, and liabilities that define national regulations on environment and health, which can then be brought more nearly into accord. In the absence of such an agreement, groups within nations will continue to advocate the use of regulations as disguised protectionism, or loosening standards of environmental quality in the name of greater competitiveness.

In GATT, a long and complex process is under way to harmonize health, safety, and environmental regulations under the heading of "sanitary and phytosanitary" measures. These efforts are highly significant, but have been given less national and international attention than they deserve. By drawing attention to the broader policy problems of which they are a part, GATT can help to prevent protectionism from masquerading as health and safety standards.

Finally, much greater sophistication is needed in gathering data on chemical agents in use and particularly on their health effects, together with policy-driven research into the design of mechanisms to reduce the problems outlined above. However, one should not wait for this data to begin the design process. Failure to act promptly will result in continuing environmental "beggar-thy-neighbor" policies. A historic opportunity exists to define the future in a way consistent with both enhanced trade and an improved global environment.

## REFERENCES

Baanante, C. A., B. L. Bumb, and T. P. Thompson. 1989. *The Benefits of Fertilizer Use in Developing Countries*. Muscle Shoals, AL: International Fertilizer Development Center.

Batie, Sandra S. 1988. "Agriculture as the Problem: The Case of Groundwater Contamination." *Choices*, third quarter, pp. 4–7.

Benbrook, Charles M. 1988. "The Environment and the 1990 Farm Bill." *Journal of Soil and Water Conservation* 43:440–443.

Food and Agriculture Organization. 1987a. *Agriculture: Toward 2000*. Rome, Italy: Economic and Social Development Series.

———. 1987b. *Introducing Codex alimentarius*. Rome, Italy: FAO/WHO Food Standards Program.

James, Jeffrey. 1982. "Product Standards in Developing Countries." In *The Economics of New Technology in Developing Countries*, eds. Frances Stewart and Jeffrey James, pp. 256–271. Boulder, CO.: Westview Press.

Larson, G. A., G. Roloff, and W. E. Larson. 1988. "A New Approach to Marginal Agricultural Land Classification." *Journal of Soil and Water Conservation* 43:103–106.

Leonard, H. Jeffrey. 1989. "Remedies are Available for Latin America's Environmental Ills." *Conservation Foundation Letter*, No. 2. Washington, DC: Conservation Foundation.

Nolan, Richard, and C. Ford Runge. 1989. "Trade in Disservices: Environmental and Health Damages in International Trade." Staff Paper P89-8, Department of Agricultural and Applied Economics, University of Minnesota, St. Paul.

Repetto, Robert. 1985. *Paying the Price: Pesticide Subsidies in Developing Countries*. Washington, DC: World Resources Institute.

Runge, Carlisle Ford. 1987. "Induced Agricultural Innovation and Environmental Quality: The Case of Groundwater Regulation." *Land Economics* 63:249–258.

Runge, C. Ford, James P. Houck, and Daniel W. Halbach. 1988. "Implications of Environmental Regulations for Competitiveness in Agricultural Trade." In *Agricultural Trade and Natural Resources: Discovering the Critical Linkages*, ed. John D. Sutton, pp. 95–117. Boulder, CO, and London: Lynne Rienner Publishers.

Swanson, Jeffrey A., and Dale C. Dahl. 1989. "The U.S. Pesticide Industry: Usage Trends and Market Development." Staff Paper P89-5, Department of Agricultural and Applied Economics, University of Minnesota, St. Paul.

World Commission on Environment and Development. 1987. *Our Common Future*. New York: Oxford University Press.

# TEN

# International Trading Arrangements, the Intensity of Resource Use, and Environmental Quality

MICHAEL D. YOUNG

The effects of international trade on the intensity of resource use and environmental quality have not been well researched and are ripe for detailed study. In particular there is a need for empirical study. Over the last decade attention has been given almost exclusively to the impact of alternative trading arrangements on opportunities for economic growth and production. Ignoring environmental considerations, most studies have forcefully demonstrated the benefits of moving toward more liberal trading arrangements. This chapter examines environmental aspects of the agricultural economics profession's claim that free trade is better. It also seeks to identify how conventional resource and environmental policy recommendations are modified by trade considerations. It has a practical, example-based orientation. Readers interested in the theory of this topic, particularly the efficiency of resource use, are directed to the collection of papers in Sutton (1988).

International interest in the environment is increasing. Among other things, the World Commission on Environment and Development's (1987) report *Our Common Future* has had a major impact on international rhetoric. Sustainable development has become a catch-cry. The World Bank has established an environment department. Articles on the greening of the OECD are being written. Governments have been falling over themselves to be seen discussing the environment in an international context.

## TRADING ARRANGEMENTS

Theoretically trade occurs whenever it is to the advantage of the parties and countries involved. Most governments hold monopoly power over the rules that govern trade between their producers and other countries. Trade barriers and production subsidies often have been used for short-term political advantage. The costs of intervention for economic growth can be high. The costs in terms of the misuse of resources also can be high. These latter costs, however, are less well understood.

Most bilateral and multilateral trading arrangements take the form of import quota and/or concessional tariff arrangements. Because the benefits of protection generally flow to a few, these arrangements are politically attractive. Usually the costs of protection tend to be invisible, dispersed among many people and often over several countries. In all cases these policy measures distort resource values, input costs, and prices. Most of the short-term costs of the support are paid by consumers. But in the longer term, other costs emerge as supply mechanisms adjust to the distortions. In the case of the environment the costs are often delayed for 5 to 10 years and become apparent only after considerable structural adjustment and investment in the distorted economy has occurred.

A considerable number of international agreements complement the above-mentioned bilateral and multilateral agreements. The most widely known of these is the General Agreement on Tariffs and Trade. Many others exist. Those with important environmental dimensions include the International Tropical Timber Agreement (ITTA)[1] and the Convention on Trade in Endangered Species (CITES).[2] Each of these agreements set precedents that could flow through to a future GATT round and also to other international agreements.

## PRINCIPAL ECONOMIC RELATIONSHIPS

Agricultural trade barriers raise home prices and depress prices elsewhere. In response, farmers increase the intensity[3] of resource use, the quantity of inputs they use per acre, and the area of land they use for production. They also facilitate the implementation of most other agricultural policies that affect the supply of agricultural products.

The implications of increases in intensity for environmental quality are not linear. Diminishing returns to increased application rates mean that agricultural pollution increases expediently with agricultural price support.[4] In addition, there are important correlations between inputs. As fertilizer application rates increase, for example, pesticide use becomes more profitable. Once the capacity of the environment to assimilate the residuals not absorbed into the products is reached, pollution occurs and adverse environmental effects begin to accumulate. Wildlife diversity and density is diminished. Pest species diversity may increase. Short-term control measures may result in further adverse environmental effects and problems with crop residues.

Market forces are restricted by trade barriers from allocating resource use and production across nations to locations that have the greatest competitive advantage. Farmers also begin to produce in areas and to use resources that in a free market, would be used for different purposes. With time the environmental effects of this secondary adjustment response to trade barriers can overshadow the first-round effects associated with increases in production intensity.

Tariff barriers also facilitate the introduction of guaranteed prices. Risk is reduced and risk-averse farmers spend more on inputs. Farm and regional specialization is encouraged. The result is the emergence of monocultures. The amenity value of the landscape declines. The number of niches necessary to ensure species preservation are reduced. Risk-averse farmers also rationally can spend more on inputs. Application rates, particularly in climatically reliable areas, increase. Further pollution from agricultural production results.

Guaranteed prices also prevent the market from sending producers signals about the quality of the products they produce. It makes it possible for producers to continue to produce average and low-quality products which, without the guarantee, would attract a much lower price.

Although not dependent on tariff barriers for their maintenance, input subsidies also create environmental problems and by reducing production costs give the recipients a competitive advantage. In Australia, subsidized irrigation water is recognized as one of the principal causes of salinity. Farmer resistance to the introduction of marginal cost pricing and/or transferable water rights is high. Downstream water users and the environment pay the costs of the resultant overuse of water resources (Bureau of Agricultural Economics, 1987).

Input price subsidies also have adverse environmental effects in less developed countries. For example, in Indonesia a subsidy for the pesticide Sevin has led to a resurgence of brown planthopper and the accelerated evolution of resistant biotypes. Eventually the resistance of two rice varieties to brown planthopper was destroyed and the resistance of a popular high-yielding variety diminished. Before the introduction of this subsidy, natural predators successfully controlled the brown planthopper (Repetto, 1988).

Investment is also distorted by the artificially high output prices, which result from tariff barriers and other forms of support to agriculture. Over time, inappropriate technologies are developed and inappropriate regional adjustment occurs. Production and environmentally inappropriate distortions become entrenched in the economy. The conservation reserve program in the United States, for example, is restricted at a regional level so it does not remove "too much" highly erodible land from production in any one region.

Bizarre production patterns and pollution problems emerge as supply mechanisms adapt to the distorted market signals. Under a series of preferential tariff agreements cassava and soya can be imported into the European Community at low and zero tariff rates. Tariff and price support policies maintain corn prices at artificially high levels. An incentive was created to lower feed transport costs by moving to and expanding the European Community's intensive animal production around Rotterdam. The result was a 224 percent increase in the Dutch pig population between 1970 and 1985 and the emergence of massive pollution problems. Over 50 percent of Dutch animal feed is now imported from outside the European Community. The ammonia from the manure produced is causing significant numbers of trees to die.

Domestic water sources are being closed, and manure banks are being constructed to stockpile the manure, which cannot be spread on surrounding land (Organization for Economic Cooperation and Development, 1989; Young, 1989). The social costs of these externalities are high. Elsewhere, in countries like Thailand where the cassava is grown for this European market, serious soil degradation is occurring (von Meyer, 1988). Taking advantage of these agreements, 50 percent of Dutch animal feed is now imported from outside the European Community. Although the world market price for corn has generally been cheaper per calorific value than cassava and soya, inside the EC the situation is reversed (von Meyer, 1988). Ironically, if an equal tariff applied to all feed imports, corn would be cheaper per calorific value than soya and cassava and the problems would not have arisen.

In summary, trade barriers stimulate the adoption of environmentally inappropriate practices and concentrate production in areas that have less unused capacity to assimilate the waste associated with agricultural production.

## THE EFFECTS OF AGRICULTURAL
## PROTECTION ON THE ENVIRONMENT

### Developed Countries

Most support to agriculture is provided through a mixture of price support and supply control mechanisms. Rates of protection have been so high that in many countries they have virtually determined the nature and location of agricultural production. In 1986 the average producer subsidy equivalent was 36 percent in the United States and 50 percent in the European Community (U.S. Department of Agriculture, 1988).[5] The effects of agricultural protection on the landscape in developed countries has been considerable. Among other things, the result of these high rates of protection has been the emergence of widespread drinking water contamination in many key production areas, losses in landscape quality, and a reduction in species diversity (Organization for Economic Cooperation and Development, 1989; Young, 1989).

There is also a body of opinion that suggests that production incentives slow the rate of structural change and modify the character of the adjustment that occurs. Structural adjustment is less imperative. Although most of the benefits from these incentives go to large, efficient farms, small inefficient ones can remain in production. In the short term, certain traditional agricultural practices of environmental advantage for tourism and regional development objectives are retained (Young, 1988). In the long run, however, the structural adjustment and the loss of traditional practices still occurs. In England, Germany, and France the Common Agricultural Policy has prevented the clearing of hedgerows, and schemes that pay farmers to retain hedgerows have proved necessary.

In other developed countries where agriculture is not protected, the environment has probably gained from agricultural protection in competing countries. Nevertheless, in most of these countries one could reason that the remaining unused assimilative capacity of the environment is generally greater than it is in those countries where agriculture is protected. For example, the social costs of significantly expanding cereal production in Australia are probably minimal in comparison with an expansion in Europe where widespread examples of water pollution associated with crop production exist. These observations suggest a need for models that, recognizing social costs, take account of the differing amounts of unused assimilative capacity of the environment that exist among nations.

## Less Developed Countries

The effects of price support and other production incentives on LDCs are controversial and vary from country to country in a manner that makes generalization difficult. Price support within the European Community, the United States and other developed countries, backed by tariff barriers and import restrictions, distort input prices. By creating new markets, production incentives have encouraged a significant number of LDCs to specialize in the production of agricultural inputs, and to become more dependent on the developed countries that maintain the incentives, hence becoming less self-sufficient.

Preferential trade agreements, particularly in association with production incentives, have had significant adverse effects on the environment. These agreements have tended to further distort markets in the importing country and also cause environmentally undesirable structural adjustment within the countries that benefit from them. George (1988) described the resultant dependence on the economies of one or two trading partners as a "fate worse than debt."

The best known example of the adverse effects of preferential trade agreements is the European Community policy that permits cassava, mainly from Thailand, and other cereal substitutes to be imported either duty free or at a low rate of duty. This has led to excessive soil degradation in Thailand and severe air and water pollution from intensive animal production in and around the Rotterdam area. Other examples include land degradation associated with sugar production in ACP countries (former British and French colonies in Africa, the Caribbean, and the Pacific) and desertification associated with beef production in Botswana (von Meyer, 1988). Such agreements are almost always bound up with negative consequences for the environment in the LDCs involved (von Meyer, 1988). Often these problems are exacerbated by the lack of institutional arrangements to facilitate the conservation of resources. Land tenure conditions, for example, often discourage investment. All demonstrate that the environmental effects of trade distortions do not stop at national borders and, through market mechanisms, can be transmitted to distant countries.

Studies that highlight the likely gains of trade liberalization to LDCs include those by the Centre for International Economics (1988) and Tyers and Anderson (1988). Both these studies conclude that the liberalization of trading conditions would significantly increase farm income in most LDCs. Increased investment in conservation and other measures could be expected to follow.

## THE ENVIRONMENT AND TRADE LIBERALIZATION

The likely effects of a move to free trade are different for developed countries and LDCs. Demand for environmental quality is higher in developed countries, and the agricultural support systems are different. Most developed countries use tariff barriers and other support mechanisms to raise prices. In contrast, many LDCs use national marketing systems to suppress prices. These countries prefer to keep the cost of food in urban centers down. Income is transferred from rural to urban areas. Input subsidies are then used to (a) offset some of the adverse effects of price suppression on farm income; and (b) encourage farmers to use modern technology.

### Developed Countries

To interpret the likely effects of a move toward freer trading conditions on the environment in developed countries, information is needed on the likely changes in farm size, farm structure, and regional prices. Most empirical models suggest that the result would be a fall in the prices received by protected producers and a rise in the world price for the protected products. The extent of these changes depends on the nature of the move. Generally, the farm income effects of a multilateral move are more favorable than those of a unilateral move. In many cases, however, the environmental benefits from a unilateral move could be greater.

In countries where producer subsidy equivalents are high, the results of trade liberalization in key and marginal production areas would be different. Most of the serious agricultural pollution in developed countries is located in key production areas where input use is intensive. Nitrate pollution of drinking water supplies, pesticide contamination of ground water, salinity, and heavy metal accumulation are the most common problems in these areas. Studies indicate that a move to less agricultural protection in these areas would eventually lead to reduced pesticide and fertilizer application rates and improved water quality.[6] Crop rotations would become more complex and the landscape more diversified.

In the United States the use of set-aside policies as a supply control measure complicates the analysis. For example, in 1988 U.S. cotton and wheat farmers had to set aside approximately 25 percent of their land to qualify for a deficiency payment. Trade liberalization probably would bring the set-aside land back into production. The acreage reduction program, for example, probably would be abandoned. With a unilateral move to free trade, fertilizer and pesticide application rates per hectare of cropped land would decline but the return of set-aside land to production could increase the total quantity of inputs used per farm and region. Nevertheless, as the quantity of inputs applied per hectare would be more in line with environmental capacity, reductions in water pollution could be expected. With a multilateral move to free trade, however, only a small price fall is expected and hence the environmental benefits could be limited to increased landscape amenity value.

In marginal areas, if the result is a significant fall in farm income, the transition to world market prices could create transitional soil erosion and land degradation problems. Portugal's experience is relevant; its wheat prices are double European Community prices, and one of the conditions of membership is a 50 percent reduction of the prices offered to farmers. Farmers in marginal areas have decided to exploit the last remaining productive capacity and not maintain existing soil conservation works (Organization for Economic Cooperation and Development, 1989). Soil erosion problems are increasing in these areas. It must be pointed out, however, that these areas are the source of most existing soil erosion problems. The ultimate result from the reversion of these lands to grazing and forest production is likely to be a significant gain in water quality.

Substantial landscape change can be expected also in marginal production areas. In Denmark, A. Dubgaard (personal communication, 1987), Institute of Agricultural Economics, expects that as European Community milk prices are reduced, marginal dairy land will shift to sheep production. In England and Wales the Centre for Agricultural Strategy (1986) has compared the environmental implications of continuing with the Common Agricultural Policy versus a move to world prices. Dividing these countries into eight regions and using a weighted index of indicators, the Centre has concluded that continuing with the Common Agricultural Policy would lead to a substantial loss in four regions and gains in two regions. Moving to free trade, however, would result in considerable structural change and environmental improvement in all regions.

In summary, trading arrangements affect, and in many developed countries virtually determine, the prices received by farmers and the cost of the inputs they use. Trade barriers, price support, and other production incentives have encouraged producers to specialize and to increase production intensity. In most developed countries where agriculture is protected there has been a decline in the amenity value of the landscape and an increase in agricultural pollution. Lower world prices have meant that those developed countries with little agricultural protection probably have a less polluted environment but have lost significant development and trade opportunities.

## Developing Countries

The conclusion that support of agriculture has been of environmental advantage to free-trade–oriented developed countries cannot be extended to LDCs where income levels are much lower and, hence, the demand for environmental quality is lower. Property markets, infrastructure, investment, and wealth conditions are different. In several LDCs, trade barriers and monopoly marketing structures have enabled governments to keep agricultural prices and, hence, the cost of food in urban areas artificially low. These policies reduce the incentive for farmers to invest in soil conservation and cause land degradation and soil erosion to occur (Walford and Pearce, 1987). In these countries there is a growing body of opinion that suggests that the exposure of developing country farmers to freer trading conditions would significantly improve farm income and national economic growth.

LDCs that export agricultural products would benefit from a recovery in world market prices. LDCs that import agricultural produce would be encouraged to base their economic development on more solid ground and to strengthen their own farm sector (OECD Ministerial Press Communiqué, May 13, 1988). If this does occur, longer term investments would be made, soil conservation would become profitable, and landscape quality would improve. Institutional changes, such as improvements to land tenure, could follow.

A move toward freer trading conditions would also reduce the political need for input subsidies. The environmental costs associated with the overuse of inputs would decrease. Land use would be more diversified and greater use would be made of livestock manure and leguminous plants.

Opponents to this view usually begin by pointing out that some countries have benefited from existing market distortions and the sale and/or donation of surpluses to them. Lower world prices for some agricultural products, such as rice and wheat, have meant that it is cheaper for some countries to import these products (Matthews, 1985). The counterargument is that this "static view" has hindered development, increased dependence upon other countries, and reduced development opportunities in rural areas.

## PREFERENTIAL TRADE AGREEMENTS

### Comparative and Competitive Advantage

The terms "competitive advantage" and "comparative advantage" dominate the free trade debate in many countries and are used interchangeably. Freebairn (1986) defined competitive advantage as the ability of a producer to deliver a product to a market at an equal or lower price using resources at their opportunity cost. The implied emphasis in this definition is on the assessment of the private marginal costs of resource use. Johnston (1989) suggested that in assessing producer subsidy equivalents, emphasis should be given to comparative advantage: the social cost of resource use. If this is done, then interesting questions arise about the environmental standards each country should adopt to maximize opportunities for real economic growth.[7] Many of the answers to these questions depend upon the rules that govern international trading arrangements. Different rules will impose different costs on producer countries and establish different markets for export products.

Recognizing the linkage between environmental policy and competitive advantage, the OECD in 1972 developed the Polluter-Pays Principle. Under this international agreement countries are expected to ensure that, after an appropriate transition period, all government expenditure on pollution prevention and control is recovered from those who create the need for the expenditure. It is a partial internalization principle designed to prevent governments from using environmental policy as a means to provide a trading advantage to their producers. In application the agreement reduces the gap between comparative and competitive advantage. It facilitates compensation for the initial taking of property rights but opposes the apparent tendency of governments to commit themselves to paying compensation in perpetuity. Ultimately, and if the principle were enforced, production would shift toward those countries and regions that have a comparative advantage and result in a decline in the global extent of agricultural pollution.

Hiding behind an argument about the impossibility of applying this principle to nonpoint sources of pollution, however, most OECD countries do not apply the Polluter-Pays Principle to agriculture. Several European countries, however, are now beginning to apply it through various input levy frameworks (Organization for Economic Cooperation and Development, 1989). Countries such as the United States and Australia, which continue to pay farmers to adopt soil conservation measures, are clearly violating this principle. Adaptation of the U.S. conservation reserve program to retire land permanently from production would be consistent with the transition exception to the principle.

## THE ENVIRONMENT AND FUTURE TRADE NEGOTIATIONS

At a GATT meeting early in 1989 countries agreed not to increase agricultural subsidies, nor to raise tariff barriers, nor to introduce other similar protection measures. A ceiling will be placed on effective rates of protection. Such an agreement, or a more progressive one that seeks to reduce levels of protection, could draw attention to the use of input subsidies and regulations as a means to support, artificially, agricultural production. Attention is now turning to other agreements such as the GATT Standards Code, the FAO Codex Alimentarius and the OECD Polluter-Pays Principle.

If interest in the international aspects of the environment continues, pressures could arise for the development of a code to require that resources be used on a sustainable basis. Serious discussions about this latter option are already being held for coal, chloroflurocarbons, and tropical hardwoods. At a trading block level and as a strategy to restrict trade, discussions about a code to guide agricultural practices could follow.

## Input Subsidies

Most OECD countries provide some input subsidies to farmers. Of all of these, the most significant are the government financing of agricultural research and extension and the provision of concession loans, income tax concessions, and subsidized water for irrigation. If each of these inputs were provided to agriculture at their full opportunity cost, then the true competitive advantage of each country would become clearer to consumers. The United States producer subsidy equivalent calculations (U.S. Department of Agriculture, 1988), for example, do not include the annual $85 million of water price subsidies given to U.S. farmers each year by the Bureau of Reclamation (Moore and McGlukin, 1988). Consideration of the trade-offs between soil erosion and international trade also warrant attention. Ignoring several intangible factors, the cost of soil erosion in the United States has been estimated at $2–13 billion per annum (Clark et al., 1985). Thus the total cost of agricultural pollution in the United States could be equivalent to as much as 25 percent of the value of U.S. exports in 1985 (US$40 billion).

As pointed out by the OECD Group on Natural Resource Management, the introduction of full marginal cost pricing for these resources would lead to a significant reduction in pollution from agricultural and other water-using industries. Greater economic growth and regional development could also be expected (Organization for Economic Cooperation and Development, 1987).

If an agreement emerges from the current GATT round of discussions, then it is likely that countries will begin to stress the need for greater harmony in the provision of input subsidies and restrictions on the use of natural resources. The OECD Polluter-Pays Principle has been widely accepted throughout secondary industry, and some northern European countries are beginning to apply it to agriculture. The result could be a move toward a position where those countries that do not apply this principle to agriculture may face new environment-related trade barriers.

## Bilateral and Multilateral Trade Agreements

The United States and Canada ratified a bilateral trade agreement in 1988. The environmental implications of this agreement are complex and, to some extent, still unclear. Significant features of the agreement include:

- The acceptance of the EPA pesticide residue limits, rather than the arguably higher Canadian limits, for traded food products
- The 10-year phased reduction of all tariffs and the removal of all import restrictions (Normile and Goodloe, 1988)[8]

Both countries have a similar competitive advantage in wheat production. The likely result of this agreement will be a reduction in the ability of the United States to use acreage set-aside and conservation reserve programs for supply control. After 1998 Canadian farmers can be expected to derive great pleasure in offsetting any U.S. supply control and enjoying the benefits of any production incentives offered at either taxpayer or consumer expense. Unlike the European Community common agricultural policy, there is no provision within the agreement between the United States and Canada to jointly finance supply control measures.

The result of the U.S.-Canada agreement and other free-trade agreements, such as that between Australia and New Zealand, is that agricultural support policies are unlikely, even in the medium term, to remain an effective means of achieving environmental and other related objectives. With time, the use of supply control policies are unlikely to remain part of North American agriculture policy. Irrespective of the Polluter-Pays Principle, options to pay farmers not to erode soil and pollute water supplies will be reduced. Failure to recognize this could result in the loss of all the gains made in reducing agricultural pollution in recent years.

## Optimal Trade-Related Environmental Policy

Free-trade agreements also raise the important question about the optimal amount of unused environmental capacity to retain and the optimal standards to set within a country. As countries move toward freer trade, the need for integrated policies that facilitate appropriate trade-offs between agricultural, environmental, and other related objectives will become more important. The OECD (1989), for example, has noted that "As measures to reduce production and, in particular, to limit price supports are realized, major opportunities to achieve these objectives and simultaneously improve the environment can be expected to emerge." Countries need to design agricultural policies so that the external costs of agricultural pollution can be internalized, the waste assimilative properties of the environment are maintained and essential environmental services such as the production of oxygen are preserved (Barbier, 1989).

An international framework that makes a clear distinction between pollution prevention and control programs and those that seek to enhance environmental quality also will be important. Strong efficiency arguments exist for programs to reward farmers who provide positive externalities such as the improvement of the tourist value of a landscape. The provision of a subsidy to bribe farmers into the nonproduction of negative externalities, however, is inefficient. The OECD Polluter-Pays Principle provides the framework for such an international agreement. It facilitates input subsidies and other payments to encourage farmers to produce positive external benefits. Conceptually, its framework is similar to the equivalence standards approach for pesticide residues and food quality standards (Organization for Economic Cooperation and Development, 1989).

Failure to seek and adopt such principles could lead to a position whereby environmental enhancement and pollution control strategies are used as a mechanism to continue support to agriculture and reduce opportunities for an improvement in world trading conditions.

## Input and Residue Standards

Input and residue standards can be used to create nonprice barriers to trade. Moreover, once the use of price barriers is restricted, environment and other nonprice barriers are likely to receive increasing attention. In an attempt to reduce the adverse effects of such a development, an adjunct to the GATT Standards Code has been developed. Under this code, equivalence provisions facilitate the resolution of a trade-related problem associated with the use of different but "equivalent" standards. For example, one country may prohibit crop spraying immediately before harvest whereas another may set maximum residue standards. In court, it could be argued that the cancer risk to consumers of these two approaches is equivalent.[9]

Two examples of input standard trade disputes are the use of hormones in the production of U.S. beef exported to the European Community[10] and the detection of organo-chlorines in Australian beef exports to the United States, which forced Australia to then ban organo-chlorines in agriculture.[11] From an environmental and health viewpoint, this latter experience provides an example of the power of a large trading partner to force environmental improvement in another country.

Both examples also highlight the potential effects of differing input standards on international trade. Such nonprice barriers to trade can be both country and product specific and can be used as important weapons in a trade war. In both cases, the result was an improvement in environmental quality. Moreover, while the dispute was in progress new markets opened up for those countries that already met the higher standard.

Arguments for harmonized standards are often presented. A risk with this approach, however, is that the outcome will be a low compromise standard that is difficult to change. As all countries adjust to the common standard, the total unused assimilative capacity of the environment and the provision of environmental services throughout the world would be reduced. However, an equivalent standards approach, backed by appropriate mechanisms to deal with disputes, permits each country to pursue its own environmental, health, and other objectives.

Many countries are now in the process of reviewing their management of agricultural chemicals. Exporting countries have three issues to consider.

1.  What is the risk that they will be excluded from markets because they use chemicals that are not registered by the countries to which they export?
2.  What agricultural chemical registration standards will maximize their trading opportunities? Higher standards will reduce competitive advantage but raise comparative advantage. If they can successfully persuade their trading partners to accept only products grown at high standards, they could increase their market share. Countries with extensive production systems could gain from higher standards as they tend to use fewer manufactured chemicals.
3.  What are the optimal standards to set in order to maximize national welfare? The higher the standards, the less the heatlh risk and the lower the agricultural pollution. The registration costs associated with high standards, however, could be prohibitive for small nations. To avoid these costs, a risk-averse, free-rider approach could be taken. Any product that is deregistered by a trading partner could be withdrawn from use immediately. Expensive review and registration procedures would then be required only for products not registered elsewhere. Generally, the higher the standards the fewer the externalities, but higher standards increase registration costs.

## Management Practices

Away from the arena of agricultural politics, the principle of compliance with certain management practices as a precondition to trade is well established. In the area of wildlife management, for example, over half of the 994 species listed in the U.S. Endangered Species Act are found outside the United States and its territories. The import of threatened species is permitted only when the U.S. Fish and Wildlife Service has determined that a management plan ensures the survival of the imported species. For example, to export kangaroo hides to the United States, Australia must prepare a kangaroo management plan that is acceptable to the U.S. Fish and Wildlife Service. Under the International Tropical Timber Agreement, similar management plan arrangements could soon apply to trade in tropical hardwoods.[12] The extension of this management approach to agriculture and other natural resources could be expected to emerge in the near future.

In the past, Canada has taken a lead in negotiating the international conventions that facilitate a number of these agreements. As the world's largest trading bloc, the United States and Canada are now in a position to strengthen the acceptance of international conventions, together with the use of management plans and other measures, to improve the environment.

Equivalence in management practices designed to protect the environment is a logical progression from the above framework. In Denmark, the introduction of stricter standards for minimum poultry cage area have caused a significant proportion of Danish production to shift to neighboring countries (A. Dubgaard, personal communication, 1988). Membership within the European Community prevents Denmark from banning imported poultry products grown under less stringent animal welfare conditions in neighboring countries. If this were possible, the ultimate result would be the full transmission of the cost of these animal welfare measures through farmers to consumers.

Recognizing the likely impact of increasingly stringent controls on fertilizer use, Danish farmers are now arguing forcefully that these controls should be introduced at the European Community level rather than at a national level. Most of their agricultural exports go to other European Community countries and they are concerned that their competitive advantage will be eroded unless a European-Community–wide approach is taken to the resolution of environmental problems.

An interesting example of the growing recognition of the interdependence of trading conditions and the sustainable use of resources has arisen in Australia. Under Section 92 of Australia's constitution, barriers to trade between states are prohibited. Yet, after 50 years of defense of this section, the Australian High Court has recently decided that the state of Tasmania can prohibit the import of crayfish that do not meet the minimum size requirements of that state. The case arose because South Australian crayfishermen are permitted to harvest smaller crayfish than Tasmanian crayfishermen. The High Court decided that Tasmania could prohibit the import of crayfish that did not meet their standard irrespective of the situation in other states (Arch and Fisher, 1988). The issue at stake is clearly related to resource management. The political steps toward equivalent animal welfare standards and soil conservation policies now seem much smaller.

As these issues emerge, all exporting countries will need to consider where they wish to position themselves in the debate and what strategies they should pursue. Possibilities include:

- Simply wait until each problem arises and then develop reactive policies to deal with them.

- Encourage major trading partners to take a common approach to this problem.
- Begin to increase input standards, so that when disputes between other countries emerge, they are well placed to capture the new market as others are excluded.

Trade policy reform is a long, painful process. In matters relating to the environment, it could be argued that those who move early stand to gain the most. Even if the trade-related opportunities do not emerge, by internalizing the national externalities associated with agricultural production, increased economic growth and national welfare is likely. If disputes over the use of input subsidies and differing environmental standards escalate, an international convention on agriculture and the environment could be appropriate.


## CONCLUDING COMMENTS

The literature on international trade and the intensity of resource use, which has been excellently reviewed by Segerson (1988), contains several weaknesses.

1. There is a lack of attention to the role that product differentiation plays in international trade. Products free from residuals are not the same as those that contain them. Opportunities exist to explore the net benefits of a country setting very high standards to enhance its market prospects.

2. There has been a lack of attention to the role of structural change in affecting the use of agricultural resources. These second-round, post-adjustment effects often have a greater impact on resource use and environmental quality than those that are first observed. Too often inappropriate policies cause structural adjustment to progress a long way before the lagged environmental costs become apparent.

3. There has been a failure to explore trade-related issues in a strategy framework. Real policy in the international trade arena is more about strategy than about black and white options. For exporting countries, advice is needed about the environmental policy changes that should be made to maximize their chances in future trade wars. Perhaps game theory could contribute.

4. The case for the development of codes of practice to define acceptable production practices for traded agricultural commodities warrants attention. Should one trading country be permitted to out-trade another by polluting its ground-water supplies? Does the other, which makes its farmers pay the costs of pollution prevention and control, have a right to recourse?

5. More work is needed on the optimal amount of unused environmental capacity to retain, the optimal standards to set, and the optimal amount of

landscape amenity value to retain. Recognition of the *real* costs of resource use and degradation should be an important part of these considerations. Evaluation of the most appropriate balance among export income, environmental quality, and national welfare is needed.

## NOTES

1. The International Tropical Timber Agreement is administered by the International Tropical Timber Association in Japan. Although still in its infancy, one of its objectives is "To encourage the development of national policies aimed at the sustained utilization and conservation of tropical forests and their genetic resources, and at maintaining the ecological balance in the regions concerned." A code of conduct in exploiting timber and a levy on all trade in tropical timber are under discussion (Hpay, 1986).

2. The CITES Agreement, as it is commonly known, provides that countries that sign and then ratify the agreement must restrict trade in protected species. In particular, a country may permit the import of a protected species only when the appropriate scientific and administrative bodies in the exporting country have approved the export of that species (Emonds, 1981).

3. There are at least three measures of intensity: input use per cropped area, input use per farm, and input use per region. In countries where land set-aside policies operate, changes in these three indicators are not always in the same direction.

4. This is known as the law of diminishing returns. One implication of this is that substantial reductions in application rates have little effect on the gross margin received by farmers. It also means that short-term responsiveness (elasticity) of input is not as great as some people expect.

5. The averages are for the 13 EC and 12 US most commonly produced agricultural commodities. For Australia's 9 most commonly produced agricultural commodities, the average producer subsidy equivalent was 13 percent.

6. Because the short-term price elasticities for most agricultural inputs in key production areas are low, the initial gains would be slow. Structural adjustment would be a necessary prerequisite to the realization of these benefits.

7. The emphasis should be on real economic growth that, through a natural resource accounting or similar approach, recognizes that income generated through the consumption of resources without replacement or a reduction in unused environmental capacity is the liquidation of capital assets, not the generation of income (Lutz and El Serafy, 1989).

8. Under certain conditions, Canada may retain fruit and vegetable tariffs for 20 years. Both countries may also reintroduce grain import quotas if there is a significant change in the trade balance for these commodities.

9. Surprisingly, Australia only has observer status and is not a signatory to the GATT Standards Code. The only other OECD countries that have not signed are Ireland and Turkey. Australia has not signed the code because it has been unable to resolve the federal-state administrative problems associated with acceding to the code

(Australian Department of Industry, Technology and Commerce, 1987).

10. On the first of January 1989 the European Community banned imports of beef grown using growth-stimulating hormones. The reasons for this ban are complex and involve both animal welfare and supply control considerations. Two large trading bodies are involved and, as yet, there is no clear outcome.

11. In 1987, the U.S. government moved to ban beef imports that contained DDT, dieldrin, or heptachlor residues. The U.S. government argued that because they had banned the use of these chemicals in the United States, their consumers should not be exposed to organo-chlorine residues from imported beef. Australian farmers still used these chemicals on a regular basis. U.S. beef producers would gain as local prices increased and the Australian beef industry would lose its principal market. Upon announcement of the intended ban, as several shipments of beef were at risk, Australia quickly banned all organo-chlorine use in agriculture, recalled all stocks, and introduced a major testing program. Livestock from all properties that tested positive were quarantined (Australian Department of Primary Industries and Energy, 1988).

12. In 1987, 18 producer and 22 consumer countries were parties to the International Tropical Timber Agreement. The preamble to the agreement recognizes "the importance of, and the need for, proper and effective conservation and development of tropical timber forests with a view to ensuring their optimal utilization while maintaining the ecological balance of the regions concerned and of the biosphere." Article 1(H) contains an objective "to encourage the development of national policies aimed at the sustainable utilization and conservation of tropical forests and their genetic resources, and at maintaining the ecological balance in the regions concerned" (Hpay, 1986). Jointly the signatories are responsible for 95 percent of tropical forest resources and trade (Freezailah, 1987).

## REFERENCES

Arch, A. M. J., and W. W. Fisher. 1988. *Agricultural Marketing Section of the Commonwealth Constitution*. Melbourne: Australian Agricultural Economics Society (Victoria Branch).

Australian Department of Industry, Technology and Commerce. 1987. *Report of the Committee of Review Standards, Accreditation and Quality Controls Assurance*. Canberra: Australian Government Publishing Service.

Australian Department of Primary Industries and Energy. 1988. *Annual Report 1987–88*. Canberra: Australian Government Publishing Service.

Barbier, E. B. 1989. *Economics, Natural-resource Scarcity and Development: Conventional Views and Alternative Views*. London: Earthscan Publications.

Bureau of Agricultural Economics. 1987. *Submission to the Industries Assistance Commission Rice Industry Inquiry*. Canberra: Australian Government Publishing Service.

Centre for Agricultural Strategy. 1986. *Countryside Implications for England and Wales of Possible Changes in the Common Agricultural Policy*. University of Reading, Reading, England.

Centre for International Economics. 1988. *Macro-economic Consequences of Farm Support Policies*. Canberra: Centre for International Economics.

Clark, E. H., J. A. Haverkamp, and W. Chapman. 1985. *Eroding Soils, the Off-Farm Impacts*. Washington, DC: The Conservation Foundation.

Emonds, G. 1981. "Guidelines for National Implementation of the Convention on International Trade in Endangered Species of Wild Fauna and Flora." Gland, Switzerland: International Union for Conservation of Nature and Natural Resources.

Freebairn, J. 1986. "Implications of Wages and Industrial Policies on Competitiveness of Agricultural Industries." Paper presented at the Australian Agricultural Economic Society Policy Forum, Canberra, Australia.

Freezailah, B.C.Y. 1987. "The International Tropical Timber Organization." *Unasylva* 39:61–64.

George, S. 1988. *A Fate Worse than Debt*. Middlesex, England: Penguin.

Hpay, T. 1986. "The International Tropical Timber Agreement: Its Prospects for Tropical Timber Trade, Development and Forest Management." International Union for the Conservation of Nature and Natural Resources/International Institute for Environment and Development Tropical Forest Policy Paper, No. 3, London.

Johnston, B. 1989. "Long Run Competitiveness in U.S. Agriculture." Washington, DC: U.S. Department of Agriculture, Economic Research Service.

Lutz, E., and S. El Serafy. 1989. "Environmental and Resource Accounting: An Overview." In *Environmental and Resource Accounting for Sustainable Development*, eds. Y. J. Ahamad, S. El Serafy, and E. Lutz. Washington, DC: World Bank.

Matthews, A. 1985. *The Common Agricultural Policy and the Less Developed Countries*. Dublin, Ireland: Gill and Macmillan.

Moore, M. R., and C. A. McGluckin. 1988. "Program Crop Production and Federal Irrigation Water." In *Agricultural Resources: Cropland, Water and Conservation Situation Outlook*. Washington, DC: U.S. Department of Agriculture, Economic Research Service.

Normile, M. A., and C. A. Goodloe. 1988. "U.S.-Canadian Agricultural Trade Issues: Implications for Bilateral Trade Agreement," Economic Research Service Staff Report No. AGES880209. Washington, DC: U.S. Department of Agriculture.

Organization for Economic Cooperation and Development. 1987. *Pricing of Water Services*. Paris, France.

———. 1988. *Report on Monitoring and on Outlook of Agricultural Policies Markets and Trade*. Paris, France.

———. 1989. *Agricultural and Environmental Policies: Opportunities for Integration*. Paris, France.

Repetto, R. 1988. "Economic Policy Reform for Natural Resource Conservation," Environment Department Working Paper No. 4. Washington, DC: World Bank.

Segerson, K. 1988. "Natural Resource Concepts in Trade Analysis." In *Agricultural Trade and Natural Resources: Discovering the Critical Linkages*. ed. J. D. Sutton, pp. 9–34. Boulder, CO and London: Lynne Rienner Publishers.

Sutton, J. D., ed. 1988. *Agricultural Trade and Natural Resources: Discovering the*

*Critical Linkages*. Boulder, CO and London: Lynne Rienner Publishers.

Tyers, R., and K. Anderson. 1988. "Liberalizing OECD Agricultural Policies in the Uruguay Round: Effects on Trade and Welfare." *Journal of Agricultural Economics* 39:197–216.

U.S. Department of Agriculture. 1988. *Estimates of Producer and Consumer Subsidy Equivalents: Government Intervention in Agriculture, 1982–86.* Washington DC: Economic Research Service..

von Meyer, H. 1988. "European Common Agricultural Policy and Its Effects on Resource Use." Unpublished paper prepared for the World Wildlife Fund, Washington, DC.

Walford, J., and D. Pearce. 1987. "Research Issues in Environment and Development: A Key Note Paper." Washington, DC: World Bank, Environment Department.

World Commission on Environment and Development. 1987. *Our Common Future.* Oxford, England: Oxford University Press.

Young, M. D. 1988. "The Effects of Agricultural Supply Control Polices," *CAP Briefing*, 15–17:5–13.

———. 1989. *Agriculture and the Environment: OECD Policy Experiences and American Opportunities.* Washington, DC: U.S. Department of Agriculture, Economic Research Service.

# Index